D1008800

"Crude Politics is a fine piece of investigative reporting. This heavily foot-noted book reveals the administration's road map for a piece of foreign oil interests benefitting special-interest groups at the expense of American security."

—STEVE ELSON, former Navy SEAL and former member of the elite Red Team that tests security for the FAA

"Crude Politics is very interesting reading. The Bush administration has a tin ear for the appearance of conflicts of interest, and they fail to appreciate how it undermines their world standing."

—TOM FITTON, president of Judicial Watch Inc.

"Crude Politics is typical Paul Sperry reporting: tough, well-researched, courageous and thought-provoking."

—I.C. SMITH, FBI counterintelligence veteran

CRUDE POLITICS

HOW BUSH'S OIL CRONIES
HIJACKED THE WAR ON TERRORISM

PAUL SPERRY

WND BOOKS

Nashville

www.WNDBooks.com

Published in Nashville, Tennessee, by WND Books.

Library of Congress Cataloging-in-Publication Data

Sperry, Paul E.
    Crude politics : how Bush's oil cronies hijacked the war on terrorism / Paul Sperry.
    p. cm.
    Includes index.
    ISBN 0-7852-6271-7 (hardcover)
    1. United States—Foreign relations—Afghanistan. 2. Afghanistan—Foreign rela-
tions—United States. 3. United States—Foreign relations--Pakistan. 4. Pakistan—
Foreign relations—United States. 5. United States—Foreign relations—2001-
6. Bush, George W. (George Walker), 1946- 7. Bush, George W. (George Walker),
1946—Friends and associates. 8. Oil industry and trade—Political aspects—United
States. 9. Petroleum pipelines—Caspian Sea Region. 10. War on Terrorism, 2001—
Economic aspects. I. Title.

E183.8.A3S68 2003
327.73'009'0511—dc21   2003004265

Printed in the United States of America
02 03 04 05 06 BVG 5 4 3 2 1

For the families of the victims of the September 11 massacre, who trusted the politicians in Washington to just this once put aside hidden agendas and ulterior motives and do the right thing for their country, to swiftly bring to justice al-Qaida's leaders and effectively protect the American people they vowed to protect; and also for my own family—my wife, Amy, and daughters—who helped me to still smile through the gnawing cynicism about the state of American politics and leadership.

CONTENTS

INTRODUCTION

TREATING DONKEY BITES
While al-Qaida Strikes—Again

There's still a lot of work to do in Afghanistan to achieve our dreams.

—PRESIDENT BUSH

"WE'VE REALLY ACCOMPLISHED A LOT," A BEAMING PRESIDENT Bush told Afghan dignitaries gathered for a White House ceremony commemorating the anniversary of the "liberation" of their country from the "brutal" Taliban regime.[1] During the October 2002 event, held in the Presidential Hall of the Eisenhower Executive Office Building, Bush spent close to thirty minutes going over all the highlights. Before the war on terrorism, he noted, girls over the age of eight couldn't even set foot in an Afghan school under the "oppressive rule" of the Taliban. Now, thanks to American liberation, they are going to class for the first time. "And our country has provided them, as well as the boys, with millions of new textbooks." America also is helping to feed, clothe, and vaccinate them. "We got the Taliban gone," Bush crowed. "We'd like to get disease and hunger gone, as well." He then recognized a U.S. soldier who traveled around the destitute country providing medical care. "He treated broken bones. He treated gunshot wounds. He treated cuts and diseases," the president gushed. "He treated a small child who was bitten by a donkey."

A touching story, to be sure. But while Bush was celebrating the liberation of the Afghan people from the Taliban, hunger, and rabid donkeys, the real enemy was still killing Americans. In fact, the day after his self-congratulatory speech, al-Qaida terrorists car-bombed a night club in Bali, killing close to two hundred people, including Americans. Three days earlier, al-Qaida snipers killed a U.S. Marine and wounded another in Kuwait; and a week earlier, a group linked to al-Qaida killed a Green Beret in the Philippines in one of a series of bombing attacks there. An al-Qaida–tied gunman in Jordan closed out the bloody month by fatally pumping at least seven bullets into a sixty-year-old American diplomat who worked at the U.S. Agency for International Development, the same group Bush had praised for "spearheading our back-to-school" efforts in Afghanistan.

In the speech, which attracted little media coverage, Bush glossed over the lingering al-Qaida threat, focusing instead on the importance of "liberating" the Afghan people from the clutches of the Taliban, who sheltered al-Qaida.

"It's very important for our fellow Americans to remember that— keep in mind about the Taliban. They were the most brutal and oppressive [of] governments—one of the most brutal and oppressive governments in modern times," he said. "It's hard for us to understand in America, but these are people who attempted to control every mind and every soul in the country."

He added, "Thanks to America, the oppressive rule has been lifted. They're no longer in power. They're on the run—along with a bunch of other ones over there, too."[2]

One of them being Osama bin Laden, a name Bush now studiously avoids mentioning in public. However, the al-Qaida leader and his top deputy, Ayman al-Zawahiri, were heard on audiotapes released the previous month calling for new attacks on Americans at home and abroad.[3] Just the day before Bush's speech, remarkably enough, the State Department cited "credible indications" of new al-Qaida attacks in issuing a six-month-long "Worldwide Caution" that advised Americans abroad to avoid "facilities where Americans are generally known to congregate or visit, such as clubs, restaurants, places of worship, schools or outdoor recreation events."[4] An update to the warning added hotels, resorts, and beaches to the list of unsafe places—in effect restricting expatriates to their offices and homes.[5] A few weeks later bin Laden took credit in another audiotape for the resurgent terrorist acts of bloody October—which included a deadly Chechen hostage-taking in Russia and an attack on a French supertanker—confirming that he had survived the administration's bombing campaign in Afghanistan. He issued more threats against Americans, and State had to update its terror alert again, this time citing "the statement released by Usama bin Laden."[6]

Yet Bush in his speech suggested that al-Qaida was a withering threat—and one still primarily contained within Afghanistan. "There's still some al-Qaida killers roaming around Afghanistan," he casually acknowledged to his honored guests, who included Afghanistan's new ambassador to the U.S. and new education minister—as well as a shadowy White House figure from Afghanistan who has been advising Bush throughout the war. (The president fondly, albeit briefly, recognized him as "Zal.") But not to worry, Bush said, U.S. forces would take care of them as part of mop-up operations—as if bin Laden and his top henchmen were still in Afghanistan, and not in neighboring Pakistan, the Taliban sponsor and al-Qaida breeder that Bush enlisted as a partner in the war on terrorism.

He changed the subject with another heartwarming anecdote, this one lauding an army captain who "got the equipment necessary to start the first post-Taliban baseball league" in Afghanistan. "He brought me a ball—two balls signed by the Eagles—the Eagles, the Eagles, the mighty Eagles of Afghan baseball," he said. "And they practice—they're practicing now, and the games are held once a week."[7]

This was a man after his own heart, declared the president, who is a big fan of the sport, and of compassion in general. "Our soldiers wear the uniforms of warriors, but they are also compassionate people. And the Afghan people are really beginning to see the true strength of our country," he said, adding that the same captain had helped supply Afghan students with thousands of pens and pencils. "I mean, routing out the Taliban was important, but building a school is equally important."

While Bush was waxing sentimental about catchers' mitts and No. 2 pencils, his CIA director was warning that al-Qaida, despite being run out of Afghanistan, had regrouped. "They've reconstituted. They are coming after us. They want to execute attacks," George Tenet testified before Congress a week after Bush's speech. "You see it in Bali, you see it in Kuwait." He added, "The threat environment we find ourselves in today is as bad as it was last summer—the summer before 9-11," when some three thousand people were slaughtered by al-Qaida.[8]

In other words, the "liberation of Afghanistan" essentially changed nothing, except the government of Afghanistan.

Never mind that. "There's still a lot of work to do in Afghanistan to achieve our dreams," Bush assured his Afghan guests at the White House. The country basically has to be rebuilt. "We're currently implementing more than $300 million worth of reconstruction and recovery projects," he said, including new hospitals, schools, bridges, and highways.

Curiously, he left out the biggest projects of all: trans-Afghanistan oil and gas pipelines—long a "dream" of Bush's cronies, including his behind-the-scenes Afghan adviser, Zal, but one that had been held up by the Taliban.

Until now.

THE PLAYERS AND
POWER BROKERS

GEORGE W. BUSH: President and commander in chief of the United States. A former Texas oil executive, he received more donations from the oil-and-gas industry in the 2000 campaign than any other federal candidate over the previous decade. Close to Saudi royal family.

DICK CHENEY: Vice president and key member of war cabinet. Headed White House's controversial energy task force. Former president and CEO of Dallas-based energy-services giant, Halliburton Co., adviser to the U.S.-Azerbaijan Chamber of Commerce, a Washington lobbying group for energy development in the Caspian Sea state, and member of the Kazakhstan Oil Advisory Board. Prosecuted Gulf War as defense secretary.

CONDOLEEZZA "CONDI" RICE: Bush's national security adviser, nicknamed the "Warrior Princess," who closely monitored war cabinet meetings after September 11. Longtime director of Chevron Corp., now ChevronTexaco, the Caspian Sea's largest energy producer. The oil giant named a tanker for her.

ZALMAY "ZAL" KHALILZAD: Bush's top Afghanistan adviser. Reports directly to Rice as senior director for Southwest Asia, Near East and North African affairs on the National Security Council. Also Bush's special envoy to Afghanistan, and special envoy and ambassador at large to the Iraqi opposition. Headed Bush-Cheney transition team for the Defense Department, and counseled Defense Secretary Donald Rumsfeld. Founding director of the Afghanistan-America Foundation, a

Washington lobbying group. One-time consultant to Unocal Corp., another Caspian producer.

RICHARD "RICH" ARMITAGE: Deputy secretary of state and influential war cabinet aide who reports directly to Secretary of State Colin Powell, an old pal. Former president of Armitage Associates L.C., a Washington lobbying group with Caspian oil clients. One of his partners worked with Khalilzad on defense transition. Also former cochairman of the U.S.-Azerbaijan Chamber of Commerce. A colorful fireplug of a man, Armitage was former President Bush's first choice for secretary of army, but his ties to the Iran-contra scandal while a senior Pentagon official scuttled his nomination. He instead became the elder Bush's ambassador to the newly independent Russian republics.

WENDY CHAMBERLIN: Bush's former ambassador to Pakistan, who met with Pakistan's oil minister soon after September 11. She also served as Mideast security adviser to Bush's father when he was president.

CHRISTINA ROCCA: Assistant secretary of state for South Asian affairs, including Afghanistan and Pakistan, who works closely with Armitage. Longtime CIA intelligence officer and most recently a top foreign-policy adviser to Senator Sam Brownback (R-Kan.) specializing in South and Central Asia, the Caucasus, and the Mideast.

SENATOR SAM BROWNBACK: The Kansas Republican chairs a key Senate Foreign Relations subcommittee and is cofounder and cochairman of the Silk Road Caucus, set up after September 11 to develop legislative policy for promoting trade and investment in the Caspian region. Trustee of the U.S.-Azerbaijan Chamber of Commerce board.

GEN. PERVEZ MUSHARRAF: President of Pakistan who seized power in a 1999 military coup. Recruited by Bush as an "ally" in the war on terrorism.

USMAN AMINUDDIN: Musharraf's oil minister who met with Chamberlin.

SHEIKH BADR AL-AIBAN: Chairman and CEO of Saudi Arabia's Delta Oil Co., a partner in a major Caspian production group with

Unocal. Signed deal with Unocal to develop a multibillion-dollar Caspian gas pipeline across Afghanistan and Pakistan. Father was a trusted adviser to Saudi Crown Prince Abdullah. Raised as a member of al-Saud household.

HAMID KARZAI: Pashtun tribal leader and reformed Taliban official who rose to become president of Afghanistan. Courtly, English-speaking leader easily recognized by his cape and lambs-wool hat covering a bald dome. One-time Unocal consultant.

QUYAM KARZAI: Hamid's older brother and closest adviser. An Afghan-American like Khalilzad, who lives in the Washington area, he is also a member of the Afghanistan-America Foundation's international advisory board.

JUMA M. MOHAMMADI: Afghanistan's minister of mines and industry, and Aminuddin's counterpart in Kabul. Former World Bank official.

ASHRAF GHANI: Afghan finance minister and Karzai's chief adviser on reconstruction projects. Former World Bank official and Johns Hopkins University professor.

FREDERICK STARR: Chairman of the Central Asia-Caucasus Institute, a Caspian-boosting group funded in part by Unocal and Chevron. It's part of Johns Hopkins University in Washington. Starr is also an adviser to the Afghanistan-America Foundation.

THOMAS E. GOUTTIERRE: Director of the Unocal-funded Center for Afghanistan Studies at the University of Nebraska at Omaha, the only such center in the world. Former adviser to the UN Special Mission in Afghanistan. Founding director and vice president of the Afghanistan-America Foundation. Calls Khalilzad an old friend. The two met when Khalilzad attended high school in Afghanistan.

JOHN "JACK" MARESCA: Former Bush administration diplomat specializing in the former Soviet republics, who turned Unocal vice president and Caspian lobbyist.

LT. GEN. BRENT SCOWCROFT: National security adviser to former President Bush who mentored Rice, then an aide specializing in Russian affairs. President of the Scowcroft Group Inc., a Washington lobbying firm with Caspian oil clients. Honorary cochairman of the Afghanistan-America Foundation, and adviser to the U.S.-Azerbaijan Chamber of Commerce. He now serves as chairman of the President's Foreign Intelligence Advisory Board, a post that gives him regular access to top-secret intelligence and to Bush's top foreign-policy advisers.

HENRY KISSINGER: The former secretary of state is chairman of Kissinger McLarty Associates, a Washington lobbying firm, and is also an adviser to the U.S.-Azerbaijan Chamber of Commerce. He, too, consulted for Unocal. Kissinger was Bush's first choice to head the commission investigating September 11.

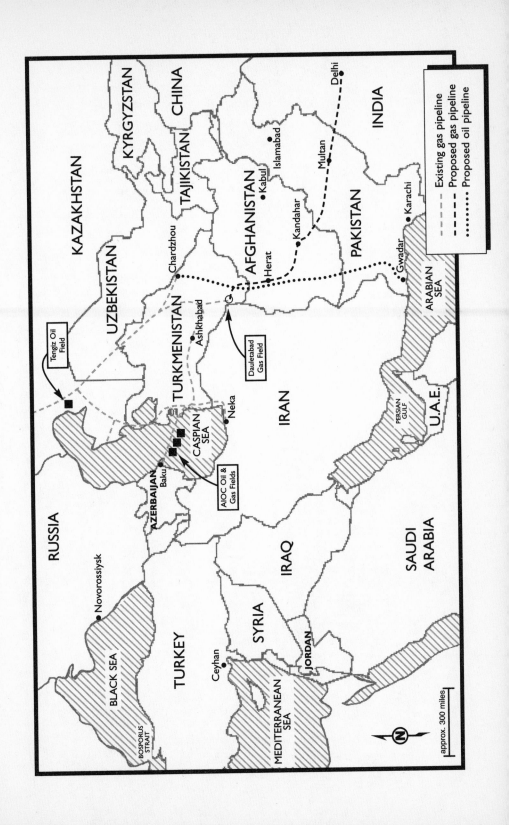

THE PIPELINES

A Chance to Clear the Path

Construction of our proposed pipeline cannot begin until a recognized government is in place that has the confidence of governments, lenders and our company.

—JOHN J. MARESCA, former Unocal Corp. vice president

IMAGINE A LAKE CLOSE TO THE SIZE OF CALIFORNIA AND similar in shape. You have just pictured the Caspian Sea of Central Asia, the largest inland body of water in the world. Buried beneath its seabed, and the former Soviet republics that ring it, is a trove of hydrocarbons so rich and vast that it rivals the oil and gas deposits found in Alaska and the North Sea, and possibly even Saudi Arabia.[1] Trillions of dollars in black gold wait to be mined there. The presence of blubbery seals in its tideless, but somewhat salty, waters has led some scientists to believe the lake was once linked to the Arctic Ocean. But now it has no natural outlet to any ocean.

And therein lies the problem with the Caspian's legendary untapped reserves: they're landlocked—and essentially worthless until moved. Exporting them to energy-hungry markets, particularly those of South and East Asia, is the trick.

Enter pipelines.

The pipeline infrastructure in the region had been dominated by a Soviet-era system designed to bring oil to the Moscow area. Lines tend to head north and west from the Caspian. A consortium of U.S. and foreign oil companies recently completed a pipeline from the northern Caspian east to a Russian port in the Black Sea. But from there, the crude has to be moved by tankers through the narrow Bosporus Strait, then out to the Mediterranean Sea. To bypass the Bosporus bottleneck, another consortium plans to build a Caspian pipeline directly to a Mediterranean port in Turkey. The shortcoming of both pipelines is that they run east-west and serve chiefly the European market, which is not only already supplied by numerous competitors, but also growing slowly. Energy demand in South and East Asia, in contrast, is soaring. And that makes a southern pipeline, running from the Caspian Basin to the Indian Ocean, more attractive. One potential route is across Iran, but sanctions foreclose that option to U.S. companies.

That leaves Afghanistan.

A route through Afghanistan, and on south through Pakistan to its coastline, is the shortest to the sea, where tankers could ship oil to hot Asian-Pacific markets. It also has the fewest technical obstacles, making it the cheapest in terms of transporting Caspian crude. The World Bank, in a study done last decade, found that a trans-Afghanistan pipeline would provide more favorable "netback" values to Caspian oil producers than alternative routes.[2] Netback, simply put, is the price producers receive for oil or gas at the wellhead after backing out all the transportation costs. For a producer in oil-rich western Kazakhstan, for example, the all-important netback value would increase by more than $1 a barrel by going south to Asia, as opposed to going west to the Mediterranean and Europe via the Black Sea, according to the World Bank's analysis of a trans-Afghan oil pipeline project proposed by Unocal Corp.[3]

Capacity is another plus. Even with the additional Mediterranean pipelines, Caspian oil producers are not expected to have enough total capacity to transport all the reserves anticipated to flow from the region in the future. A southern route through Afghanistan would provide "a sort of pressure-relief valve" to the south of the Caspian Basin, as one Chevron Corp. executive put it.[4] Chevron, which now has longtime board member and Caspian-policy expert Condoleezza Rice in the West Wing, is developing huge reserves in Kazakhstan. With its recent Texaco merger, it is far and away the Caspian's biggest producer and investor.[5]

The Game Plan

Unocal anticipated that four or five pipelines would eventually be needed to handle the volume from the region.[6] The giant oil producer, which also specializes in pipelines, but is best known for its Union 76 gas stations, proposed an initial 1,040-mile-long crude oil pipeline that would start near the town of Chardzhou in northeastern Turkmenistan—where it would gather oil from existing pipeline infrastructure there and in Kazakhstan, Uzbekistan, and Russia—and drop almost straight south through the western sections of Afghanistan and Pakistan to the port of Gwadar on the Arabian Sea, where an export terminal would be built to load the oil onto tankers bound for Asia and other world markets. The Central Asia Oil Pipeline, or CAOP, would use a forty-two-inch-diameter pipe capable of moving a million barrels of oil a day—about a fourth of the oil that Central Asia is projected to be capable of exporting by 2010. The estimated cost of the megaproject, which would be similar in scope to the Trans-Alaska Pipeline, would be about $2.5 billion.[7]

Unocal also proposed laying a natural gas pipeline across Afghanistan. The 790-mile-long Central Asia Gas Pipeline, dubbed CentGas, would originate at the Turkmenistan-Afghanistan border, and extend south through Afghanistan's western territory along the old Herat-to-Kandahar highway—which the Bush administration has committed to rebuild, having already pledged $80 million for its construction. From there, the forty-eight-inch-diameter pipeline, which would carry gas at a rate of up to 2 billion cubic feet a day, would cut southeast across Pakistan's border in the vicinity of Quetta, and connect to that country's gas-distribution grid in Multan. Estimated cost: $1.9 billion. A proposed 400-mile extension to India would move gas to the power-starved New Delhi area, adding about $600 million to the price tag. On the other end, a 105-mile extension financed by Turkmenistan would link the pipeline from Afghanistan to the vast Dauletabad gas field in southeastern Turkmenistan.[8]

In 1997, Unocal signed up a large group of international companies to develop the gas pipeline. It initially took a 46.5 percent stake in the CentGas project, handing off development management to a subsidiary, and later increased its stake to a majority share of 54.1 percent. It gave minority stakes to Japan's Itochu Oil Exploration Co., Japan's Indonesia Petroleum Ltd., South Korea's Hyundai Engineering & Construction Co., and Pakistan's Crescent Group, as well as Turkmenistan's government. It reserved a 10 percent cut for Russia's RAO Gazprom, but the natural gas conglomerate did not bite, viewing the project as a threat at the time. Unocal's main partner in the deal, however, was Saudi Arabia's mysterious Delta Oil Co. Ltd., which held a 15 percent equity stake.[9]

The energy giant heralded its trophy project as "the foundation for a new commerce corridor for the region, often referred to as the Silk Road for the 21st century."[10]

Both pipeline proposals had the blessing of the governments of Turkmenistan and Pakistan. Just one thing stood in the way: Afghanistan's ruling Taliban militia, which only a handful of countries, among them Pakistan and Saudi Arabia, formally recognized as the official government of Afghanistan. Unocal couldn't negotiate a contract with an unrecognized government, even if the radical Taliban clerics were amenable to the idea, nor could it obtain international commitments to fund and underwrite the costly project. "Construction of our proposed pipeline cannot begin until a recognized government is in place that has the confidence of governments, lenders and our company," John J. "Jack" Maresca, Unocal's then vice president of international relations, told Congress in 1998.[11]

Unocal executives solicited export-credit agencies and multinational-lending groups like the World Bank, but were told that, while the pipeline projects were feasible, they couldn't get backing until an internationally recognized government was established in Afghanistan.[12] Commercial banks, which rarely make big loans for long-term projects in unproven, unstable markets, were complete nonstarters. Without debt financing for the projects, the rates of return required by equity investors for the perceived risk of an otherwise unfundable project would force pipeline tariffs higher—resulting in either lower netback values for producers or higher prices for consumers. In other words, it was international financing or nothing. And that wasn't going to materialize unless the U.S. and the United Nations recognized the Taliban.

So $7 billion-in-sales Unocal turned to Washington for help, hiring Maresca and others to lobby on behalf of its trans-Afghan pipelines.

Maresca knows Caspian politics. A State Department official in the first Bush administration, he had worked closely with the government of hydrocarbon-engorged Azerbaijan, where Unocal has been active since 1991, when the country declared its independence from Russia. He is close to Richard L. Armitage, the deputy secretary of state who was one of the biggest voices in the Bush administration arguing for the overthrow of the Taliban via Northern Alliance proxy forces. Armitage, part of Bush's war cabinet, is past cochairman of the U.S.-Azerbaijan Chamber of Commerce, which promotes investment in the oil-rich Caspian country. He urged the Clinton administration to get Russia to butt out of Azerbaijani economic affairs, allowing Unocal and other U.S. oil producers to get a better foothold there, as detailed later in Chapter 10.

What's more, both Armitage and Maresca, a Yale alumnus like Bush and his father, lobbied to have restrictions on U.S. economic aid to Azerbaijan repealed. The Clinton administration left the 1992 ban in place, but President Bush, with help from a key oil ally in the Senate, has quietly lifted it, citing the war on terrorism. Armitage, who also worked for the first Bush administration, served on the Washington-based Azerbaijan chamber's board with executives from Chevron and Unocal, before resigning in early 2001. Vice President Dick Cheney also resigned as a chamber officer when he rejoined the federal government.[13] Cheney headed Halliburton Co., a Dallas-based oil services firm with major contracts, including ones involving pipeline construction, in Azerbaijan and other Caspian states.

Playing to the Taliban

Joining Unocal's Maresca in the Washington lobbying effort was Zalmay M. Khalilzad (pronounced ha-LEEL-zod). He was another old Bush hand—the "Zal" mentioned by the president in his October 2002 remarks on regime change in Afghanistan, and the same aide who is now coordinating regime change in Iraq. As a Unocal consultant, he, too, appeared on Capitol Hill to testify in support of the pipelines. The Afghan native also penned articles to promote them. At least initially, he called for the U.S. to engage, rather than isolate, the Taliban, and offer support for "economic reconstruction" projects—namely, the pipelines—as an incentive for them to reform their draconian ways.

"We should be willing to offer recognition and humanitarian assistance and to promote international economic reconstruction," Khalilzad wrote in the *Washington Post* in late 1996. "We should use as a positive incentive the benefits that will accrue to Afghanistan from the construction of oil and gas pipelines across its territory."[14]

He argued the following year in an article for the *Journal of International Affairs* that the "Taliban seem to be in the strongest position" of all the warring factions in Afghanistan to establish a single authoritative government that could be recognized by the U.S.[15] Though he knew that might mollify some of the international lenders' concerns about "instability," if recognition were to happen, he also stated that the Taliban mullahs would have to "establish a government that is broadly acceptable to various ethnic groups"—particularly ones in the north, where opposition was greatest—and improve their medieval human rights record, which was particularly abysmal regarding women. Otherwise, all bets were off for the pipeline projects, which Khalilzad noted would be developed and managed by a U.S. company: "An American company, Unocal, in partnership with the Saudi firm Delta Oil, announced plans for building two pipelines, one for oil and one for gas, to bring Central Asian gas and oil to markets through Afghanistan."[16]

Though the Taliban were the only option at the time in Kabul, there was no denying the group was a hard sell politically and diplomatically back here, and would need a serious makeover to earn Washington's recognition—a critical imprimatur for securing institutional financing for the pipelines.

So Unocal, with help from the well-educated and urbane Khalilzad, played Pygmalion, flying the Taliban troglodytes to America in the hope that some exposure to Western culture would soften their hard Islamic line. First stop: Houston, where Unocal's Central Asian operations are based.

In December 1997, company officials led by Vice President Marty F. Miller, the point man for the pipelines, welcomed eight bearded men in flowing robes to Unocal's modern glass office building in Sugar Land, Texas, just west of Houston. The Taliban delegation—which included one-eyed foreign minister at the time, Mullah Mohammed Ghaus, and minister for mines and industry, Ahmed Jan—was shuttled to NASA headquarters and the Houston zoo for tours. The Talibs were also heli-coptered to Unocal oil rigs in the Gulf of Mexico. No visit to America, of course, would be complete without a trip to the mall, where the mul-lahs spent several hours shopping. At a Target store, they went on a spree, stocking up on toiletries, such as toothpaste, combs, and soap—no doubt to the delight of their hosts, who paid for the excursion.[17]

Unocal spared no expense, putting the guests up at a five-star hotel in Houston during their four-day visit. One night featured a swanky dinner party at executive Miller's mansion,[18] where the mullahs beheld his swimming pool and Christmas tree—oddities in war-torn, Islamic Afghanistan.[19]

Khalilzad helped Unocal entertain the Afghan visitors during their Houston stay.[20]

The company then whisked them off to Omaha, Nebraska, where they spent two days at the University of Nebraska's commuter campus.[21] There, they hooked up with Thomas E. Gouttierre, director of the university's Center for Afghanistan Studies, which had begun heavily promoting the trans-Afghan pipelines after receiving a nearly $1 million grant from Unocal.[22] Professor Gouttierre, who has testified in Congress in support of the pipelines, alongside his old pal Khalilzad, took his turn at feting the ruling Afghan mullahs. "It was part of an effort to show them what America looks like," said Gouttierre, who has lived in Afghanistan. "Also to have them understand that people in America could get along even with women."[23]

Alas, the American experience did not rub off. The last stop on the Taliban delegation's tour was a high-level meeting in Washington that Unocal had arranged with President Clinton's assistant secretary of state for South Asia and other diplomats.[24] It was a golden chance for the Taliban leaders to repair their image—and ask for recognition, which they did. But when officials brought up their strict Islamic laws treating women and ethnic and religious minorities as second-class citizens, they practically drew back bloody stumps.

"This is God's law. This is the way it's supposed to be," the mullahs bellowed. "Leave us alone."[25]

Even the charming Khalilzad's gentle guidance concerning their treatment of women was rebuffed over dinner at the luxury Houston hotel.[26]

Undaunted, Unocal worked through State Department channels to arrange for a return trip in the summer of 1999, this time sending Taliban officials, as well as opposing Afghan parties, on a sight-seeing tour that included Mount Rushmore and spanned five weeks. The University of Nebraska, flush with Unocal and State Department grant money, picked up the tab. Gouttierre, fluent in Dari, hosted parties for them in Omaha. On July 9, 1999, he gathered the leaders of the Taliban regime and opposition factions in a room for two hours, and tape-recorded the debate for one of several classified briefings he filed with the State Department, which was closely monitoring continued civil unrest in Afghanistan.[27] Unocal, for its part, wanted to open up dialogue with opposition leaders in the north, who later formed the Northern Alliance, as a hedge against the Taliban, still reluctant to play the game. It was not their first encounter. In July 1997, Miller had visited their stronghold in Mazar-e-Sharif, Afghanistan,[28] in addition to the Taliban headquarters in the south,[29] to help win their support. And while Unocal gave the Taliban gifts, such as a fax machine and a generator,[30] it also handed out medical supplies to other factions in a bid to win friends on all sides.[31]

Working through the University of Nebraska center, moreover, Unocal sponsored a program to train Afghans in the skills necessary for pipeline construction.[32] Some 450 men were taught pipe-fitting and welding, as well as carpentry and wiring, at a school in Kandahar, the southern Afghan city on the gas pipeline route. Using the money from Unocal's generous grant, the center rebuilt more than a dozen one-story buildings on a fifty-six-acre plot there.[33]

Unocal got help from other think tanks it has supported as well. One is the Central Asia-Caucasus Institute, run by S. Frederick Starr, who has championed federal underwriting of Caspian oil projects and testified on Capitol Hill with Unocal official Maresca. The Washington-based institute's corporate sponsors include both Unocal and Chevron.[34] The two energy giants, incidentally, are heavy contributors to the Republican Party and were major donors to the Bush-Cheney campaign. Starr, it turns out, sits with both Khalilzad and Gouttierre on the international advisory board of the Washington-based Afghanistan Foundation (recently renamed the Afghanistan-America Foundation), which is a big booster for American investment in Afghan reconstruction projects.[35] Khalilzad, one of the foundation's charter directors, drafted its position paper urging Washington to help Kabul form a broad-based, stable government to lay the groundwork for a "valuable" energy corridor through Afghanistan, among other things.[36]

Even if Unocal could have succeeded in getting the Taliban recognized, there was no guarantee they would have signed a contract with Unocal's consortium. Taliban leader Mullah Mohammed Omar, now a fugitive, played Unocal off Argentina oil giant Bridas Corp., a BP Amoco partner, which was also bidding for the gas project. Omar refused to give a firm commitment, holding out for higher transfer fees. Unocal had offered 15 cents per 1,000 cubic feet for the pipeline across his territory, but Omar wanted more.[37]

At that point, Unocal figured it needed better diplomatic channels in the Pakistani capital of Islamabad, which had given birth to the Taliban and maintained some control over the group. The Taliban kept representatives there. Islamabad at the time was fully on board Unocal's pipeline projects, and had even sent an intelligence agent with the Taliban on the Houston trip,[38] but the company needed officials there to massage the Taliban more. So it added Robert Bigger Oakley, former U.S. ambassador to Pakistan during the first Bush administration. Unocal hired him as a consultant after he left government.[39] Texas-born Oakley is also an Afghanistan-America Foundation adviser.[40]

The company added an Afghan native by the name of Hamid Karzai to its payroll[41] to help establish dialogue with former Afghan leaders who might someday be in a position to replace the Taliban. Karzai, a one-time Kabul diplomat who is close to Khalilzad, moved to Quetta, Pakistan, during the Afghan civil wars of the early and mid-1990s. A moderate, he thought the Taliban clerics were too harsh in their application of Islamic law, though he supported their leadership in the beginning. It was Karzai, in fact, who helped arrange the 1999 powwow at the University of Nebraska between the Taliban and the opposing Afghan parties, reveals Raheem Yaseer, assistant director of the Center for Afghanistan Studies there. He told me that Karzai had visited the center "several times" last decade. "He initiated that meeting here" in 1999, said Yaseer, an Afghan native who met several times last year with Karzai, the new U.S.-backed leader of Afghanistan. "He picked up a group of people from various parts of Afghanistan and sent them to Omaha for dialogue, which was conducted here for five weeks."[42] INS records show Karzai entered America twice on business in 1999, the second time coinciding with the Taliban's visit to the University of Nebraska and Mount Rushmore.[43] He also testified in Congress in 2000, and visited Washington several times before that, immigration records show, including in late 1997 when the Taliban clerics were making a bad impression at the State Department.

Unocal even retained the help of international power broker Henry A. Kissinger, who early on made a trip to the United Nations in New York on behalf of the gas pipeline deal.[44] Bush last year named the eighty-year-old former secretary of state, interestingly enough, to head the special commission investigating the September 11 attacks. Kissinger, who runs an international consulting firm, soon stepped down, however, citing a reluctance to publicly disclose his client list.

All in all, it was an impressive lobbying campaign.

But in August 1998, Unocal reluctantly shelved its plans for both oil and gas pipelines after the Clinton administration pumped about sixty cruise missiles into largely empty al-Qaida terrorist training camps in Afghanistan in retaliation for the U.S. embassy bombings in Africa. The El Segundo, California–based company made the announcement the next day.[45] The strikes made it obvious the Taliban were, at a minimum, sheltering Osama bin Laden, meaning Unocal could kiss good-bye any hopes of project financing. And certainly no international insurer would underwrite multibillion-dollar pipelines that could be blown up by missiles or by terrorists as payback for such strikes. More, the strikes made the Taliban even bigger pariahs in the court of world opinion, turning Unocal's past courtship of them into a mini public relations disaster. Disengaging the Taliban, at least for the time being, was a no-brainer.

But then the oil-friendly Bush administration took power, and suddenly, the Taliban were reengaged, though this time not so gently. Bush officials firmly reminded them that sanctions against Afghanistan would not be lifted until they complied with UN resolutions to improve human rights and part company with terrorists.

Back in the Game

On August 2, 2001, senior State Department official Christina Rocca, a former veteran CIA agent, met in Islamabad with the Taliban ambassador to Pakistan, Abdul Salam Zaeef.[46] As Bush's assistant secretary of state for South Asia, Rocca is the key emissary for White House policy on Pakistan and Afghanistan. She is also a former top aide to GOP Senator Sam Brownback, one of Capitol Hill's biggest Caspian oil boosters, as well as biggest recipients of campaign cash from big oil, including Unocal. Brownback cofounded the Silk Road Caucus to promote U.S. business investment in the Caspian Basin, and has hosted hearings for Unocal executives and consultants such as Khalilzad.

On September 12, 2001, the day after the al-Qaida attacks on New York and Washington, D.C., Deputy Secretary of State Armitage—Rocca's boss, who also happens to be a former Caspian oil lobbyist—met at Foggy Bottom with the Pakistani intelligence chief who put the Taliban in power, Gen. Mahmoud Ahmad.[47] Ahmad wasn't flown in after the September 11 attacks. He had been in town the previous week, meeting with other top Bush administration officials. The full agenda and list of participants are still shrouded in secrecy, but this much is known: Armitage asked that Pakistan sever ties with the Taliban.

Then, two days after Bush ordered U.S. forces to begin bombing Taliban targets in Afghanistan, his ambassador to Pakistan at the time paid a visit to Pakistan's oil minister. Diplomat Wendy Chamberlin—who was a key Mideast adviser on former President Bush's National Security Council during the Gulf War—sat down in Islamabad with Usman Aminuddin, Pakistan's federal minister for petroleum and natural resources, to discuss "matters pertaining to Pakistan-U.S. cooperation in the oil and gas sector," according to Pakistan's official news agency.[48] The dust was still settling at Ground Zero from a massive attack that traces back to Pakistan as much as Afghanistan, yet terrorism was not on Chamberlin's agenda that day. In their October 9, 2001, meeting, she and Aminuddin discussed, among other energy issues, reviving the proposed trans-Afghanistan gas pipeline, which would connect near bankrupt Pakistan, as well as Afghanistan, to the Caspian fortune. Aminuddin remarked that "this project opens up new avenues of multidimensional regional cooperation, particularly in view of the recent geopolitical developments in the region," according to an English-language newspaper published by the Pakistani government in Peshawar, a city near the Afghan border.[49]

The same oil minister would, one year later, meet in the "liberated" Afghan capital of Kabul with newly installed President Karzai's own oil minister and World Bank officials to discuss, in earnest, both gas and oil pipelines.[50]

MISSION CREEP
Liberating and Rebuilding Afghanistan

We went into Afghanistan to free people.

—PRESIDENT BUSH

BY THE WINTER OF 2000, ZAL KHALILZAD HAD HAD A CHANGE of heart. Seeing that the ruling Taliban mullahs were yoked to Osama bin Laden, the trans-Afghan pipeline adviser concluded that simply "engaging" (Washington-speak for reprogramming) them would not work. The radical Islamic clerics had proved too intransigent—making it plain that, for all his lobbying, Washington would never help underwrite an energy corridor through Afghanistan with the mullahs in power. The "valuable corridor," as the Afghan-born Khalilzad called it, would benefit not only his energy clients, but also his impoverished former countrymen. So he argued instead for "more muscular forms of pressure to influence" the ruling clerics. "Washington must weaken the Taliban" by backing anti-Taliban forces such as the Northern Alliance. "The United States should offer existing foes of the Taliban assistance," Khalilzad asserted in a long article in the *Washington Quarterly*, an influential foreign policy journal.[1]

In a stunning reversal, he pronounced the Taliban a "rogue regime" for refusing to turn over outlaw bin Laden and restore human rights, and he chided "pragmatists" among the Clinton diplomatic corps for thinking the Taliban could be rehabilitated. "Some administration officials tacitly favored the group when it emerged between 1994 and 1995, underestimating the threat it posed to regional stability and to U.S. interests," he said.[2]

Of course, Khalilzad was one of the very pragmatists he condemned. Four years earlier, after the Taliban seized Kabul in September 1996, he had argued publicly for reaching out to the militia's leaders—even vouching that they were not "hostile" to the U.S.[3] Three years earlier, the energy analyst had helped his client Unocal wine and dine Taliban leaders in Houston.

And just two years earlier, he had told a Senate Foreign Relations Subcommittee that the Taliban and other Afghans "have not been involved in terrorism," and couldn't really be held responsible for the actions of al-Qaida's mostly Arab terrorists, who had moved there from Saudi Arabia.[4] "The Taliban just inherited some of these people," he testified, and in effect they were bribed to look the other way. "Bin Laden, in my judgment, is a source of finance."[5] If the U.S. could offer an alternative source of finance in the form of support for "economic reconstruction" projects, such as the proposed oil and gas pipelines, perhaps the Taliban would shun bin Laden, Khalilzad suggested to the panel's powerful chairman, Republican Senator Sam Brownback, who listened intently.

But in the *Washington Quarterly* piece he wrote during the 2000 presidential campaign, Khalilzad portrayed the Taliban as the locus of evil and the lifeblood of al-Qaida. He argued that the U.S. should focus more on the Taliban's "radical leadership" than on bin Laden, even going so far as to pooh-pooh bin Laden's power to hurt America on his own. "Clearly, bin Laden is a dangerous terrorist who must be captured and prosecuted," Khalilzad wrote. "Yet the U.S. focus on him, rather than on the trend he represents, is misguided. Bin Laden is a wealthy, capable and dedicated foe, but hardly an evil genius or charismatic leader who single-handedly is waging war against the United States."[6]

He argued, "To stop bin Laden's network, Washington must gain the support of the governments that host it. As long as the Taliban's radical leadership remains in power, however, a true crackdown is not likely."[7]

In other words, target the Taliban first, then bin Laden. Until the Taliban are replaced, he added, Afghanistan will continue to be plagued by the "instability" that has scared off oil investors and international lenders.

"The importance of Afghanistan may grow in the coming years, as Central Asia's oil and gas reserves, which are estimated to rival those of the North Sea, begin to play a major role in the world energy market," Khalilzad stressed. "Afghanistan could prove a valuable corridor for this energy as well as for access to markets in Central Asia. In addition, Afghanistan can serve as a trade link between Central and South Asia."[8] He was describing Senator Brownback's and Unocal's vision for a new Silk Road for the twenty-first century.

"Instead," Khalilzad continued, "Afghanistan has proven an obstacle to the development of this region, as outside investors fear the strife that emanates from Afghanistan."[9] Which is to say, Afghanistan's government—the Taliban—was an obstacle to the proposed pipelines, and it had to be removed. September 11 offered a convenient pretext for such action.

The next year, not long after he was sworn in as president, Bush made Khalilzad one of his top White House assistants—and his Afghan adviser's plan effectively became policy after the September 11 attacks. As the National Security Council's senior director for Southwest Asia, the Near East, and North Africa, Khalilzad reports directly to National Security Adviser Rice, whose decade of work on Caspian issues for Chevron so endeared her to its board of directors that it named an oil tanker after her. After Afghanistan was "liberated" from the Taliban, Bush appointed Khalilzad special envoy to America's temporarily adopted country. He reports to the president through Secretary of State Colin Powell, but he will continue to also report to Rice, Bush's closest adviser in the war on terrorism.

Parts of Khalilzad's plan were already being put into effect before the war. The State Department, at the behest of Deputy Secretary Armitage, lifted the previous administration's objections to arming the Northern Alliance in the spring. And by September, Rice had signed off on a plan that would give the CIA as much as $200 million a year to arm the anti-Taliban forces. She drafted a presidential directive for Bush to sign September 10, 2001.[10] What's more, Armitage in the summer said the administration had decided to provide $124 million to feed the Afghan "refugees who are victims of mismanagement and bad government of the Taliban."[11] The humanitarian aid package, which Armitage described as "very robust," reflected another component of Khalilzad's strategy. "Humanitarian aid should be used to weaken the Taliban," he wrote in the *Washington Quarterly*, by channeling it to troubled ethnic communities through the Taliban's opponents.[12]

Then al-Qaida struck New York and Washington, and the White House had to decide how to respond. As Bush and his advisers put their heads together in those first four long weeks of National Security Council meetings in the White House and at Camp David, their talk focused almost exclusively on taking out the Taliban. Practically from the start, it was decided that U.S. retaliation had to be broader than punishing the al-Qaida perpetrators. The mission had to also include overthrowing the Taliban regime harboring them. Armitage, Rice, and Vice President Cheney recommended strengthening the Northern Alliance, and Bush agreed. The president signed off on a plan to forward-deploy CIA operatives with bundles of cash to make sure the anti-Taliban forces were supplied with enough food and weapons to advance on dug-in Taliban forces. U.S. bombers would then take out Taliban command-and-control assets, and soften their military positions along the northern front. In agreeing with the broader plan, Bush remarked, "This is an opportunity. We have to think of this as an opportunity."[13] Borrowing a page from Khalilzad's playbook for undermining local support for the Taliban, the president also ordered humanitarian airdrops of food rations, medicine, and clothing to coincide with bombing missions over Afghanistan, cautioning that supply drop points should avoid Taliban strongholds. Ousting the Taliban was the first priority. The anti-Taliban hawks ruled the day.

Bin Laden on a Platter?

Weeks after the al-Qaida attacks, Bush summarily rejected an offer from the Taliban to turn bin Laden over to a neutral third country, and pressed ahead with plans to bomb Taliban targets in Afghanistan. The president can be forgiven for not trusting the Taliban to keep their word. They had played games in the past. He figured, reasonably, that they were more than likely stalling for time, knowing full well that U.S. aircraft carriers and warplanes were headed toward Afghanistan. The offer also fell short of Bush's earlier demand to turn bin Laden over to U.S. authorities.

But it turns out that Talib offers of giving up bin Laden were both more numerous and more serious than the White House has let on.

Several months before al-Qaida struck America, a Taliban envoy by the name of Rahmatullah Hashimi boarded a plane in Afghanistan bound for Washington. The official arrived bearing a gift carpet for Bush, and a letter from Taliban chief Mohammed Omar proposing ways to bring bin Laden to justice.[14] And up until one month before the attacks, Taliban officials held secret talks with State Department officials over bin Laden's fate; they met in Islamabad, Pakistan, where Taliban delegates kept offices at the time. Taliban offers to give up the al-Qaida overlord were repeatedly rebuffed, however. One overture proposing bin Laden be turned over to a panel of three Islamic jurists—two picked by Afghanistan and Saudi Arabia, and one by the U.S.—was dismissed out of hand. But the Talibs countered that they would settle for only one Islamic jurist on the panel, a source close to the Taliban leadership told the *Washington Post*. The paper also quoted a former CIA station chief, who oversaw U.S. covert operations in Afghanistan in the 1980s, as saying that he had "no doubts they [the Taliban] wanted to get rid of" bin Laden, and that Washington was missing the Taliban's signals. Their counterproposal, which still let bin Laden avoid immediate U.S. custody, also was rejected.[15] Bush, in his September 20, 2001, speech before Congress, demanded the Taliban turn bin Laden over to "United States authorities."

But Bush official Christina Rocca was less particular about where bin Laden was brought to justice in her August 2, 2001, meeting with the Taliban ambassador to Pakistan. The assistant secretary of state for South Asia said she told Abdul Salam Zaeef, among other things, that United Nations sanctions against the regime might be dropped if it "simply complied with the [UN] resolutions by closing terrorist training camps and sending Osama bin Laden to a country where he can be brought to justice."[16]

Before joining the Bush administration, Rocca worked in the Senate as Brownback's chief foreign policy adviser. The Kansas Republican, influential head of the Senate Foreign Relations Subcommittee covering Central and South Asian issues, is a fan of the trans-Afghan pipeline projects, following in the footsteps of his predecessor on the panel, ex-Senator Hank Brown (R-Colo.), who once let Unocal fly in Afghan speakers for one of his hearings.[17] Brownback is also closely tied to former Caspian oil lobbyist Armitage, Rocca's new boss. Rocca helped her old boss provide Unocal executives and consultants, including Khalilzad, Gouttierre, and Karzai, with a public forum before his committee. Before advising Brownback, she served fifteen years in the CIA working, among other things, as staff operations officer for the Directorate of Operations. In the 1980s, she helped coordinate secret deliveries of Stinger missiles to the Afghan mujahideen.[18] The shoulder-fired rockets helped the U.S.-backed holy warriors—who included a young, wealthy Saudi mercenary named Osama bin Laden—drive the Soviet invaders out of Afghanistan. Khalilzad was the State Department official at the time who convinced the White House to arm the mujahideen with Stingers.

Whether the Bush administration sent the Taliban mixed messages regarding bin Laden's extradition is open for debate. It is also anyone's guess whether the Taliban would have delivered on promises to hand him over (although an aide to Omar's foreign minister, who's in U.S. custody, now says they wanted to get rid of bin Laden in July 2001 after learning he was planning a "huge attack" on targets inside America—information he claims to have passed on to a U.S. consular official in Pakistan and UN officials in Kabul).[19]

But one thing is clear: Bush didn't wait to find out if the Taliban would turn over bin Laden. On October 7, he ordered U.S. forces to start bombing Taliban targets, and he continued the campaign even as the Taliban tendered one last, desperate proposal to surrender bin Laden. "The Taliban will pay a price," the president said in his televised address that day from the White House.

"At the same time, the oppressed people of Afghanistan will know the generosity of America and our allies," he was quick to note. "As we strike military targets, we will also drop food, medicine and supplies to the starving and suffering men and women and children of Afghanistan."

In that historic 954-word address, Bush did not mention Osama bin Laden once, a switch from his earlier congressional speech on the war. And he cited the Taliban twice as many times as al-Qaida.

The president played down bin Laden and al-Qaida even more over the next few months as the mission crept into broader and broader areas— from government overthrow to nation building to occupation. Amazingly, Bush and his speechwriters and political handlers managed to reframe the September 11 conflict as one between the "oppressive" Taliban regime and the Afghan people, as much as one between al-Qaida and the American people. Given that the Washington press corps for the most part have gone along with the spin, it's a rhetorical feat of Orwellian distinction.

Losing Osama

After the Afghanistan capital of Kabul and the Taliban stronghold of Kandahar fell to U.S.-backed anti-Taliban forces, Bush actually began boasting of the "success" of the military strategy, even though bin Laden had survived. On December 28, he held a press conference at his Prairie

Chapel Ranch in Crawford, Texas, to do a bit of chest puffing for reporters. He brought along Gen. Tommy Ray Franks, the commander who led the Afghanistan campaign. Franks grew up in Bush's hometown of Midland, Texas, which is located in the heart of the vast fifty-four-county Permian Basin of West Texas, a geological region producing about 70 percent of the oil in Texas. In fact, Franks went to Midland Lee High School with First Lady Laura Bush. The president strutted out to the microphones in his cowboy boots and took some wood to naysayers.

"You know, a couple of months ago, a lot of people said that this administration and our military really weren't sure what we were doing," he said in his breathy drawl. "But I had confidence all along . . . confidence in the success of what we set out to do."

He then turned the mikes over to Franks. Oddly, the four-star general seemed more interested in talking about the political, rather than the military, side of the mission. He praised the nation-building effort already under way, particularly the installation of Hamid Karzai as interim leader of post-Taliban Afghanistan.

"We also had a chance to attend the installation ceremony in Afghanistan, where we saw Mr. Karzai and members of that team form an interim government in Afghanistan, where for the first time in decades more than 26 million people will have an opportunity to have their way represented in that government," Franks said, apparently not realizing such news would be cold comfort to the 285 million people in America who remain in bin Laden's crosshairs.

Then a reporter dared to ask Bush the obvious question: "What's your reaction to bin Laden's tape?" The videotape, aired in full the previous day by the Arab television network Al-Jazeera, showed a gaunt bin Laden wearing green combat fatigues and speaking outdoors in rugged terrain. He praised the hijackers for causing economic losses of "a trillion dollars," and he threatened to "hit the U.S. economy" again. It convinced U.S. intelligence officials that the September 11 mastermind had survived at least the initial U.S. bombing raids.[20]

"Oh, the tape, yeah. I didn't watch it all," Bush frostily replied. "I saw snippets of it on TV. You know, it's—who knows when it was made?

"Secondly, he is not escaping us. I mean, this is a guy who three months ago was in control of a country," Bush insisted, as if the battle were over geography and not a network of nomadic terrorists. "Now he's maybe in control of a cave.

"He's on the run. Listen, a while ago I said to the American people, our objective is more than bin Laden. But one of the things for certain is we're going to get him running and keep him running, and bring him to justice. And that's what's happening. He's on the run, if he's running at all. So we don't know whether he's in a cave with the door shut, or a cave with the door open. We just don't know. There's all kinds of reports and all kinds of speculation.

"But one thing we know is that he's not in charge of Afghanistan anymore," Bush said.

Later, the president emphasized that a large part of the remaining mission in Afghanistan "is to make sure that Afghanistan is a stable country." He did not describe the efforts to take out bin Laden and his top henchmen.

On January 5, Bush traveled to Oregon to give a speech at Parkrose High School in Portland. In his progress report on the war, he trumpeted the removal of the "repressive" Taliban, as if their treatment of Afghans had anything to do with September 11 and Americans' ongoing nightmare.

"We led a coalition that liberated women and children," Bush gushed. "A coalition that brought down a government that was so incredibly repressive it's hard for those of us who live in America to understand.

"Some of my finest memories thus far of this war against terror was the joy that came on people's faces when they realized that the Taliban would no longer hold them hostage to an outdated, outmoded, dictatorial point of view," Bush added, apparently forgetting the still-tortured faces of the family members who lost loved ones because of al-Qaida's leaders, more than two-thirds of whom are still at large.

He also praised the humanitarian part of the mission in Afghanistan.

"While we dropped bombs, we also dropped food and medicine and clothing to make sure that the innocents in Afghanistan could survive the brutal winter in that part of the world," Bush said, failing to explain why humanitarian aid, while noble and compassionate, was dispensed *before* the enemy was eradicated, unlike in World War II and other conflicts.

He called the military plan in Afghanistan a "good strategy." Bin Laden got no mention in his 2,842-word speech.

Workers at the Port of New Orleans in Louisiana got the same message from Bush on January 15. "The Taliban no longer rules in Afghanistan," he intoned. "We met that objective, and in doing so, we liberated a group of people that had been terrorized. We liberated women and children."

In that speech, which contained 2,972 words, Bush again found no room for bin Laden, U.S. public enemy no. 1.

On January 17, Bush sat down with NBC News anchor Tom Brokaw in the Oval Office to discuss the war. Astoundingly, he said he wasn't focused on bin Laden. Here's the exchange:

> BROKAW: You ever leave here at night saying to yourself, "OK, Osama bin Laden, where are you now?"
> BUSH: No, I don't, because Osama bin Laden is not my focus. My focus is terror at large.

His State of the Union address two weeks later hit on the same anti-Taliban themes while glossing over the unfinished business of al-Qaida and bin Laden. On January 29, speaking from the House chamber, Bush said the military in Afghanistan, in addition to capturing or killing "thousands of terrorists" and destroying terrorist training camps, "saved a people from starvation, and freed a country from brutal oppression.

"The last time we met in this chamber, the mothers and daughters of Afghanistan were captives in their own homes, forbidden from working or going to school," he said. "Today women are free and are part of Afghanistan's new government.

"The American flag flies again over our embassy in Kabul," he proclaimed, as if any American outside the Beltway even knew—or much cared—that the U.S. embassy in Afghanistan had been closed for more than a decade. Bush then vowed to help rebuild Afghanistan.

The president mentioned *Afghanistan* or *the Afghan people* fourteen times in the speech. Osama bin Laden's name, in contrast, did not come up once. Bush cited *al-Qaida* one time, and only in passing, to recount the Richard Reid shoe-bomb incident.

The bin Laden omission was glaring, and the Washington media, which normally love to flyspeck State of the Union speeches, would have made more of it. But Bush had added three new major enemies to the war on terrorism, effectively shifting the fulcrum of debate even farther from al-Qaida. He claimed that Iraq, Iran, and North Korea, as terror-sponsoring regimes allegedly developing weapons of mass destruction, pose a grave and exigent threat to America and world peace. Left unchecked, this so-called axis of evil could arm terrorists with such weapons, Bush warned.

New Targets

The sudden focus on the three rogue states seemed to come out of nowhere and was largely unexpected. Politics and, once again, commercial interests explain a good part of it, however.

It turns out that, in the case of Iran, the president was just as concerned about the threat the Islamic republic posed to the stability of Afghanistan as to the security of America. The White House decided to put Iran on notice, administration officials told me, after it received reports out of Kabul that Tehran was trying to undermine the new U.S.-backed government in Afghanistan. In particular, the Iranian government was fomenting unrest in the western city of Herat, which is on the proposed route for the gas pipeline. Indeed, some two weeks before Bush's speech, his special Afghan envoy, Khalilzad, had claimed that Tehran was sending units from within the Iranian Revolutionary Guard and other subversive elements, such as Afghans trained in Iran known as Mohammed's Soldiers, across its border to stir up trouble in western Afghanistan. He also said Iran was providing financial support to its favorite factions and warlords, namely Ismail Khan of Herat, in that strategic Afghan region.[21] (Kahn in 2001 returned from Iran to help evict the Taliban, who had seized Herat from him six years earlier.) Khalilzad complained to Gen. Franks at U.S. Central Command about the western incursion.[22] Tehran views a trans-Afghan energy corridor as a threat to its Persian Gulf monopoly. It has discussed with Turkmenistan running its own pipelines south through its territory. The proposed trans-Afghan oil pipeline would also run through Afghanistan's western region, where Tehran is trying to destabilize the new government. The Iranian government also fears growing Pakistani influence in the region. An energy corridor connecting Caspian reserves through Afghanistan to Pakistan would greatly enhance Pakistan's economic and political leverage in the region. By targeting Iran in his speech, Bush was sending a warning to Tehran to cancel its plans not only for development of nuclear weapons, but also for insurrection in western Afghanistan, officials said. The president singled out Iran again for rebuke in this year's State of the Union speech. And his administration recently warned Iran, dominated by Shia Muslims, to stop fomenting unrest among Iraq's Shia majority, and then accused it of sheltering al-Qaida operatives—which, if true, would be remarkable given that al-Qaida is comprised of Sunni Muslims who hail mainly from Sunni-dominated Eygpt, Saudi Arabia and Pakistan.

Meanwhile, targeting Iraq set the stage for a new battlefront, one that involves oil (next to Saudi Arabia, Iraq boasts the world's largest proven reserves). It also provided a hot new topic of debate that has raged in the media ever since. The steady drumbeat over Baghdad—which has been using its oil exports as a weapon to manipulate oil markets—drowned out most criticism of Bush's failure to decapitate the al-Qaida leadership. And Saddam Hussein became a handy fig leaf for the embarrassment of bin Laden's escape, even though the Iraqi dictator's ties to September 11 are tenuous at best. Consider this exchange:

NBC's *MEET THE PRESS* HOST TIM RUSSERT: Do we have any
evidence linking Saddam Hussein or Iraqis to this operation?
CHENEY: No.

Yes, the interview was conducted September 16, 2001. But the administration has managed to come up with only sketchy al-Qaida links since then. And it reportedly has pressured analysts at the CIA and U.S. nuclear weapons research laboratories to cook up reports backing Bush's assertion that Iraq is developing weapons of mass destruction. For example, his allegation last year that Iraq was trying to import hardened aluminum tubing to help enrich uranium for nuclear weapons was viewed as a stretch by the U.S. intelligence community. "Basically, cooked information is working its way into high-level pronouncements, and there's a lot of unhappiness about it in intelligence, especially among analysts at the CIA," said Vincent Cannistraro, the CIA's one-time chief of counterterrorism operations.[23]

When Bush gave his September 20 speech outlining steps for retaliation, he, like Cheney, knew there was no evidence tying Iraq to September 11. That's why he did not finger Iraq. He fingered al-Qaida and bin Laden as the perpetrators. Invading Baghdad was no more the original war mandate than was rebuilding Afghanistan. Or feeding Afghan children. Or freeing Afghan women from the oppression of Taliban clerics. Though Bush expressed sympathy for Afghans in that speech, he never told the American people he would use the U.S. military for such nation building.

Yet a year later, he bragged of meeting these false objectives.

"We went into Afghanistan to free people, because we believe in freedom," Bush said. "We believe every life counts, everybody has worth, everybody matters, whether they live in America or in Afghanistan."[24] He added, "And so we are helping the people to now recover from years of tyranny and oppression."[25]

Despite the White House's demonization of the Taliban and, later, after bin Laden escaped, Saddam Hussein, Americans knew who the real enemy was from the start. A whopping 83 percent of them blamed bin

Laden for the September 11 attacks, according to a Gallup poll taken several days after Washington and New York were hit.[26] Even after the Taliban were ousted, half of Americans said the war could not be successful if bin Laden remains on the loose.[27]

CIA analysts knew who the real enemy was as well. They put bin Laden–buster symbols on each page of the Top Secret briefing booklet distributed to members of Bush's war cabinet four days after the attacks.[28]

Same for the FBI. Bin Laden was, and still is, first on the bureau's list of Most Wanted Terrorists, while Taliban leader Omar never appeared on the list.[29]

Pentagon counterterrorism experts also knew. Officials there told me on the afternoon of September 11 that they were already busy looking at targets to take out bin Laden.[30]

The secretary of state had no doubts, either. "It is becoming clear with each passing hour, with each passing day, that it is the al-Qaida network that is the prime suspect," said Powell just a few days after the attacks. "And all roads lead to the leader of that organization, Osama bin Laden."[31]

Even the commander in chief knew. On September 17 Bush told reporters, "The focus right now is on Osama bin Laden, no question about it. He's the prime suspect and his organization." Then in a fit of bravado, he said he wanted bin Laden "dead or alive." In his September 20 war speech before Congress, moreover, he singled out al-Qaida as the culprit. "Americans are asking, 'Who attacked our country?' The evidence we have gathered all points to a collection of loosely affiliated terrorist organizations known as al-Qaida." Its leader, he went on, is "a person named Osama bin Laden."

It was plain to all, early in the crisis, that bin Laden and his al-Qaida network were the chief targets.

"Our war on terror begins with al-Qaida," Bush declared on September 20. That is what the president told America that night. But that was not the plan.

WAR BY PROXY

Farming Out the Hunt for Osama

America failed to kill or capture any of the al-Qaida
leadership.

—OSAMA BIN LADEN[1]

TESTIFYING BEFORE POLITICIANS IS USUALLY A TENSE AFFAIR
for military brass. But this hearing was different. The country was in the
middle of a very personal war, and there was good news from the
Afghanistan theater—four months after U.S. forces launched Operation
Enduring Freedom. Fortunate for the general, who took his seat at the
witness table in Room 216 of the Senate Hart Office Building, patriotic
giddiness had replaced the usual tension. The only things missing were
the ticker tape and miniature flags. It was a chance for Gen. Tommy
Franks to bask in what everyone was calling a victory. The hearing was
basically an invitation to tick off all the accomplishments—the Taliban
routed out of Kabul and Kandahar, a population liberated from tyranny
and starvation, al-Qaida camps and caves destroyed, relatively few civilian casualties, and even fewer U.S. casualties.

But the fawning senators beat him to it.

"We have seen our armed forces conduct not only combat sorties, but humanitarian food drops, reflecting America's compassion for the suffering Afghan people alongside our determination to bring terrorists to justice," gushed Senator Carl Levin (D-Mich.), then chairman of the Senate Armed Services Committee, in his opening statement. "We have seen small teams of special operations forces serving alongside Afghan opposition forces—twenty-first-century warriors on horseback coordinating attacks and calling in precision airstrikes against Taliban and al-Qaida targets. We've seen precision-guided munitions more often than ever before."

He attributed "the excellence and innovation of our forces in and around Afghanistan" to a "good plan" executed by Franks.

Senator John Warner, the ranking Republican on the committee at the time, echoed Levin's praise, adding that Franks would take his "place in a long line of distinguished senior combat commanders in American military history." He commended the lanky, jug-eared general: "Well done, sir."

"Thank you, sir," said Franks, who ran the Afghan war with his top commanders from the U.S. Central Command headquarters (CentCom) at MacDill Air Force Base near Tampa, Florida.

Senator Mary Landrieu (D-La.) also was impressed with the high-tech show that Franks put on in Afghanistan. "We've won this war with some of the most extraordinary precision weapons," she marveled. Landrieu happens to cochair Brownback's Silk Road Caucus.

Indeed, nearly 60 percent of all the bombs used in Afghanistan were precision guided, compared to about 10 percent during the high-tech Gulf War a decade earlier.[2]

Franks put a finer point on it. "My view is that this has been the most accurate war ever fought in this nation's history," he boasted in his Texas drawl. "I believe that the precision of this effort has been incredible."

Senator Jim Bunning had heard enough.

The no-nonsense Republican from Kentucky let some air out of the room—and Franks's shirt—with a sharp-edged question. If the air strikes were so accurate, and the war was such a success, "Why were so many people able to flee Afghanistan that were al-Qaida and/or Taliban?" he quizzed, not even knowing for sure at the time that bin Laden, the main quarry, had also escaped.

Franks sat there a while with his face flapping before finally admitting that "some have certainly left Afghanistan," crossing the border into Pakistan. But he assured the senator that Pakistan, as a partner in the war on terrorism, would seal off the border and intercept the fleeing al-Qaida enemy.

But Bunning—a Hall of Fame pitcher who way back in September 1993 called Bill Clinton "the most corrupt, the most amoral, the most despicable person I've ever seen in the presidency"—was not mollified.[3]

> BUNNING: I think you've done a good job in Afghanistan as far as the replacement of an illegitimate government with a temporary [one]. And I think the Afghan people are legitimately pleased that that has happened. But I'm not pleased, and I don't think any Americans are pleased that we haven't done a better job on al-Qaida, the terrorist group that attacked the New York Trade Center and planned it and did those things.
>
> FRANKS: Sir—
>
> BUNNING: So I think we're halfway there.
>
> FRANKS: Sir, I agree with you. I think we're halfway there.

It was a stunning admission, but one that was lost in all the White House–generated hoopla over the liberation of Afghanistan and exile of the Taliban's leaders. In so many words, the war's commander was acknowledging that the core mission of bringing to justice the more dangerous al-Qaida leaders—who hatched the September 11 plot and conspired to murder three thousand people—had not been accomplished in the Afghanistan operation.

So what went wrong? Simple: al-Qaida was not the priority going in.

Letting al-Qaida Go

The military strategy that President Bush approved on October 2, 2001, and launched October 7, centered on helping the opposition Northern

Alliance drive the Taliban out of Kabul. There was no early strategy in southern Afghanistan, where bin Laden and other al-Qaida leaders were based, other than to bomb Taliban targets and pump Tomahawk cruise missiles into al-Qaida terrorist training camps—twenty-six days after America was attacked. Most of the camps were already empty by then, and the expensive bombs merely pounded a lot of sand. U.S. forces also dropped cave-busting bombs on the Tora Bora area of the White Mountains in southeastern Afghanistan, where U.S. intelligence had pinpointed bin Laden's location early on. But the intelligence was dated by the time they acted. Bin Laden had already begun his escape from the cave complex there. U.S. Special Operations Forces weren't even used for early cave hunting, the more critical part of the battle. They took a back-seat to local Afghan tribesmen, some of whom helped the enemy escape. Special Forces teams were relegated to spotting bombing targets for the proxy fighters—and were not at all happy about it, I have learned. But more about that later.

Here are the sobering facts:

- As much as 90 percent of the sorties flown in the first month of battle supported anti-Taliban opposition forces, mostly in the Northern Alliance outpost of Mazar-e-Sharif.[4]
- Bin Laden was not even on the list of targets in the opening volley of U.S. air and missile strikes in Afghanistan.[5]
- From the time the first U.S. bombs began pounding Taliban positions, CentCom waited thirty-eight days for U.S.-backed warlords to take Kabul, and an additional twenty-four days for them to take Kandahar, where Taliban chief Omar conducted most of his business—allowing bin Laden and his henchmen more than enough time to find better hiding places and escape routes and, ultimately, to slip across the southeastern border into Pakistan.
- The U.S., along with coalition forces, dropped some 24,000 bombs during the campaign,[6] yet it committed just 316 Special Forces

soldiers and 110 CIA officers,[7] most of whom worked with anti-Taliban rebels in northern Afghanistan.[8]

- And it wasn't until early December, when bin Laden is believed to have escaped, that elite U.S. and British commandos—just one hundred strong at their peak—were deployed in Tora Bora to work with local Afghan foot soldiers hunting bin Laden.[9]
- Yet U.S. intelligence had drawn a bead on bin Laden in early November, tracking his movements that month from Kandahar to Oruzgan to Jalalabad and finally to Tora Bora, from where he retreated into Pakistan in the first ten days of December.[10]
- American and Pakistani troops did not try to block mountain border trails leading out of the Tora Bora area until well after the torrent of bombing ceased.

The Bush administration, however, insists that its Afghan military strategy dealt a punishing blow to al-Qaida by destroying its sanctuary in Afghanistan. The terrorist network has been decentralized, and its leader bin Laden has been denied a "home base," argued Rice, the national security adviser who rode herd on the strategy sessions in the White House. The terrorist leader no longer has a "command-and-control" center, she said at a November 15, 2002, White House press conference, fending off questions about bin Laden's reemergence.

But that argument assumes two things: (1) that bin Laden does not have a new home base in Pakistan; and (2) that he needs a sophisticated command-and-control center to issue orders to al-Qaida operatives. His means of communication have always been laptop computers, the Internet, satellite phones, mosques and, more recently, tapes delivered to the Arab TV network Al-Jazeera. His cave complexes in Afghanistan may have been more elaborate than first thought, but NORAD they were not. And the Taliban communications system that U.S. forces knocked out was not exactly state-of-the-art.

Asked at the Senate hearing what damage had been done to al-Qaida's network, Franks replied, "Well, we know that al-Qaida, as an operating network, is not conducting operations within Afghanistan, because the connectivity, the ability to plan and think inside Afghanistan has been taken away." Apparently, Franks is unaware that many of al-Qaida's planners and thinkers live in Pakistan. Parts of the September 11 plot were hatched in Pakistan, as well as Germany and Malaysia, and financed through a bank in the United Arab Emirates. If Franks thinks that scattering al-Qaida terrorists with one-ton bombs in Afghanistan would prevent them from re-forming and restriking, he has never taken a stick and stirred up a red-ant hill as a kid living in Texas. They can recolonize practically overnight. And that is what al-Qaida agents, who have the single-minded purpose of angry red ants, have already done, judging from the recent surge in terrorist attacks. If destroying al-Qaida's sanctuary in Afghanistan destroyed its members' ability to plan, think, and strike, someone forgot to tell the al-Qaida terrorists who since then have killed Americans and others in Saudi Arabia, Jordan, Indonesia, Kuwait, the Phillipines, Russia, Yemen, Kenya, and elsewhere. Furthermore, al-Qaida plans its large plots years in advance. So another attack on the scale of September 11, or worse, may already be in the pipeline, just waiting for bin Laden's order to activate sleeper cells to carry it out.

Franks's remarks are about as comforting as Bush's refrain that he's got bin Laden "on the run." When has he *not* been on the run? He's always been moving—from Saudi Arabia to Afghanistan to Sudan and back to Afghanistan. And now he's in Pakistan. The man travels with his wives and elite guards in caravans of four-wheel-drive pickup trucks, pack mules, and horses. He is a nomad. Reconstituting strength is second nature to him and his footmen.

Homeland Security Director Tom Ridge tried a different angle: "We've disrupted their training facilities in Afghanistan."[11] In fact, U.S. forces "destroyed Afghanistan's terrorist training camps," as the president pointed out in his 2002 State of the Union address. "Our military has put the terror training camps of Afghanistan out of business." While true, at least at the time he said it, its impact is largely symbolic. Bin Laden's camps in Khost and elsewhere were used largely to train Kashmiri fighters for Pakistan's border conflict with India,[12] not anti-American terrorists such as the nineteen hijackers, who trained for their September 11 mission at U.S. flight schools and martial arts gyms. (The FBI, however, says Zacarias Moussaoui, the alleged twentieth hijacker, trained at the al-Qaida–affiliated Khalden Camp in Afghanistan.)[13] Besides, the camps were largely empty when the missiles hit them.[14] Ironically, Bush used the same antiseptic tactic that Republicans ripped Clinton for employing in 1998 to punish bin Laden. They both just pounded sand with missiles launched from afar.

Thinking as Westerners, Bush and his military advisers are hung up on infrastructure. But it is not as big a factor in al-Qaida operations as they think. Al-Qaida is a spiritual base, not a physical one—an international brotherhood of Islamic supremacists, powered by the fiendishly unconventional ideas of a handful of militant gurus they call "sheikhs," supreme among them bin Laden. The way to disrupt the network is to cut off the flow of ideas—the planning of attacks and the spiritual justification for them—from the top. And the way to do that is to decapitate the leadership.

There's been some progress on that key front, but not nearly enough.

Four months into the war, Bush said U.S. forces had "rid the world of thousands of terrorists" in Afghanistan, an impressive-sounding number at the time.[15] Nearly six hundred of them were being held at U.S. bases in Guantánamo, Cuba, and others at Bagram, Afghanistan. Subsequent interrogations there, however, revealed the detainees were mostly grunts. No al-Qaida leaders were among them. "Some of these guys literally don't know the world is round," one U.S. intelligence official told the *Los Angeles Times*.[16]

To be sure, some big al-Qaida fish have been caught.

Captured: Ramzi bin al-Shibh, an al-Qaida planner and a roommate of hijacker ringleader Mohamed Atta; Abu Zubaydah, a senior al-Qaida operations chief and terrorist coordinator; Omar al-Farouq, Southeast

Asia operations chief; Abd al-Rahim al-Nashiri, Persian Gulf operations chief; and Abu Zubair al-Haili, an operational planner.

Killed: Mohammed Atef, thought to be bin Laden's second in command and al-Qaida's military chief; Qaed Salim Sinan al-Harethi, a top associate of bin Laden who helped plan the bombing of the USS *Cole* in Yemen with al-Nashiri, an explosives expert; Mohammed Salah, a military operations planner; and Tariq Anwar al-Sayyid Ahmad, also involved in military operations.

Tellingly, most of the al-Qaida militants were brought to justice *after* the Afghanistan bombing campaign. Atef, Salah, and Ahmad were killed in Afghan air strikes. But Zubaydah was captured in March 2002 in Pakistan, followed by Al-Farouq, who was seized in June 2002, along with al-Haili. Then in September 2002, Bin al-Shibh was captured in Pakistan. And finally, al-Harethi was killed in November 2002 in Yemen, the same month al-Nashiri was caught. Al-Nashiri was not even caught by the U.S., as the president has implied. "People who love freedom are one person safer as a result of us finding this guy," Bush bragged at a November 22, 2002, press conference with Russian President Vladimir Putin. "We did bring to justice a killer." But it was the United Arab Emirates that arrested the Saudi-born al-Qaida lieutenant and then handed him over to U.S. authorities, as the small Arab nation disclosed in December.

At the same time, however, more than half of al-Qaida's leaders have not been killed or captured.[17] One important arrest that came during the writing of this book was that of Khalid Shaikh Mohammed, about thirty-eight, a Kuwaiti-Pakistani believed to be one of the chief planners of the September 11 attacks. Besides bin Laden, the ones still on the loose include the following:[18]

- Ayman al-Zawahiri, age fifty-one, an Egyptian surgeon thought to be bin Laden's doctor, deputy commander, and spiritual adviser.
- Saif al-Adel, around forty, an Egyptian national believed to be bin Laden's security chief and new chief of military operations.

- Midhat Mursi, an Egyptian national believed to be al-Qaida's researcher for weapons of mass destruction.
- Saad bin Laden, early twenties, the supreme leader's Saudi-born son.

It's possible all of them are hiding with bin Laden in the Afghanistan-Pakistan border region. Also still at large are bin Laden's spokesman, personal aide, chief training camp commander, and several of al-Qaida's other financiers, recruiters, spiritual advisers, and operational leaders.[19]

Democratic Senator John Kerry, a Vietnam war hero who plans to make a bid for Bush's job in 2004, is disappointed in the war results so far. "I think there are problems with the war on terror," he says. "I mean, look, Target No. 1, Osama bin Laden. Target No. 2, al-Qaida. Target No. 3, Mullah Omar. All three of them are still loose."[20]

The Massachusetts senator questions the strategy Bush used to hunt down the al-Qaida criminals who, he notes, "remain very powerful." Kerry argues, "We had al-Qaida and we had, you know, Osama bin Laden in the mountains of Tora Bora. I think we made a bad decision in how we fought that particular encounter. I think we repeated the mistakes in [Operation] Anaconda subsequent to Tora Bora. So mistakes have been made."[21]

Kerry's criticism could easily be dismissed as political. But Special Forces commandos who did tours in Afghanistan also questioned the strategy. They were unhappy with the decision to use Afghan proxy soldiers to ferret out bin Laden in southeastern Afghanistan instead of sending in U.S. ground troops.

"They were champing at the bit to go in. They wanted to see action, but were held back," said a Special Operations technician who helped with battlefield reconnaissance in the mountains of southeastern Afghanistan.[22]

CentCom confined the elite units to setting precise targets for bomber pilots, who were able to place 2,000-pound "cave-busters" in entrances from altitudes of 15,000 feet to 20,000 feet. Two types of high-tech bombs were used: laser-guided bombs, which follow a laser beam "painted" on the target by soldiers on the ground using hand-held "designators"; and joint direct attack munitions, better known as J-DAMs, which are guided to targets by ground personnel relaying latitude and longitude coordinates from GPS devices. Some 13,000 of the bombs used in the Afghanistan theater were precision guided.[23]

"Afghanistan proved that expensive precision weapons defeat the enemy and spare lives, and we need more of them," Bush said in his 2002 State of the Union speech.

They might have helped defeat the Taliban, but not al-Qaida, the enemy that actually attacked America. And for all their precision, the bombs could not zero in on bin Laden and his top lieutenants, who survived the massive shelling of their Tora Bora base. Bush repeated the mistakes of the Soviets, who thought big bombs would kill bin Laden and other mujahideen fighters holed up in the deep underground caves of Tora Bora. They spent years doing it, even dropping fuel-air bombs that blast sideways into cave openings—but to little effect. Flushing out al-Qaida militants from the caves required attacking and searching them by foot, yet U.S. commandos were not allowed to do that, at least not in the early going. They were relegated to providing rear support for local rebels, who had little interest in doing America's bidding once the Taliban were ousted from power.

Subletting the War

Even some CentCom brass expressed doubts about subcontracting such critical fighting. They say ground troops should have been deployed in Tora Bora in November 2001 to seal off border escape routes, and then to surround and eventually strangle off bin Laden and his top lieutenants and guards.

"There could have been one or two infantry divisions, or at least brigades, doing this job," said one senior officer at MacDill involved in the Afghanistan operation. "They are perfectly qualified to check out caves."[24]

Afghan surrogates not only failed to do the job, but also looked the other way as sympathetic tribal leaders and local villagers helped bin Laden and his top lieutenants escape. Some U.S.-backed fighters joined in the smuggling—for a price.

AP correspondent Chris Tomlinson was in Jalalabad at the time. He reported December 18, 2001, that senior Afghan tribal leaders helped top al-Qaida commanders, their families, and hundreds of al-Qaida militants flee to safety in Pakistan. Citing accounts by Sorhab Qadri, an intelligence officer with anti-Taliban forces in Tora Bora, and another Eastern Alliance official, Tomlinson said that two of the region's most respected tribal elders—Din Mohammed and Younis Khalis—helped organize escape routes through an aide, Mohammed Amin, who was the main liaison between bin Laden and the two tribal leaders. Qadri said some of Khalis's men delivered al-Qaida leaders and their families from the Tora Bora area to safe houses in Jalalabad, some thirty miles away, before escorting them to the border.

Tomlinson discovered that even anti-Taliban militias there were sympathetic to al-Qaida. "Almost all say their primary goal is to drive out al-Qaida, not necessarily to destroy it," he reported. "Before the September 11 terrorist attacks, many Afghan fundamentalists—some of whom are members of the post-Taliban *shura* [Islamic council]—saw al-Qaida members as honored veterans of the war against the Soviet occupation in the 1980s," he explained. "They became liabilities only when the United States launched its military campaign."

Other correspondents who interviewed anti-Taliban fighters also found their loyalties divided. "In candid moments, most of the anti-Taliban soldiers admitted that they'd rather see the terrorists flee than have to slaughter them," Megan K. Stack of the *Los Angeles Times* reported April 25, 2002, from Tora Bora.

Even U.S. officials complained anonymously that their anti-Taliban allies betrayed them, citing a cease-fire ruse. "Rebels under the command of warlords in Tora Bora called a surprise cease-fire at the height of the

U.S. bombing to allow al-Qaida forces to escape, probably across the mountains into Pakistan," Jonathan Weisman and Jack Kelley of *USA Today* reported February 5, 2002. "Plain and simple, the United States was hoodwinked," they quoted Qadri as saying. One commander, Hajji Zaman, was accused of taking a large al-Qaida bribe to help organize a halt to the bombing.[25]

Zaman wasn't alone. Many other Afghan allies reportedly took bribes of cash, as well as new Kalashnikov semiautomatic rifles, from wealthy al-Qaida leaders to help them escape.[26] Al-Qaida even outbid inducements given to new U.S. recruits. One of the key Tora Bora warlords the U.S. enlisted in the battle, Hazret Ali, paid a lieutenant named Ilyas Khel to take his men and block the main escape routes into Pakistan, something U.S. forces should have done from Day One. But al-Qaida leaders paid him more, and Khel ended up laying down cover fire for escaping al-Qaida, according to *Christian Science Monitor* correspondent Philip Smucker, who filed an eye-opening report from Tora Bora on March 4, 2002.

All the villagers in and around Tora Bora and Jalalabad, meantime, sneezed at the whopping $25 million bin Laden bounty offered by the U.S. The Bush administration blamed the lack of interest on poor villagers' inability to grasp the value of such a high sum, rather than on the bond of Islam between Afghans and Arabs such as bin Laden and his al-Qaida fighters. Yet listen to what one local commander allegedly on the U.S. side of the battle confided to Smucker: "We are not interested in killing the Arabs. They are our Muslim brothers."

Hitching America's security to the whims of Afghan warlords made little sense at the time, frustrated U.S. military officials told me. They had one thing in mind—seizing power from the Taliban. Once that happened, they had little incentive to hunt down fellow Muslims like bin Laden.

"All of the people at a tactical level knew better than to let Afghan rebels and former Taliban actually do any hunting or scouting," said a military intelligence officer involved with CentCom operations.[27]

The official, who is aware of the pipeline projects bounding ahead in Afghanistan, blames politics for bin Laden getting away.

"There's no problem with the combat arms commanders. It's the politicians that make the decisions that cost us this way," he said. "There's no real good reason that UBL [bin Laden] got away."[28]

While Franks has not admitted misjudging the agendas of Afghan proxies in Tora Bora, he did put more American boots on the ground in a subsequent al-Qaida battle to the south, known as Operation Anaconda.

But even then, the hard lessons of Tora Bora were not completely learned. Franks once again let Afghan warlords do the initial heavy lifting, and once again he got burned. The March 2002 offensive stalled when Gen. Zia Lodin, one of three Afghan commanders, backed away. His fighters never arrived, and Special Forces troops and soldiers of the 10th Mountain and 101st Airborne Divisions had to scramble to move on the enemy in what should have been a surprise attack. But al-Qaida was ready for them, raising U.S. officers' suspicions that Afghan allies tipped off al-Qaida about the plans. "Anaconda was a bit of an eye-opener. We didn't think the resistance would be as bad as they found. Al-Qaida were well-entrenched and prepared to fight," a senior Pentagon official and former Green Beret told me. "Locals supported al-Qaida in many ways. Afghans often play both sides of the fence, and the senior officers have to be cautious."[29]

Further hamstringing U.S. commandos, Franks initially set strict rules of engagement that required them to first seek permission from CentCom before launching air strikes and ground action on al-Qaida targets. Reason: he didn't want to risk the deaths of Afghan refugees making their way back inside Afghanistan from Pakistan, who could be mistaken for the enemy. In one instance, army Special Operations troops were forced to reposition twice while tracking about two dozen al-Qaida fighters before they got the OK from Tampa to launch an attack. During the first two months of bombing, Franks reportedly nixed al-Qaida–rich targets because they were too close to civilian areas.[30]

"Politically, it may have been a good move," the U.S. recon specialist told me. "But it was another tactical blunder."

A U.S. Army officer knocked Franks as a politician in uniform. "He's not a snake-eater, a warrior," said the officer, who also will have to remain nameless. "He's more of a politician. A smooth talker." He added, "Basically, Franks tried to run the war like a video game from Florida."[31]

U.S. forces also were betrayed by Afghan proxies in their pursuit of Taliban chief Omar, who is still on the lam after having been driven out of Kandahar in December 2001. Local warlords, who share Omar's Pashtun ethnicity, had surrounded him north of the city about a month later, but then he escaped again with his guards during surrender negotiations allowed by Franks.[32] The one-eyed Omar is said to be holed up in his native Oruzgan province—and appears to be quite safe there, judging from the lack of local interest in the $10 million reward that the U.S. is offering for his capture.[33]

So, both prized quarry of the highly acclaimed Afghanistan campaign—bin Laden and Omar—remain at large.

Career military officials have told me that the Tora Bora battle was the most critical of the war, offering the best chance to kill or capture al-Qaida's leaders. They also agree its prosecution was bungled. Focusing on the Taliban and relying on Afghan proxy forces, they say, virtually guaranteed bin Laden's escape.

Publicly, Bush has expressed no regrets. He and members of his war cabinet, in defending their decision to use local forces, have said they didn't want to relearn the lessons of Vietnam, which became a quagmire resulting in more than fifty thousand American casualties. Committing American ground troops to Afghanistan, with its mountain hideouts, high altitudes, and bitter-cold winters, would be courting disaster. "We learned some very important lessons in Vietnam," Bush said a few days after launching Operation Enduring Freedom.[34] In short, they were worried about footage of body bags leading the evening news.

But a large majority of Americans were ready to accept casualties to win this war, tragic as any death might be. This war was nothing like Vietnam; this time Washington was sending the nation's sons and daughters to defend America, not a far-off foreign country few can even find on a map. According to a *USA Today*/CNN/Gallup poll of 1,032 adults taken September 14–15, 2001, at least 65 percent said they would support retaliation if it involved ground troops and the loss of 1,000 soldiers or more. All told, fifty-two American servicemen and women were killed in the Afghanistan campaign, and less than half of them in combat.[35] The largest number of casualties came March 4, 2002—long after bin Laden had fled—when seven soldiers were killed during Operation Anaconda, the biggest ground assault of the war.

Administration officials also have said they didn't want to "Americanize" the war. Anti-American sentiments were already running high in the Muslim world. Taking more than a custodial role in battling an enemy inside a Muslim country might aggravate tensions and risk fraying Bush's coalition, which included many Muslim nations, they reasoned. They couldn't afford jeopardizing the cooperation of Saudi Arabia and Pakistan, most of all. Therefore, it was critical for the world to see Afghans, rather than Americans, fighting Afghans and Arabs. Bush officials worried that putting a lot of boots on the ground might look to Afghans like a Soviet-style occupation rather than a liberation.

Of course, if there's any war the world would forgive America for Americanizing, it's this one. And if the goal was—and is—to keep America's profile as low as possible, why is the U.S. military essentially occupying Afghanistan right now and engaging in nation building—something Bush slammed the Clinton administration for doing? Bush claims he doesn't want to leave a vacuum there that could be filled all over again by terrorists. "We've got to work for a stable Afghanistan," he said, "one that doesn't become yet again a haven for terrorist criminals."[36]

Those are the stated reasons, anyway, for farming out the fighting to Afghans.

But they are only part of the story. Recall that Bush's top security adviser on Afghanistan, Zal Khalilzad, brought to the table an anti-Taliban plan he had drafted during the 2000 election. It called for using the Northern Alliance and other opposition factions to dislodge the Taliban, and then rallying them to create a U.S.-friendly government that could provide a more stable environment for a trans-Afghan "energy corridor"—that is, the proposed oil and gas pipelines. The blueprint also advised undermining local support for the Taliban by funneling food and other assistance to blighted areas in Afghanistan neglected by the Taliban. On the first day of bombing, tellingly, U.S. planes also dropped food rations—from 18,000 feet to avoid Taliban antiaircraft fire. In fact, U.S. and coalition forces airdropped more humanitarian rations in just the first day—about 37,000—than all the bombs dropped throughout the Afghan campaign, which totaled about 24,000.[37]

"A major humanitarian effort is required. We need to develop a humanitarian campaign and get in the swing next week," Rice told principals just prior to the bombing offensive, borrowing a page from her aide Khalilzad's playbook. "We need to clarify out of our president's mouth that there is going to be a major effort to help the Afghan people."[38]

Needless to say, Khalilzad and his ideas figured prominently in the military planning. The former Pentagon official, who headed Bush's transition team for the Defense Department, at one point spoke two or three times a week with Gen. Franks about Afghanistan operations.[39] Now Bush's special envoy in Kabul, Khalilzad needed the cooperation of the Afghan tribal leaders in both the north and the south to form the new government. To get that cooperation, they would have to be given big stakes in the war, which they got—along with millions of dollars in CIA cash.

But putting the fate of bin Laden and Omar in their hands, rather than those of gung-ho American soldiers, backfired. Their loyalties proved more parochial than expected. While Bush and his cronies were busy installing a puppet regime in Kabul, bin Laden was allowed safe passage through snow-packed mule trails running alongside the mountainous

Khyber Pass to remote northern Pakistan, where he enjoys strong support among tribal leaders.

Bush officials tap-danced around the issue of bin Laden's escape for more than a year, claiming that they didn't know whether he was alive or dead. Even when a resurfaced bin Laden issued new threats against America, Franks seemed dangerously distracted by plans to oust Saddam Hussein. "I don't know where bin Laden is, alive or dead," he said with a shrug before quickly changing the subject to Iraq.[40] Off the record, officials played up rumors that bin Laden was dead and played down credible reports that he was alive. Some senior officials at the White House and Pentagon flatly asserted, anonymously, that bin Laden was dead.

But the November 12, 2002, tape recording of bin Laden praising the previous month's rash of al-Qaida terrorism proved once and for all that rumors of his death were greatly exaggerated. Both the CIA and the National Security Agency concluded from their own technical and linguistic analyses that the recording, first aired on Al-Jazeera, was authentic.[41] Despite fresh threats from bin Laden on the tape, the White House refused to elevate its public terror alert from yellow to orange (high risk), even as government facilities worldwide were put on a heightened state of alert. The Homeland Security Office explained that it had received no "specific" threats—though that didn't stop it from elevating the advisory to orange the day before the September 11 anniversary. Also, the president never addressed the very serious issue of bin Laden's survival-cum-threats to the American people, even though he had told them more than a year earlier that bin Laden was the "evil one" responsible for the September 11 massacre. He offered Americans no new plan for hunting him down. For that matter, he has yet to publicly acknowledge that bin Laden escaped. Just a couple of months earlier, Bush had claimed to be "very mindful of my job as the American president to do everything we can to protect the American people from future attack."[42] Unfortunately, he was referring to Saddam Hussein—not bin Laden—when he made the remark.

It wasn't until bin Laden issued another tape-recorded message expressing solidarity with Iraq that the Bush administration publicly acknowledged his survival. Cynically, it seized on his February statement to help justify its preemptive war against Iraq, and only then raised the terrorist threat level.

The news of bin Laden's survival merely confirmed a string of credible, yet largely overlooked (thanks to White House damage-control efforts), press reports concluding the same thing over the previous year. Here is a sample, beginning with one filed several days after bin Laden escaped in early December 2001:

- From interviews with two Afghan tribal leaders in Jalalabad, the Associated Press reported December 18, 2001, that "hundreds of al-Qaida family members escaped, and top al-Qaida commanders may have been among them . . . possibly even including top terror suspect Osama bin Laden."

- "Mohammed Habeel, spokesman for [new Afghan] Defense Minister Mohammad Qasim Fahim, said 'reliable intelligence sources' reported that bin Laden had crossed from the Tora Bora region of eastern Afghanistan in Pakistan," Agence France-Presse reported December 28, 2001.

- "In a major setback to the war on terrorism, CIA analysts have concluded bin Laden escaped from the Tora Bora cave complex in eastern Afghanistan around the first week of December, intelligence officials said," ABC News reported January 15, 2002.

- "We have high confidence that [bin Laden] was there [in Tora Bora around December 3], and also high confidence that he got out," the *Washington Post* on April 17, 2002, quoted a U.S. intelligence official as saying. "We have several accounts of that from people who are in detention, al-Qaida people."

- "We are sure Osama bin Laden escaped through this road to the Pakistani tribal areas," said anti-Taliban commander Haji Khalan Mir in Tora Bora, as quoted by the *Los Angeles Times* on April 25, 2002.

- "While intelligence officials are not certain whether Osama bin Laden is alive or dead, they have found a tantalizing document that suggests he was living at least as recently as the last days of December," Lisa Beyer wrote June 30, 2002, for *Time*. "That would mean bin Laden survived last year's American bombardment of Afghanistan, including the assault on Tora Bora."

But common sense dictated as much. The idea that air strikes had killed bin Laden without any hue and cry never passed the smell test. If he had died, word would have spread rapidly throughout the Middle East, and his followers would have mourned him as a martyr. And that spike in Arabic chatter would have been picked up by the National Security Agency (NSA) in its monitoring of signals intelligence. If the White House had solid intelligence that bin Laden were dead, moreover, it's highly unlikely Bush's top political adviser, Karl Rove, would have passed up the chance to make great hay of the news during the 2002 midterm election campaign. Bin Laden is the war's trophy, whether or not White House officials want to admit it. And of course they won't, at least not publicly, while he's still free. For his part, Bush insists, in so many words, that bin Laden is "only part of the objective," and that "the war on terror is about more than one man"—talking points that have now become a mantra around the White House, sources there tell me. Around the anniversary of the September 11 attacks, Cheney parroted the lines in an interview with NBC's *Meet the Press* host Tim Russert.

"Does it bother you, bug you, that you have not captured Osama bin Laden in over a year?" Russert asked.

Cheney, after weakly suggesting he may be dead, insisted, "He's not the sole objective of our operations here . . . One man all by himself isn't likely to be able to do much by way of damage to the United States."[43]

No? Bin Laden launched a terrorist attack that toppled the Twin Towers, destroyed four jumbo jets, bankrupted a major airline, sent Wall Street into a tailspin, blew away a wedge of the Pentagon, and wiped out some three thousand lives—all in a morning's work. And the attack was just the latest in a series of attacks he's launched against America over the past decade, each one increasingly ambitious and brazen. In denying bin Laden the grudging respect he's due, the vice president is engaging in damage control, or he's seriously underestimating the enemy. The man all by himself poses a monumental threat to the security of America—like no terrorist, or even dictator, before him.

Formidable Foe

America-hating terrorists have been around for decades. But until bin Laden declared holy war on America, no terrorist has been able to inflict as much damage and death on America and its assets around the world. No one has been able to marshal such a disciplined cadre of killers. Or pull off such sophisticated and well-coordinated attacks.

Bin Laden is different. He is low-key, patient, and careful—not a hot-head, which is a departure from past Islamic terrorists. He is educated. Having studied civil engineering, he knows how to bring down structures. He is diabolically clever, able to turn jetliners into weapons of mass destruction. He studies our systems. He can make big things happen with simple means: the toppling of the Twin Towers began with box cutters and mace. He is wealthy, at one point worth some $300 million, which makes him hard to corrupt and compromise. And he is charismatic.

Yet he does not appear to be a madman. We do not know his true motives, but by all accounts, bin Laden is not driven by ego. He is driven by faith in a sacred book that he believes justifies his jihad against the "unbelievers"—most notably Americans, who he contends are contaminating holy soil in Saudi Arabia, site of Mecca and Medina. Recall that he issued his *fatwahs* only after former President Bush left U.S. airmen in Saudi Arabia to baby-sit Saddam Hussein, the aggressive dictator next door that the senior Bush left in power at the end of the Gulf War. Major anti-American attacks by al-Qaida, Arabic for "the base," all began after that—from the first World Trade Center attack in 1993, to the bombing of U.S. Air Force barracks in Saudi Arabia in 1996, to the U.S. embassy bombings in Africa in 1998, to the USS *Cole* blast in 2000, to the September 11, 2001, attacks.

Indeed, if bin Laden were a megalomaniac, he would have statues made of himself and palaces built in his name, as Saddam has done, and certainly would not live for long spells in caves. No, he seems to be a true believer, and that makes him exceedingly dangerous. His acolytes respect him immensely for it. They see him "fighting in the cause of Allah," not himself, as the Koran commands, and they cannot wait to sign up for his next mission. That explains why no one has sold him out for the $25 million bounty on his head. And that's why he has been able to appeal to Muslims of so many nationalities—al-Qaida terrorists operate in more than sixty countries. Their Islamic faith drives them, and bin Laden's purity inspires them. It is a cult within a cult, and the combination is extremely powerful—and lethal.

Bin Laden is the most formidable foe—in terms of a single personality, as opposed to, say, a nuclear state enemy—that America has faced since Hitler, and Hitler never attacked New York or Washington. In fact, bin Laden is such a proven threat that he may never have to actually attack us again to hurt our economy, one of his main goals. All he has to do is mouth a threat on Al-Jazeera, and shoppers will take cover and stock investors will twitch. We simply cannot afford to take him lightly after what he did to us September 11.

The good news is, according to FBI counterterrorism experts I have interviewed, there is really no up-and-coming leader who can fill bin Laden's shoes, though some say his closest aide al-Zawahiri garners as much respect. Once he is gone, the network will likely disintegrate and become much less effective in carrying out major terrorist attacks, particularly in the United States. Gradual impotence has generally been the rule for other terrorist groups that have lost charismatic leaders.

"As long as bin Laden is unaccounted for, his followers will look upon him as invincible, and from their standpoint, one who has divine protection," FBI counterintelligence veteran I.C. Smith warned. Likewise, former FBI counterterrorism chief Bob Blitzer told me: "He was and is the leader of thousands of terrorists bent on the destruction of the West. This will not diminish as long as he is out there." They note that major al-Qaida attacks typically come in two-year intervals, triggered by bin Laden's orders.

That said, the White House must redouble its efforts to capture or kill bin Laden, and quit trying to rationalize its failure to take him out when it had the chance in southeastern Afghanistan in the weeks after September 11. It must do everything possible to decapitate him from his body of followers. Anything less is a dereliction of duty.

"The only thing that's going to devastate al-Qaida would be to find the top leadership—bin Laden and Ayman al-Zawahiri," said former CIA terrorist expert Kenneth Katzman. "They are the charisma, they are the ethos behind the organization."[44]

Unfortunately, the White House is leaving that job largely up to the Pakistani military, which reveres bin Laden.

4

UNHOLY ALLIANCE

Trusting Pakistan, Harvard of Terror

Our enemy is a radical network of terrorists and every
government that supports them.

—THE BUSH DOCTRINE

CARVED FIFTY-SIX YEARS AGO FROM MUSLIM-DOMINATED
areas of India, Pakistan is a nation founded on Islamic fundamentalism.
Its very name means "land of the pure"—as in pure Islam. If you are a
practicing Christian in Pakistan, you take your life into your own hands
virtually every day. Blasphemy laws there are some of the harshest in the
Islamic world. A Christian accused of "blasphemy against Islam" can get
the death penalty—on the flimsiest evidence. Most charges are filed by
Muslims disputing Christians over land. "Some 2,500 people are said to
be in jail or to face charges for blasphemy," said historian Serge Trifkovic,
author of *The Sword of the Prophet: Islam History, Theology, Impact on the
World*. "Christians charged with blasphemy have been murdered by fundamentalists before their cases reached the courts."

Churches are no sanctuary in Pakistan. In October 2001, Islamic terrorists armed with Kalashnikov rifles mowed down eighteen Protestants
in a church in Bahawalpur. The massacre was followed in March 2002 by

a grenade attack on a church in Islamabad's diplomatic enclave that killed five, including a U.S. embassy worker and her daughter.

Hostility toward America runs deep in Pakistan—in fact, deeper than in most other Muslim countries. In a revealing poll of attitudes in Islamic nations taken a few months after September 11, the Gallup Organization found that 68 percent of Pakistanis dislike the U.S., the highest negative opinion among the nine nations polled—higher even than Iran. Other countries surveyed were Saudi Arabia, Indonesia, Turkey, Lebanon, Morocco, Kuwait, and Jordan. Together, only a slight majority—an average 53 percent—view America unfavorably. What's more, 86 percent of Pakistanis deny Arabs were involved in the September 11 attacks. And 80 percent feel America had no moral justification for taking military action in Afghanistan.[1]

The anti-American resentment is stirred up in Pakistan's mosques and madrassas, the strict Islamic schools where boys are taught to memorize the Koran and act out on its violent passages exhorting Muslims to fight unbelievers in the cause of Allah. The large coastal city of Karachi is the mecca of the fundamentalist movement in Pakistan. The Binori Mosque there runs a madrassa that includes among its alumni exiled Taliban chief Mullah Omar and the fiery founder of an al-Qaida–affiliated terrorist group in Pakistan. The madrassa is said to be a veritable hatchery for young Islamic militants. The school follows the so-called Deobandi movement, which arose in British India as a revival of hard-core Islamic values. It forms the backbone of the Taliban, though Omar and his clerics made it more extreme by aligning it with the supremacist Wahhabi creed practiced by bin Laden and his ilk. The Binori school in 1997 sent some six hundred of its students to Afghanistan to join the Taliban (which means "students of Islam"),[2] and in more recent years, some Binori students in Karachi have been seen sporting assault rifles.[3]

The Binori school preaches "strict interpretation of the Koran, intolerance of other religions, a puritanical way of life and jihad against Jews and Americans," said Professor Masood Kahn of Lahore University in

Pakistan. "Death during jihad is considered a sure-fire ticket to heaven according to its teachings."[4]

Karachi is not fringe. Most of the military pooh-bahs who control Pakistan's government in Islamabad subscribe to the Deobandi brand of Islam.[5] In fact, the military's powerful intelligence wing—the notorious ISI, or Inter-Services Intelligence—helped put the Taliban in power. The ISI supplied as much as half of the Taliban's military equipment and personnel, according to *Jane's Defence Weekly*.[6]

Seedbed of Terror

The Taliban's main patron had been former ISI chief Lt. Gen. Mahmoud Ahmad, who led Gen. Pervez Musharraf's military coup.[7] Musharraf overthrew the civilian government of Prime Minister Nawaz Sharif on October 12, 1999, in the first ever military coup in a country with nuclear weapons. Musharraf anointed himself president of Pakistan. The coup reportedly was partly a result of mounting fear among generals that Sharif might bow to U.S. pressure and cut Pakistan's ties to the Taliban. Following the 1998 al-Qaida attacks on U.S. embassies in Africa, Sharif came under increasing pressure from the U.S. and the UN to rein in ISI support for the Taliban, then sheltering bin Laden.

Support for the Taliban accelerated under Musharraf, triggering an unprecedented rebuke from the State Department, which for the first time singled out Pakistan as a hub of terrorism. "The United States remains concerned about reports of continued Pakistani support for the Taliban's military operations in Afghanistan," declared the department's 2000 report on global terrorism. "Pakistan is providing the Taliban with materiel, fuel, funding, technical assistance and military advisers." The report added another troubling item: "Pakistan has not prevented large numbers of Pakistani nationals from moving into Afghanistan to fight for the Taliban."[8]

Bush's Deputy Secretary of State Armitage reportedly asked Lieutenant General Ahmad to sever ties with the Taliban when he happened to be in Washington the week of September 11. And reportedly, Musharraf agreed with the request when Ahmad took it back to Islamabad. As the story goes, Musharraf then dispatched Ahmad to Kandahar, Afghanistan, to meet with Omar and other Taliban leaders to try to persuade them to hand over bin Laden to the U.S., or else lose Pakistani support.[9]

But Ahmad disobeyed Musharraf, and instead assured Omar that the Taliban could count on continued backing from the ISI. Musharraf, in turn, sacked Ahmad and two other hard-line ISI generals who resisted turning out the Taliban.[10] That is the unofficial explanation for the purge. According to Islamabad, Ahmad simply sought retirement.

However, the Indian press tells a darker story. Reporting from the Indian capital of New Delhi, the *Times of India* dropped a bombshell on October 10, 2001: "Top sources confirmed here that the general lost his job because of the 'evidence' India produced to show his links to one of the suicide bombers that wrecked the World Trade Center." According to the report, which cited unnamed New Delhi officials, the Bush administration sought Ahmad's removal after learning from the Central Bureau of Investigations, India's equivalent of the FBI, that he had facilitated the transfer of funds to lead hijacker Mohamed Atta. Agence France-Presse (AFP) seemed to confirm the story later that same day, reporting: "A highly placed [Indian] government source told AFP that the 'damning link' between the general and the transfer of funds to Atta was part of evidence which India has officially sent to the U.S." It then quoted its source as saying, "The evidence we have supplied to the U.S. is of a much wider range and depth than just one piece of paper linking a rogue general to some misplaced act of terrorism." This implied a larger conspiracy possibly involving Musharraf himself.

Asked about the report at a May 16, 2002, White House press conference, Bush's national security adviser, Condi Rice, claimed ignorance.

REPORTER: Are you aware of the reports at the time that the ISI chief was in Washington on September 11th, and on September

10th, that $100,000 was wired from Pakistan to these groups here in this area? And why was he here? Was he meeting with you or anybody in the administration?

RICE: I have not seen that report, and he was certainly not meeting with me.

Still, there is no doubt that India provided Bush administration officials, as well as members of Congress, with intelligence showing Pakistani ties to al-Qaida. A senior Senate staffer involved in foreign policy affairs told me he got a classified briefing from Indian Defense Minister George Fernandes shortly after September 11. In it, according to the Republican aide, who wished to go unnamed, Fernandes laid out the ISI's connections to al-Qaida and, by extension, September 11. Fernandes briefed a number of U.S. officials, he said.[11] The defense minister later criticized the U.S. bombing campaign in Afghanistan as an "exercise in melting the ice caps."[12]

Islamabad has dismissed India's allegations as "baseless."[13]

But it is an open secret that al-Qaida enjoys broad support in Pakistan's military intelligence, which essentially runs the government as a shadow state within the state. Bin Laden has helped fund and train thousands of Kashmiri militants fighting to bring all of Kashmir, the mineral-rich territory divided between largely Hindu India and Pakistan, under Pakistani control. An estimated twenty thousand people passed through Pakistan over the last decade to train at bin Laden's camps in Afghanistan.[14] "Bin Laden provided sanctuary and training facilities for Kashmiri militants who were backed by Pakistan, and Islamabad had little interest in drying up that support," said Ahmed Rashid, author of *Taliban*. It was the ISI, he stated, that helped introduce bin Laden to the Taliban in 1996, when it took control of Afghanistan. Fittingly, the ISI turned down Washington every time it asked for help in catching bin Laden, asserted Rashid, a Pakistani-based journalist who covered Afghanistan for the *Far Eastern Economic Review* for sixteen years.

Al-Qaida operatives with ties to Pakistan are legion. And many of them have ties to September 11 and other anti-American terrorism. Consider the following men:

Ahmed Omar Saeed Sheikh. A Briton of Pakistani descent, he is the mastermind behind *Wall Street Journal* correspondent Daniel Pearl's abduction and murder in Karachi. Pampered by the ISI, he was allowed to roam freely in Pakistan after fellow terrorists in 1999 hijacked an Indian jetliner and forced the Indian government to release him from jail, where he was being held for kidnapping tourists, including an American. Sheikh was arrested last year in Lahore, Pakistan, after the FBI became involved in the high-profile Pearl case. At one point he told investigators he met with bin Laden in Afghanistan after the September 11 attacks.[15] He also said he had met with bin Laden in Kabul in 2000.[16] The Indian press maintains that Sheikh transferred money to the September 11 hijackers with Lt. Gen. Ahmad's blessing, if not urging.[17] However, it may be confusing him with Mustafa Ahmed al-Hawsawi, who has many aliases, including Shaikh Saiid.[18] The FBI says al-Hawsawi, a Saudi national, was the main financial conduit for the hijackers, wiring money to them through a London-based bank in Sharjah, United Arab Emirates (UAE), which also recognized the Taliban government in Afghanistan.[19] Omar Sheikh, Pearl's killer, was a key fund-raiser for Jaish-e-Mohammed, or Army of Mohammed, a Pakistan-based terrorist group in league with al-Qaida. He allegedly set up money-laundering operations in Pakistan, Afghanistan, and UAE.[20] British investigators reportedly believe that Sheikh helped train the September 11 terrorists in hijacking techniques.[21]

Mustafa Ahmed al-Hawsawi. Also known as Shaikh Saiid al-Sharif, al-Hawsawi is believed by German and U.S. authorities to be the hijackers' chief paymaster.[22] He had power of attorney over the UAE bank accounts opened by one hijacker, from which several transfers totaling $114,500 were wired to Atta and another hijacker in New York and Florida. Al-Hawsawi collected the $42,608 in unspent funds that the frugal hijackers wired back to the UAE bank just before the attacks. On September 11, according to FBI records, $40,871 was prepaid to a Visa card connected to a savings account al-Hawsawi had opened at the UAE bank. That same day, al-Hawsawi fled UAE for Pakistan. Two days later, the supplemental Visa card connected to al-Hawsawi's account was used to make six ATM withdrawals in Karachi, Pakistan.[23]

Khalid Shaikh Mohammed. A Pakistani national born in Kuwait, he is believed to be one of the chief planners of the September 11 plot. And he may have participated in the plot to slay journalist Pearl.[24] Mohammed, a senior al-Qaida figure, was captured March 1, 2003, in a joint raid by CIA and Pakistani operatives on a house in Rawalpindi, Pakistan, owned by an activist of Pakistan's oldest religious party, Jamaat-e-Islami, which has close links with the ISI. The house is in the posh Westridge district of Rawalpindi, headquarters of the Pakistani Army and home of President Gen. Pervez Musharraf. Not long after Mohammad's arrest, another senior al-Qaida member, Tawfiq Attash Khallad, was nabbed in Pakistan.

Ramzi Yousef. The 1993 World Trade Center–bombing mastermind was captured last decade in Pakistan, right back where he started from. He had flown to New York City from Pakistan about six months before the first WTC attack.[25] He is believed to be Khalid Mohammed's nephew.[26] The al-Qaida operative and his uncle hatched the scuttled 1995 plot—code named "Bojinka," after the Serbo-Croatian word for explosion—to bomb twelve U.S. jetliners on the same day. Yousef is known to have visited Mohammed's Karachi home about four months after the 1993 WTC blast.[27] A coconspirator in the Bojinka plot was Abdul Hakim al-Hashim Murad, a Pakistani pilot who was arrested earlier in the Philippines. He, too, visited Mohammed in Karachi.[28]

Maulana Masood Azhar. The Pakistani is founder and leader of the Jaish-e-Mohammed (J-e-M), and Omar Sheikh's mentor. After Musharraf agreed, belatedly, to ban the group following pressure from the FBI, Azhar was put under house arrest—but then quietly let go late last year. The group has been active in kidnapping rings that raise funds for Pakistani militants fighting in Kashmir. Indian intelligence believes the group used some of the funds from ransom payments to help bankroll the September 11 strikes in America.[29] Azhar taught at the Binori madrassa with Mullah Omar and other Taliban clerics.[30] The State Department says that J-e-M is tied to al-Qaida primarily through Kashmiri training camps in Afghanistan. But al-Qaida may be trying to absorb elements of the J-e-M now that it has been banned.[31]

Richard C. Reid. Investigators have traced the al-Qaida shoe-bomber back to Pakistan as well. In 1999 and 2000, he lived in Pakistan and reportedly attended a madrassa there.[32] He also met with a Muslim cleric in Lahore.[33] Police in Paris, moreover, arrested five Pakistanis suspected of providing logistical support to Reid in Paris, from where he boarded an American Airlines flight to Miami with explosives concealed in his sneaker.[34]

Zacarias Moussaoui. FBI records show the alleged twentieth hijacker flew from London to Pakistan on December 9, 2000. He flew back to London from Pakistan on February 7, 2001.[35]

Abdullah Ahmed Abdullah. The senior al-Qaida operative left Nairobi, Kenya, on August 6, 1998—the day before the U.S. embassy bombing there—and went to Karachi.[36]

Abu Zubaydah. The senior al-Qaida operations leader was captured last year in Faisalabad, one of Pakistan's biggest cities. FBI and CIA agents recovered computer hard drives, CD-ROMs, and documents at his home there, leading to the surveillance of at least two hundred suspected al-Qaida agents in the U.S.[37]

Jose Padilla. The suspected al-Qaida agent, aka Abdullah al-Muhajir, allegedly went to Pakistan with Zubaydah to study how to make a so-called dirty bomb, attending at least two meetings in Karachi at which senior al-Qaida operatives discussed making a conventional bomb that would scatter radioactive material.[38]

Ramzi bin al-Shibh. Atta's roommate in Hamburg, Germany, who helped arrange money transfers to Moussaoui after being denied a U.S. visa, was captured late last year in Karachi.

A Pakistani official told me that if Pakistan is a breeding ground for terrorists, America has no one to blame but itself. After all, he says, the CIA worked with the ISI to fund and train many of them to fight in Afghanistan against the Soviets.

"Pakistan is close to Afghanistan. What happened there [jihadi training] did not happen yesterday. This has been happening since 1979, when the CIA and the Saudi intelligence made Pakistan the front line state [against the spread of communism] between 1979 and 1989," said Asad Hayauddin, press attaché for the Pakistan embassy in Washington. "You just don't turn off the switch and then walk away. Pakistan is not just a washing machine that you can just load your dirty laundry in and walk away.

"These are human beings, who you have trained in a certain way, and you funded them and you called them 'mujahideen' [holy warriors], which was a kosher word up until 1989," Hayauddin fumed. "Now 'jihad' is a four-letter word."[39]

While true, the U.S. turned off the "switch," as he calls it, more than a decade ago with the collapse of the Soviet Union. Yet Pakistan kept churning out jihadi militants. And terrorist activity flourished under military strongman Musharraf, according to the State Department's report on global terrorism in 2000. "Pakistan's military government, headed by Gen. Pervez Musharraf, continued previous Pakistani government support of the Kashmir insurgency, and Kashmiri militant groups continue to operate in Pakistan, raising funds and recruiting new cadre," explained the report. "Several of these groups were responsible for attacks against civilians in Indian-held Kashmir" and elsewhere. State cited Jaish-e-Mohammed, which "has publicly threatened the United States," as one of the more dangerous terrorist groups that Musharraf had allowed to remain active.[40]

In addition, State scolded the Pakistani strongman for failing to close down the madrassa terrorist hatcheries. "Islamabad also failed to take effective steps to curb the activities of certain madrassas, or religious schools, that serve as recruiting grounds for terrorism," according to the report.[41]

Musharraf's post–September 11 "crackdown" on Pakistani terrorism has not impressed FBI and Pentagon counterterrorism experts I have interviewed. Pakistan remains a relatively safe haven for terrorists. Karachi and Lahore are particular hot spots of al-Qaida activity. Here are just two examples:

In September 2002, U.S. naval intelligence working with Italian police arrested fifteen Pakistanis believed to be members of al-Qaida. Each man was carrying an open-return air ticket from Karachi.[42]

In December 2002, FBI agents working with local police arrested nine suspected al-Qaida operatives in Lahore, Pakistan. All nine were of Pakistani origin, though two were naturalized Americans.

U.S. authorities also suspect al-Qaida has Pakistani cells in America. In March 2002, four Pakistani nationals—Ghulam Qadar, Adnan Ahmed, Mohammad Nazir, and Ahmad Salam—deserted a Malta-registered cargo ship, the *Progreso*, when it docked at Norfolk, Virginia. "At this time we have reason to believe that the 4 deserters might be connected to al-Qaida," said the federal BOLO, or be-on-the-lookout, that went out to law enforcement agencies, a copy of which I obtained. INS the next month apprehended Ahmed, twenty-four, in Chicago. And Salam, twenty-seven, was arrested earlier in San Antonio. The other two appear to still be at large, likely absorbed by the huge Pakistani immigrant population in America, which totals 269,831, according to the Washington-based Center for Immigration Studies. Among Muslim countries, only Iran has a larger immigrant population in America.

The U.S. believes Pakistan, along with Afghanistan, has the world's highest concentration of al-Qaida agents.[43] It now likely shelters al-Qaida's top leaders, including bin Laden.

On September 20, 2001, Bush promised to punish any country that harbors terrorists. "Our enemy is a radical network of terrorists and every government that supports them," he told a wounded America that night. The bold statement became known as the Bush Doctrine. Under that doctrine, Pakistan would have been a legitimate target for military retaliation, at least as much as Afghanistan (and certainly more than Iraq, whose ties to September 11 are sketchy at best).

Yet Bush gave Pakistan blanket immunity. And defying all logic, he made it a key ally in our war on terrorism—which has resulted in intelligence sharing with the very ISI that aided and abetted the enemy. Then he rewarded Musharraf with a $1 billion economic aid package and other inducements such as debt relief. Enlisting a regime to help us bring to justice the terrorists it supported is odd enough.

No Choice but Pakistan?

But the unholy alliance with Pakistan also makes for strange statecraft. America, the world's greatest representative democracy, is cozying up to a military dictatorship that threatens a sister democracy right next door. India, unlike Pakistan, affords a free press and free elections. And unlike Pakistan, it has not been party to violence in foreign states. On the contrary, India has been a victim of such violence—chiefly from Pakistan—just as the U.S. has been. "For decades Pakistan has waged its own war by proxy against India through its Kashmiri surrogates controlled by the ISI, even while denying any links with or control over them," Trifkovic said.[44] In fact, just three months after Washington was attacked, Pakistani terrorists stormed the New Delhi parliament—a shocking act that brought the two nuclear states to the brink of war. India accuses al-Qaida–tied Jaish-e-Mohammed of involvement in the deadly December 13, 2001, attack, yet Musharraf won't hand over its leader to Indian authorities for questioning.

The Bush administration maintains it really had no choice but to partner with Pakistan. Afghanistan is landlocked, officials duly note, and U.S. forces needed overflight rights and bases in western Pakistan to hit targets inside Afghanistan. They also needed to evacuate wounded to Pakistani hospitals, the Senate foreign policy adviser pointed out to me. Though he admitted Pakistan is an unseemly ally, circumstances warranted the partnership.

"In World War II, we allied with Joe Stalin for crying out loud," the GOP aide said in a phone interview. "In wars, you do that."

Even so, the U.S. was given access to airspace over former Soviet republics Georgia and Azerbaijan, as well as ones bordering Afghanistan in the north and east. In addition, it was allowed to set up military bases in Kyrgyzstan, Uzbekistan, and Tajikistan, which is not far from Tora Bora, which should have been the key battleground of the Afghan war. Even after the U.S. military set up its own air base in Bagram, Afghanistan, the administration held on to the Pakistani bases nearby.

None of the Caspian countries that stepped forward to help us in Afghanistan has been accused of supporting terrorism, at least not to the extent Pakistan has. In effect, the Bush administration asked for permission to fly over a swamp in which terrorists breed to drain a swamp in which terrorists breed. Go figure.

The unholy alliance with Pakistan, as it turns out, was not just a desperate military measure, but part of a larger plan hatched by Zal Khalilzad, Bush's influential Afghan adviser, to secure an energy corridor linking the Caspian region with Pakistan.

5

THE GENERAL
Appeasing Musharraf

I would give the first priority that he is dead,
and the second priority that he is alive somewhere in Afghanistan.

—PAKISTANI PRESIDENT PERVEZ MUSHARRAF'S
advice to America regarding bin Laden

KHALILZAD'S EARLIER PRESCRIPTION FOR STABILIZING
Afghanistan also called for convincing Pakistan to disown the Taliban it
had husbanded. "Washington must weaken the Taliban, support moderate Afghans, and press Afghanistan's neighbors, particularly Pakistan, to
work against extremism in the region," he said. "As the Taliban's most
important sponsor, Pakistan bears a responsibility for its misdeeds and
can play an important role in transforming the movement.

"Ideally, Islamabad would support Washington's anti-Taliban campaign, using its influence and contacts to weaken the Taliban and encourage a more moderate leadership," he added. "More realistically, the United
States should press Pakistan to reduce its support for the Taliban."[1]

But he knew that would not be an easy task.

"The Taliban enjoys considerable support from Pakistan's military
and intelligence services and among Pakistan's strong Sunni Islamist community," explained Khalilzad, who has also spent time in Pakistan and

understands the local politics. "Furthermore, Pakistan's new government, which took power in a coup in October 1999, may prove even more supportive of the Taliban."[2]

Khalilzad, now a key adviser to Bush in the war on terrorism, also knew Pakistan had its hand out. Thanks in part to UN sanctions, foreign investment had dried up and its economy was in "shambles," he noted, and it was looking for some goodwill. Washington should use economic assistance as leverage, he advised.

At the same time, it should "make it clear to Islamabad that it understands and accepts Pakistan's legitimate interests in the region," said Khalilzad, who as a former oil industry consultant extolled the benefits of an energy corridor linking oil-rich Central Asia to Pakistan and Afghanistan in the south. "These legitimate interests include the existence of a non antagonistic Afghanistan willing to explore all mutually beneficial relationships, including the opening up of Central Asia to trade with the south and the promotion of economic development."[3]

Khalilzad had another point: "Washington must also emphasize that a stable Afghanistan that is based neither on exclusionary Pashtun dominance nor on Pakistani control of rigid and radical Islamists is far more in Pakistan's interest than the current high-risk strategy being followed."[4]

That is, Musharraf must be made to realize that supporting the Taliban does not promote Pakistan's long-term economic interests in the region. And more than anything the Taliban could offer him, a growing economy linked to vast energy resources would help the new dictator consolidate power at home and increase clout abroad, particularly with regard to rival India.

After the September 11 attacks, Khalilzad's recommendations became policy. Secretary of State Powell and his deputy, Armitage, drew up a list of seven demands for Musharraf to meet, with divorcing the Taliban key among them. The way the story was leaked to the press, however, no deal was brokered; the list was simply crammed down the military strongman's throat. Musharraf, who commands the eighth-largest army in the world and an arsenal of nuclear weapons (though no ICBMs), had to agree to all seven demands—or else. "The implicit signal to Pakistan today was that if it did not choose to cooperate with the United States, then it could find itself a target in any retaliation for Tuesday's attacks," the *New York Times* reported September 12, 2001. And that is how it was spun to the *Washington Post*'s Bob Woodward for his book, *Bush at War.* "This is not negotiable," Armitage told Pakistani military intelligence chief Ahmad as he handed him the list of demands.[5] Here they are, as recorded by Woodward:

1. Stop al-Qaida operatives at the border, intercept arms shipments through Pakistan and end ALL logistical support for bin Laden.
2. Blanket overflight and landing rights.
3. Access to Pakistan, naval bases, air bases and borders.
4. Immediate intelligence and immigration information.
5. Condemn the September 11 attacks and "curb all domestic expressions of support for terrorism against the [United States], its friends or allies."
6. Cut off all shipments of fuel to the Taliban and stop Pakistani volunteers from going into Afghanistan to join the Taliban.
7. "Should the evidence strongly implicate Osama bin Laden and the al-Qaida network in Afghanistan AND should Afghanistan and the Taliban continue to harbor him and his network, Pakistan will break diplomatic relations with the Taliban government, end support for the Taliban and assist us in the aforementioned ways to destroy Osama bin Laden and his al-Qaida network."

Musharraf agreed to all the demands. But contrary to White House spin, he did not succumb to arm-twisting. Rather, he was brought along with very expensive carrots.

Buying Pakistan

In exchange for Pakistan's so-called cooperation in the war, the Bush administration has so far provided it with some $2 billion in economic support funds, debt relief, and security assistance.[6] At the same time, it encouraged the International Monetary Fund to kick in big loans, including one for $135 million, and helped reschedule Pakistan's external debt. It even lifted long-standing economic sanctions against the rogue state stemming from its nuclear bomb testing. After the Taliban were ousted from Afghanistan, Bush's top diplomat for Pakistan and Afghanistan policy dashed over to the U.S.-Pakistan Business Council in Washington to remind investors of all the goodies.

"We greatly appreciate President Musharraf's bold and courageous decision to throw Pakistan's support firmly behind the coalition's efforts," said Christina Rocca, assistant secretary of state for South Asia. "Pakistan's support for the coalition has opened up great new vistas for enhanced economic cooperation with the U.S."[7]

The administration's "ultimate goal is to work together with the government of Pakistan to help set the economy back on track," asserted Rocca.

"In pursuit of these goals," she said, "we have:

- waived and suspended sanctions
- supported Pakistan in the IMF
- transferred to Pakistan $600 million in cash for balance of payments support
- decided to reopen a USAID [United States Agency for International Development] mission in Pakistan
- provided a $300 million line of credit for investment promotion [from the federal Overseas Private Investment Corporation, OPIC], as well as an unspecified amount of Export-Import Bank coverage
- [started] working with other Paris Club creditor nations to negotiate

a highly concessional [*sic*] debt rescheduling program for Pakistan's
bilateral debt[11]

Rocca closed by encouraging the council to "work with our embassy
in Islamabad and the Pakistan Board of Investment to attract U.S. trade
and investment in Pakistan." The oil and gas industry topped her list of
"key sectors" for investment.[8]

Toward that end, OPIC's $300 million line of credit will come in
handy. After announcing the special financing in October 2001, the president of the federal economic development agency declared that OPIC
programs, which include political risk insurance and loans for major
industrial projects, were "open for business in Pakistan.

"Pakistan's commitment to the war against terrorism becomes even
more meaningful for ordinary Pakistanis when foreign direct investment
supports the country's economic development," said OPIC President and
CEO Peter Watson.[9]

The economic package does not include the $617 million in hard
currency the U.S. so far has reimbursed Pakistan for expenses it claims it
has incurred helping the U.S. fight its war on terror.[10] And the administration has promised to sweeten the pot in the future.

Bad Buy

Has America gotten its money's worth out of Musharraf? So far he has
fully complied with only two of the seven demands he vowed to meet.

*1. Stop al-Qaida operatives at the border, intercept arms shipments
through Pakistan and end ALL logistical support for bin Laden.*

"We have deployed additional security all along the border, including,
for the first time, military troops," said Pakistani Foreign Ministry
spokesman Aziz Ahmed Khan. "We are looking for each and every one

who is crossing the border illegally. As far as we are concerned, the border is completely sealed."[11]

That is what Pakistan claimed in early December 2001 as hundreds, if not thousands, of al-Qaida fugitives escaped the Tora Bora region and other points along the Afghan border into Pakistan. Bin Laden himself is believed to have fled December 9, if not earlier (while tricking U.S. intelligence into thinking he was still in Tora Bora by leaving his monitored satellite phone with a bodyguard who continued to use the phone in Tora Bora).

Granted, Pakistan cannot be expected to "completely seal" off a 1,340-mile border, particularly one riddled with remote mountain passages, but Pakistani border guards did not even set up roadblocks opposite Tora Bora until December 17, which was like closing the proverbial barn door after the livestock had escaped. Even Defense Secretary Donald Rumsfeld complained that efforts to hunt down al-Qaida leaders along the Afghan-Pakistani border were hurt when Musharraf took troops off the border in early 2002 to confront India during renewed tensions. "They have forces along the Indian borders that we could use along the Afghan border," he noted.[12] Then the Pakistani dictator used his bogus election as an excuse for delaying action on bin Laden. "U.S. forces want permission to pursue al-Qaida forces in this area, but Gen. Musharraf has made it clear he cannot approve such action without jeopardizing an April 30 [2002] referendum on his request for five more years as president," reported *Washington Times* correspondent Arnaud de Borchgrave from Peshawar, Pakistan. "It would also provide ammunition to his opponents in October's national election."[13]

Even after roadblocks were set up, Pakistani border guards refused to stop al-Qaida leaders. "The Pakistani army would not be a problem" for al-Qaida members fleeing across the Afghan border into Pakistan, an Afghan informant in early February 2002 reported to a U.S. Special Forces adviser trying to cut off smuggling in northern Paktia province, which is close to Pakistan. "They wouldn't stop al-Qaida fugitives. A commander in the Pakistani army was arranging the cross-border movements" for senior members of the group, he said.[14]

Worse, several reports allege Pakistan's military worked with Afghan tribal leaders sympathetic with al-Qaida to help smuggle its leaders into Pakistan. Pakistani officials even bribed some tribal leaders, such as Younis Khalis, according to UPI. Khalis, who owns nice homes in Pakistan and has high-level connections there, had been given money in Pakistan to protect al-Qaida.[15] De Borchgrave interviewed a top Afghan tribal leader who said the ISI is protecting bin Laden and other al-Qaida leaders.[16]

Pakistan has vehemently denied the reports. Khan, the Foreign Ministry spokesman, called the reports "utter nonsense."[17]

But CentCom officials have told me that U.S. commanders on the ground in Afghanistan were well aware of such betrayals by the Pakistani military. "The ground commanders don't trust the Pakis any more than the Afghanis," an intelligence officer said.[18]

Musharraf angrily denies reports that the Pakistani military helped bin Laden and his wives and sons escape into Pakistan with other al-Qaida leaders. He says he is positive bin Laden is not hiding in northwestern Pakistan because the Pakistani military and police were combing the area and would have arrested him had they seen him.[19] In fact, the general tried to insist early last year that bin Laden was dead: "I think now, frankly, he is dead, for the reason he is a patient, he is a kidney patient. We know that he donated two dialysis machines into Afghanistan. One was specifically for his own personal use."[20]

If bin Laden does suffer from failing kidneys, Musharraf would know, according to at least one report. The night before September 11, Pakistani intelligence allegedly spirited bin Laden into a military hospital in Rawalpindi, Pakistan, for treatment of ailing kidneys. "On that night, they moved out all the regular staff in the urology department and sent in a secret team to replace them," an unidentified hospital nurse told CBS News. *Taliban* author Rashid said the story rings true: "There were reports that Pakistan intelligence had helped the Taliban buy dialysis machines and the rumor was that these were wanted for Osama bin Laden."[21] Others, however, maintain bin Laden suffers not from kidney failure, but from kidney stones.

Musharraf claims that if bin Laden is alive, he is still in Afghanistan. "I would give the first priority that he is dead," he said, "and the second priority that he is alive somewhere in Afghanistan."[22] Not surprisingly, his theory dovetails with Bush's. The president has assumed that if bin Laden were not dead, he would be "hiding in a cave" in Afghanistan.[23]

But that strains credulity for a number of reasons.

For one, CentCom's chief intelligence officer stopped getting daily briefings on Afghanistan in the fall of 2002, if not earlier, a U.S. intelligence official told me. "The chief intel officer for CentCom isn't even getting briefed on AFG anymore, not daily anyway," he said.[24]

Also, Maj. Gen. Franklin L. Hagenbeck, the commander of the army's 10th Mountain Division in Afghanistan, last year told the *New York Times* in an exclusive interview that virtually the entire senior leadership of al-Qaida fled the Tora Bora area and is operating with as many as one thousand non-Afghan fighters in the remote tribal areas of western Pakistan. He maintained that they were plotting terrorist attacks from Pakistan.[25]

The U.S. intelligence community, moreover, has traced al-Qaida e-mails—including recruiting messages from bin Laden's son—back to Pakistan. Much of the cyberspace activity is coming from the remote border regions of Pakistan.[26]

Other Bush officials have suggested bin Laden and his lieutenants could be in Yemen or the Philippines or Indonesia. "The al-Qaida operations in Afghanistan were destroyed. Another piece of this is to make sure that there are not other places that they can puddle or other places that they can gain the kind of foothold that they did in Afghanistan," Condoleezza Rice said. "And that's why you see us working with countries like Yemen or with the Philippines or Indonesia to try to keep that from happening."[27]

Still other officials think he may be holed up in Iran, which the Bush administration accused of being "the most active state sponsor of terrorism" in its 2001 report on global terrorism.[28] (Ironically, the administration opposes oil and gas pipeline routes through Iran as a matter of long-standing U.S. policy against conducting business with countries that sponsor, train, fund, or harbor terrorists, and that work to acquire weapons of mass destruction. But the administration supports pipeline routes through Pakistan even though it has sponsored, trained, funded, and harbored terrorists, and still harbors them, and it *already* has weapons of mass destruction.)

Rumsfeld has been all over the ballpark, speculating bin Laden could be in Sudan, Somalia, Saudi Arabia, or even Chechnya—but not Pakistan.[29]

Most recently, Bush tried to suggest he may be in Iraq. "Some al-Qaida leaders who fled Afghanistan went to Iraq," Bush claimed last fall in his speech justifying military action against Iraq. He emphasized that any state that harbors terrorists is an enemy of America, apparently not seeing the glaring hypocrisy in exempting Pakistan.[30] It is plain that Bush cannot bear to admit that America's top terrorist enemy has found safe refuge in the bosom of America's so-called vital ally in the war on terrorism. That is a messy proposition indeed.

The November 2002 recording of bin Laden offers yet another clue that the al-Qaida leader is in Pakistan. The audiotape that confirmed his survival was given to an Al-Jazeera correspondent in Pakistan (the Arab TV network is based in Qatar). An apparent al-Qaida agent met Ahmed Muhaffaq Ziedan in Islamabad and gave him a TDK audiocassette containing bin Laden's three-minute message praising last October's resurgent al-Qaida attacks. "He came to me, and said he has a tape for me from bin Laden and disappeared," said Ziedan.[31]

Musharraf insists the terrorist overlord has not found refuge in his country. But it would not be the first time he has lied.

Jim Hoagland, the *Washington Post*'s respected foreign affairs columnist, pointed out that the Pakistani president-for-life—whom he calls a "confirmed and practiced liar"—told a whopper when he said he ended terrorism in Kashmir, for example. "Musharraf lied publicly when giving pledges last spring [2002] to end cross-border terrorism—pledges he has broken," Hoagland wrote. "Musharraf even lied about whether President

Bush had talked to him about that subject in a September meeting in New York."

Yet "he has paid no price for lying to Powell about ending terrorism in Kashmir or about cooperating fully in crushing al-Qaida," he added. "The only consequences for duplicity have been rewards and protection."[32]

Meanwhile, the bin Laden manhunt moves at a glacial pace.

Despite the Pakistani military's failure to seal off the Afghan border during the Tora Bora battle, CentCom is piggybacking on its patrol of border areas rather than leading it. U.S. forces are not operating independently of the Pakistani military in the Peshawar region in deference to Musharraf, who has agreed only to let U.S. military advisers accompany Pakistani troops. In fact, U.S. troops are prohibited from pursuing al-Qaida fighters from Afghanistan into Pakistan. An American soldier who tried last December was shot in the head by a Pakistani border guard. "Absolutely not. The Americans cannot cross the Pakistani border from Afghanistan to chase what they say are vestiges of Taliban and al-Qaida," Pakistani Information Minister Sheikh Rashid Ahmed told the Associated Press after the incident. And Pakistani Foreign Minister Khursheed Kasuri drove the point home in a written statement: "From the first day, it has been absolutely clear and fully understood that operations within Pakistani territory would be conducted solely and exclusively by our own forces and in response to decisions taken by Pakistan." U.S. Major General Hagenbeck last year said the Pakistani military had developed its own plan for driving al-Qaida and the Taliban from their mountain redoubts. So U.S. forces agreed not to cross the border to pursue them.[33] Hagenbeck, however, expressed confidence that Pakistani troops would capture al-Qaida. "They are interested in ridding western Pakistan of al-Qaida," he said, even though al-Qaida has aided Pakistan's campaign in Kashmir.

Reality is, Pakistani soldiers are anything but interested in crushing al-Qaida or Taliban fugitives. "The Pakistani military were loath to risk firefights with their erstwhile Taliban clients and allies, and never went into the remote border areas," noted historian Trifkovic.[34] And if they did, they would be shooting their own. You see, the Taliban are not just in league with Pakistanis; they *are* Pakistanis. "The Taliban were born in Pakistani refugee camps, educated in Pakistani madrassas and learned their fighting skills from Mujahideen parties based in Pakistan," said Taliban expert Rashid. "Their families carried Pakistani identity cards."[35] It is not hard for al-Qaida fugitives to go underground in Pakistan, either. They have wide support throughout Pakistan, including in the military-run government.

Simply hoping Pakistan will arrest Taliban and al-Qaida leaders is not good enough. But that appears to be all the administration is doing— even though Bush vowed to step in if he sees allies dragging their feet.

"Some governments will be timid in the face of terror. And make no mistake about it: If they do not act, America will," Bush vowed in his 2002 State of the Union speech. Despite Musharraf's timidity in ferreting out al-Qaida, Bush has not acted. CentCom commander General Franks seems concerned only with making sure al-Qaida is driven out of Afghanistan.[36] And Bush's chairman of the Joint Chiefs of Staff, Gen. Richard Myers, has said he is leaving it up to Pakistani forces to find and detain any al-Qaida leaders entrenched in Pakistan.[37] In other words, the administration is trusting Muslim proxy forces to do in Pakistan what Muslim proxy forces *failed* to do in Afghanistan.

"President Musharraf has been very helpful," Bush complimented the leader. "And we believe he'll help with Mr. bin Laden, too—if in fact he happens to be in Pakistan."[38]

Such blind trust seems extremely foolish in light of Musharraf's track record with respect to apprehending bin Laden. As soon as he took power, the Pakistani dictator reportedly canceled a top-secret mission being planned with the U.S. to send commandos, using Pakistani intelligence, into Afghanistan to snatch bin Laden.[39]

2. Blanket overflight and landing rights.

Musharraf met this demand and took a lot of heat for it from the Pakistani people, who violently protested the U.S. military presence in

Pakistan. But the additional bombing sorties made possible by access to Pakistani airspace aided regime change in Afghanistan, not the far more critical goal of eradicating al-Qaida.

3. Access to Pakistan, naval bases, air bases and borders.

Musharraf provided five air bases, at least two of which the U.S. is still using.[40] Unfortunately, they have helped little in rounding up al-Qaida leaders. Teaming up with Pakistan's military has hurt those efforts. "While Mr. Musharraf's cooperation was helpful to the military campaign in Afghanistan, the Pakistani army's deliberate failure to block al-Qaida's escape routes ensured that all the big fish have safely slipped away," Trifkovic stated.[41]

4. Immediate intelligence and immigration information.

U.S. authorities were not exactly confident in Musharraf's ability to warn them of Pakistani terrorists attempting to enter the U.S. In September 2002, Attorney General John Ashcroft authorized the INS to fingerprint, photograph, and even track the whereabouts of young Pakistani men entering the U.S. on visas.

"The attorney general has determined warranting special registration of certain nonimmigrant aliens who are citizens or nationals of Pakistan, Saudi Arabia and Yemen who are males between 16 and 45 years of age," said Johnny N. Williams, executive associate INS commissioner of field operations, in a September 5, 2002, memo to INS regional directors. The four-page memo, a copy of which I obtained and posted on the independent news site WorldNetDaily.com, which broke the story, also gave INS inspectors the authority to specially register any foreign visitors who cannot credibly explain trips to Pakistan stamped in their passports.[42]

The policy, which went into effect October 1, 2002, outraged Islamabad. "You are going to fingerprint and mugshot our people as if they are common criminals," complained Pakistan embassy spokesman Asad Hayauddin. "It will certainly leave a bad taste among Pakistanis."[43]

In addition, Musharraf has refused to turn over leaders of al-Qaida–linked terrorist groups, such as Pakistan-based Jaish-e-Mohammed, to the FBI for interrogation. FBI agents have complained they have been denied access to suspects and information by Pakistani authorities.

5. Condemn the September 11 attacks and "curb all domestic expressions of support for terrorism against the [United States], its friends or allies."

In Islamic nations, words and deeds are often at variance, particularly when dealing with non-Muslims. Pakistan is a textbook example.

Musharraf quickly condemned the attacks and, a few months later, solemnly pledged to crack down on terrorist groups based in his country. "Pakistan rejects terrorism in all its forms and manifestations, and has fully cooperated with the international coalition in that spirit," Musharraf stated.[44]

But the cooperation from Musharraf has been selective at best.

Yes, he finally agreed to ban Jaish-e-Mohammed (Army of Mohammed), the Pakistan-based terrorist group tied to al-Qaida, after U.S. authorities pressured him. And, yes, he took into custody its founder and leader Maulana Masood Azhar.

But Musharraf put him under house arrest, and refused to allow U.S. and Indian authorities to question him about various J-e-M acts of terrorism. Both countries sought his extradition. And then, on December 14, 2002, the Pakistani leader very quietly had Azhar released from custody! The al-Qaida–tied terrorist leader is free today.[45] Why? Turns out Azhar has been instrumental in funding and training Kashmiri fighters for Musharraf's campaign against India. "It is quite clear that the investigation and charges against Masood Azhar have not been pursued by Pakistani authorities with any seriousness," complained a spokesman for the Indian Foreign Ministry.[46]

Musharraf also went easy on two nuclear scientists tied to bin Laden.

Sultan Bashir-ud-Din Mehmood and Abdul Majid made several trips to the Afghan capital of Kabul, where bin Laden arranged meetings with them. Mehmood spoke with bin Laden, with whom he shares the same hard-core Islamic beliefs, as late as July 2001. His son told the Associated Press in December 2002 that they discussed building a nuclear bomb. Both scientists worked for Pakistan's Atomic Energy Commission and had close contacts with Pakistan's main spy agency, the ISI. Mehmood retired and devoted his time to his charity, the Holy Quran Research Foundation, which is on the U.S. list of terrorist groups. After the U.S. made noise over their links to al-Qaida, the men were taken into custody (Mehmood reportedly was held at an ISI safe house). But in December 2001, Musharraf quietly freed both scientists, who are under a gag order from the ISI.[47] It was akin to the kid-glove treatment afforded J-e-M chief Azhar.

"Pakistan is now cracking down on terror, and I admire the strong leadership of President Musharraf," Bush said in last year's State of the Union address.

But U.S. authorities involved in counterterrorism do not share his optimism. In various phone interviews over the last year, FBI agents have expressed frustration with what they describe as the low level of cooperation Pakistani authorities have offered to bring terrorists there to justice.

Former Indian officials, moreover, tell me that Bush is being played by Musharraf, and they point to the Pearl murder case as clear proof.

Conventional wisdom says Daniel Pearl, the late financial journalist in charge of the *Wall Street Journal*'s South Asia bureau, was kidnapped and beheaded by al-Qaida–linked terrorists in Karachi, Pakistan, because he was investigating al-Qaida shoe-bomber Richard Reid's ties to Pakistan. But the conventional wisdom apparently has not read a damning report Pearl filed just three weeks before his abduction that exposed Musharraf's terrorist "crackdown" as a fraud. The article appeared on page one of the *Asian Wall Street Journal* on December 31, 2001, under the headline, "Militant Groups in Pakistan Thrive Despite Crackdown: Jaish-e-Mohammed Says It Is Still Operating After Police Detained

Some Staff; India Demands Clear Evidence of Action." Pearl, based in India, paid a visit to J-e-M's headquarters in Bahawalpur, Pakistan. He discovered that "the crackdown doesn't look so harsh.

"Members of Jaish-e-Mohammed said the group is still operating. They say provincial police officers rang the doorbell of the administrative office early last week and herded staffers into waiting vans, but left behind enough people to keep the office running," Pearl wrote. In addition, "a nearby Jaish-e-Mohammed regional center was still operating Thursday, its traditional recruiting day. The group's name had been painted over, but the posters praising holy war are still hung inside," Pearl reported. "And a bank account that Jaish-e-Mohammed uses to solicit contributions remains open, despite a November order by Pakistan's central bank freezing the group's accounts."

The intrepid investigative reporter learned that J-e-M kept an account at Allied Bank in Bahawalpur. So he sniffed around there, too, and found that no accounts had been frozen. Pearl pressed the assistant branch manager, Muslim Bhatti, about it, but the manager denied the terrorist group held an account there.

Pearl also revealed that J-e-M activists moved files and computers to a secret location four days before the police raids began. At the same time, Azhar appointed a deputy to keep the headquarters running in his absence. Azhar was placed under house arrest following the raid. The moves indicated the terrorists were tipped off about the raid.

Why would Musharraf go easy on J-e-M? Pearl thought he had the answer—Kashmir.

"Jaish-e-Mohammed was considered a favorite among the militant groups that receive unofficial Pakistani support. Its operatives drove expensive 'double-cabin' Hilux pickup trucks, some with government license plates," he reported. J-e-M enjoyed such support because it sent thousands of fighters and funds into India-controlled Kashmir "to help fuel a separatist movement there." And that would go a long way toward explaining why, as Pearl reported, police did not ask J-e-M detainees "about the group's alleged participation in recent terrorist strikes in India," including the December 13, 2001, attack on the New Delhi parliament that had rekindled border tensions. At the time Pearl filed his story, India and Pakistan were amassing troops on their borders, causing the evacuation of some border villages.

J-e-M is one of many militant groups supporting Islamabad's campaign against sworn foe India in Kashmir, groups that Bush at the time had urged Musharraf to crush. The Pakistani strongman reported to Bush that he had arrested fifty members of militant groups. But Pearl looked into it and found that officials in Pakistan "couldn't verify that claim."

The respected reporter, whose office was in Bombay, India, apparently had also gained access to a report from Indian intelligence revealing Musharraf's crackdown on terrorist groups as nothing more than window dressing designed to fool his new American benefactors, according to my Indian sources, as well as Pakistan-based journalists. And this made Pearl dangerous not only to terrorist groups like J-e-M, but also to their silent partners in Islamabad—namely, the ISI, whose main goal is to end Indian rule in Kashmir.

Indeed, former ISI officers Brigadier Abdullah, who headed the spy agency's Kashmir operations, and Brig. Ijaz Shah, the highest security official in Pakistan's governing province of Punjab, played a key role in cultivating J-e-M—and pampering Omar Sheikh, the mastermind behind the plot to kill Pearl. Sheikh was allowed to turn himself in to Brigadier Shah on February 5, 2002, in his parents' hometown of Lahore, which is in Punjab province and near Kashmir.[48] It was not until February 12 that Sheikh's arrest was announced—one day before Musharraf met with Bush in the White House with his hand out for more aid. In that intervening week, Islamabad told U.S. authorities it was still looking for Pearl's killer. The delay looked to many like Musharraf was trying to impress Bush right before their meeting. If so, it worked: Bush on February 13 offered Musharraf an additional $200 million in U.S. aid.[49]

While in Washington, the Pakistani strongman also held out hope that Pearl was still alive—when Pakistani authorities knew he had been dead since at least January 31.[50] Pearl's death was announced after Musharraf returned to Islamabad with Bush's chit for more succor safely in his pocket. Bush officials were then fooled into believing Sheikh, who had already been indicted in the U.S. for the 1994 kidnapping of an American tourist in India, might be extradited to America.

But while in protective custody in Karachi (to where he was moved from Lahore after the "arrest" was announced), it was widely reported that Sheikh blabbed about his ties to ISI and his role in the recent terrorist attacks on India—as well as his ties to bin Laden and al-Qaida operations. In the end, Musharraf refused to hand over Sheikh to the U.S. He also barred reporters from Sheikh's court proceedings. Indian officials contend Musharraf was worried that Sheikh would reveal his ISI links—and more—to U.S. investigators. The refusal was indeed suspicious in view of Pakistan's swift extradition last decade of Ramzi Yousef and other terrorists sought by the U.S. The well-connected Sheikh remains a glaring exception.

The Bush administration, for its part, seemed reluctant to draw attention to one of Pakistan's most dangerous terrorist groups. Despite early warnings from Indian intelligence about J-e-M's ties to al-Qaida, the State Department did not blacklist the organization until December 26, 2001. Britain's Home Office, by comparison, had done so nine months earlier. In a phone interview at the time, Joe Reap, spokesman for State's Office of Counterterrorism, maintained that J-e-M's ties to al-Qaida were limited to "terrorist training in Afghanistan."[51]

In spite of Pakistan's unremitting homegrown violence, Wendy J. Chamberlin, then U.S. ambassador to Pakistan, was never short on praise for Musharraf and all his "help" in the war on terror. She said he was doing a good job cracking down on terrorists with his self-described "iron hand."

Yet while he was supposedly busy smashing terrorism, Pakistani or Pakistan-tied terrorists still managed to:

- gun down eighteen Christians worshiping in St. Dominic's Church in Bahawalpur, Pakistan;
- attack the Indian parliament and come close to igniting a nuclear war;
- nearly blow up an American Airlines jumbo jet with a shoe bomb;
- attack the U.S. Information Center in Calcutta, India, killing four guards and injuring twelve others including consulate staff;
- decapitate a prominent American journalist in Karachi;
- toss grenades into an Islamabad church packed with foreigners, killing five, including two Americans;
- blow up eleven foreigners and two other people and injure twenty-three in a suicide bus-bombing outside a Karachi hotel;
- and, murder eleven people and injure forty-five in a suicide car-bombing outside the U.S. consulate in Karachi.

After the March 17, 2002, attack on the Islamabad church, which killed a U.S. embassy administrator and her teenage daughter, Chamberlin's two teenage girls were evacuated from Islamabad, where they were living with their mother in the diplomatic enclave there. Chamberlin, who at one point had to be escorted to her offices by U.S. commandos,[52] bailed out of the Pakistani capital soon afterward.[53] The Bush administration last May had to find a replacement for her on a temporary basis until the Senate could confirm the new ambassador in August 2002.

Back safe, or at least safer, in America, Chamberlin is likely rethinking her original impressions of Pakistan, which she expressed in glowing terms at her Senate confirmation hearing. "American and Pakistani people believe in many of the same core values," she testified. "We are both a deeply religious peoples. We are both ethnically diverse societies ... We both want ... our laws to protect the weak and the minorities."[54]

Islamabad insists the rash of horrific attacks in Pakistan was the result of a few bad apples. It is unfair to condemn a nation of 147 million for the acts of a "select few evil ones," argued the head of Pakistan's official news organ. "Pakistan and the United States have banded together to fight international terrorism. Pakistan has been the front-line state in the war against terrorism," said Asim Mughal, editor of the Pakistan News Service. He told me that any attempts to link Pakistan with Islamic terrorism is "racist" and "insulting," and an attempt to "undo the efforts of President Bush and President Musharraf in cementing the bonds of friendship" between our two nations.[55]

Truth is, Musharraf is a dictator running a police state. If he really wanted to put terrorist groups out of business or force banks to freeze their assets or track charity-laundered terror funds or close madrassas incubating future bin Ladens, he could have just snapped his fingers.

But he did not.

Money often is pumped into such terrorist groups through Pakistani charities, yet Musharraf has taken only mincing steps toward curbing such money laundering. The head of the Financial Action Task Force (FATF), an international body working to combat terror financing, said he was perplexed by Islamabad's failure to follow FATF's anti-money-laundering procedures.[56] As of late last year, Pakistan still had no system to track the transactions of foreign charities in Pakistan—even though about two-thirds of all groups designated as having a terrorist link by the U.S. and UN have a Pakistani connection, according to the Treasury Department.[57]

Pakistan remains in direct violation of Bush's doctrine. "From this day forward, any nation that continues to harbor or support terrorism will be regarded by the United States as a hostile regime" subject to military punishment, the president vowed before Congress on September 20, 2002.

Yet Bush keeps blowing Musharraf kisses.

6. Cut off all shipments of fuel to the Taliban and stop Pakistani volunteers from going into Afghanistan to join the Taliban.

Part of the reason Bush needed to cozy up to Pakistan is to get it to stop supplying and arming the Taliban so Afghan opposition forces would have an easier time overthrowing the regime. Pakistan did it anyway in the month after Musharraf agreed to cut off aid.

On at least October 8 and October 12, Pakistani border guards at a checkpoint in the Khyber Pass waved through convoys of trucks headed into Afghanistan. Hidden under tarps in the back of the trucks were rifles, ammunition, and rocket-propelled grenade launchers.[58] The ISI-approved military shipments, which were delivered at night to the Taliban stronghold of Kandahar, also included fuel.[59]

Islamabad let thousands of Pakistani mercenaries join the Taliban in the battle against U.S. and U.S.-backed forces. And as the Taliban forces were being overrun, the Pakistani air force flew to their rescue, airlifting them back to Pakistan—and the Bush administration reportedly let it happen at the request of Musharraf, who was concerned the Pakistani Taliban would be massacred. At least three Pakistani aircraft in mid-November were seen landing in Kunduz, Afghanistan, as the Northern Alliance prepared to storm the city.[60]

Not all Pakistanis aiding the Taliban in Afghanistan managed to escape, however. Detainees held in Guantánamo for questioning included at least fifty-eight Pakistani nationals. But even they were turned over to Pakistan later.[61]

7. *"Should the evidence strongly implicate Osama bin Laden and the al-Qaida network in Afghanistan AND should Afghanistan and the Taliban continue to harbor him and his network, Pakistan will break diplomatic relations with the Taliban government, end support for the Taliban and assist us in the aforementioned ways to destroy Osama bin Laden and his al-Qaida network."*

Even after the 1998 embassy bombings, when the Taliban continued to shelter al-Qaida, Pakistan still formally recognized it as the official government of Afghanistan. Pakistan, Saudi Arabia, and the UAE were the only countries in the world that did. The Taliban even had offices in Islamabad. Despite UN and U.S. pressure, Musharraf held fast to his pro-Taliban stand—until Bush showered him with aid in the wake of September 11. Then he finally cut ties. Appeasing the Pakistani strongman also helped shore up support for the new U.S.-friendly regime in Kabul, one amenable to the development of the proposed energy corridor. In a subtle slap, however, Musharraf nonetheless maintained diplomatic ties with the Taliban in the weeks following the American attacks, allowing its ambassador to stay in Islamabad and hold court before the world press, spewing propaganda—much to the consternation of the Bush administration.

In another act of defiance, one that has received little notice, Pakistani officials were accused of sheltering many top Taliban leaders who fled to Pakistan from their southern Afghanistan stronghold of Kandahar. They allegedly included much of Mullah Omar's cabinet, including his spokesman Syed Tayyab Agha and Justice Minister Nooruddin Turabi. Islamabad has angrily denied the allegations.[62]

Khalilzad's Game Plan

The White House's odd willingness to turn a blind eye to Musharraf's "double game in Afghanistan," as author Trifkovic called it, has started to draw suspicion—and criticism—around the world. "It was wrong to assume either that Musharraf is turning into a Pakistani Kemal Ataturk [the secular Turkish reformer], or that Pakistan itself was a stable and reliably responsible partner of the United States, let alone an 'ally' in the way Britain is, or Russia could be," Trifkovic said.[63] For that matter, during a joint news conference in Pushkin, Russia, Russian President Vladimir Putin last fall openly questioned Bush's judgment in partnering with Pakistan. In an embarrassing moment for the White House, Putin pointedly asked, "Where has Osama taken refuge?" He then cited reports that bin Laden is hiding in Pakistan, wondering aloud whether Musharraf was doing enough to help America stamp out al-Qaida.[64]

Bush continued to praise and reward Musharraf, even after learning

he provided nuclear technology to North Korea, which Bush has condemned as part of the "axis of evil." In return, North Korea gave Islamabad
ballistic missile parts to help it build nuclear-tipped missiles capable of
reaching strategic targets in India. In July 2002, while Musharraf was supposed to be devoting his military resources to hunting al-Qaida, he used
an American-built C-130 cargo plane to pick up the secret shipments of
missile parts.[65] When the *New York Times* first broke the shocking story,
quoting unnamed U.S. intelligence officials, the White House refused to
discuss Pakistan's role in aiding North Korea's nuke program.[66] In fact, it
intentionally left out the Pakistani angle in previous disclosures about
Pyongyang's secret program.[67] Powell and other State Department officials
have since tried to brush aside the problem by noting assurances from
Pakistan that it is currently not providing assistance to North Korea.
Musharraf, for his part, has categorically denied that Pakistan has provided any nuclear aid to the Communist regime *at any time*, a claim that
Hoagland adds to the list of lies from Bush's antiterror war ally.

"Pakistan's role as a clandestine supplier shatters the Bush administration's efforts to paint that country as a flawed but well-meaning member of the coalition against terror," said the *Post*'s Hoagland, who called
Pakistan "the most dangerous place on Earth" now that it is known to be
exporting nuclear technology as well as Islamic terrorism.[68]

Yet even after the disturbing revelation, Bush restored the U.S. military ties with Pakistan that were suspended in 1998 when the rogue state
tested nuclear weapons. U.S. and Pakistani forces in October 2002 conducted the first joint military exercises in four years. General Franks personally attended the maneuvers—a largely symbolic move since he fought
the Afghan war itself from Florida.[69] U.S. training of young Pakistani
officers also may be under way, a carrot that was dangled in negotiations
with Islamabad after September 11.[70]

More alarming, Bush is reconsidering the 1990 Pressler amendment
that cut off U.S. military aid to Pakistan to punish it for its nuclear
weapons development program, a move that was also hinted at in early

discussions with Musharraf, administration officials told me. Pakistan has submitted an arms wish list to the administration, including some twenty-eight F-16 fighter jets the country had ordered years ago. The warplanes were blocked by the Pressler amendment, but the administration may work to clear their delivery.[71] Smaller arms shipments are in the offing.[72] At first blush, these moves would appear to make absolutely no sense.

But they also were part of Bush adviser Khalilzad's game plan. To help persuade Pakistan to sever ties with the Taliban, he proposed "a major policy review of U.S.-Pakistan relations" that included reconsidering the Pressler amendment.

"The Pressler amendment has, if anything, proven counterproductive in stopping Pakistan's nuclear program. It has also led to a slide in U.S.-Pakistan relations," he argued. "Increasing U.S. leverage may require lifting or modifying the Pressler amendment."[73]

The promise of renewed shipment of U.S. military equipment to Pakistan would help wed the ISI to America's anti-Taliban policy, Khalilzad argued with an eye toward clearing a path for the Caspian energy corridor through Afghanistan to Pakistan.

"Particular attention should be focused on pushing the [Pakistani] intelligence service to rethink its Afghanistan policy," he said. "The military, and through it the intelligence services, could become more inclined to cooperate with U.S. initiatives if it saw the promise of gaining access to U.S. military hardware and expertise." He added, such controversial "measures require devoting more high-level attention to the difficult problem of persuading, and pressuring, Pakistan to support U.S. objectives in Afghanistan."[74]

Khalilzad knew that such attention would have to come from the Oval Office. After September 11, it did. Musharraf and the ISI were essentially bought off, and the Taliban were driven out of power without much resistance from Islamabad. Now it was up to Khalilzad to install a pliable government in Kabul to carry out those so-called "objectives in Afghanistan."

THE ROYALISTS
Sucking Up to the Saudis

What I don't like is demonizing Saudi Arabia. It's not true. They are not enemies of ours. And to come under that kind of criticism, I think, is ridiculous.

—FORMER PRESIDENT GEORGE H. W. BUSH

ADEL AL-JUBEIR WAS FURIOUS. THE THIN, BUG-EYED FOREIGN policy adviser to Saudi Crown Prince Abdullah stormed into Justice Department headquarters and demanded to know if what he had read on the Internet was true. According to a confidential government memo, Attorney General John Ashcroft had authorized INS agents to fingerprint and track certain high-risk citizens of Saudi Arabia entering the U.S. on visas. Starting October 1, 2002, male visitors between the ages of sixteen and forty-five would be subject to special registration. Al-Jubeir, who is based in Washington, complained that the Saudi royal government was "shocked" and highly offended to have its citizens added to the INS antiterrorist-tracking system with those of the five Mideast countries designated as state sponsors of terrorism. He demanded Saudis be treated no differently from other visitors. At the time, only visitors from Iran, Iraq, Sudan, Libya, and Syria were singled out for special scrutiny.

But given that the September 11 hijackers were not from those nations, and fifteen of the nineteen were from Saudi Arabia, it was only logical to expand the program. From his September 20, 2002, high-level meeting—which he managed to get the day after WorldNetDaily.com first posted the four-page Justice Department memo on its news site[1]— al-Jubeir claimed to have walked away with assurances from top Ashcroft aide David T. Ayers that Saudi visitors to the U.S. would not be finger-printed, photographed, or monitored. "The Department of Justice has informed the Kingdom of Saudi Arabia that in regard to entry into the United States, Saudi citizens will not be treated any differently than cit-izens of any other nation," the royal embassy of Saudi Arabia announced.[2] It was a face-saving effort by the Saudis, who had parsed a letter from Ayers to al-Jubeir—though it was not hard to do. The two-page letter does not actually deny the policy, but it is written in a way that could give that impression.

"It was wonderful to have the opportunity to spend some time with you on Friday afternoon," Ashcroft's chief of staff opened his September 23 letter to "Adel." "After hearing so many good words about you, I was impressed to see that you lived up to these expectations.

"During our visit, you provided me with copies of some documents from the Internet. As you may recall, I did not review these documents in our meeting. I later learned that the documents, if they were legitimate, would have been classified as law enforcement sensitive," he continued. "Therefore, it would have been inappropriate for me to comment on the specific documents which you provided from the Internet in any way."[3]

It was a nice dodge. Instead of confirming the part of the sensitive memo authorizing "special registration of certain nonimmigrant aliens who are citizens of Pakistan, Saudi Arabia and Yemen who are males between 16 and 45," Ayers just told the Saudi official what the memo, dated September 5, 2002, did *not* authorize. "All citizens of only five countries which are designated as state sponsors of terrorism will be required to be registered and fingerprinted under the National Security Entry Exit Registration System (NSEERS)," he said. "Any citizen of any nation visiting the United States can be included in the NSEERS, but all citizens of no other nation, including Saudi Arabia, will be subject to NSEERS as required by current U.S. law." Technically, he was right. "All citizens" of Saudi Arabia would not be fingerprinted. Just young Saudi men. Ayers then encouraged Saudi Arabia to share information about suspected terrorists, hinting that perhaps it had not been very forthcoming in the past. "Any intelligence that Saudi Arabia shares about specific individuals of concern will be greatly appreciated and will assist our targeting," he said, before closing with a warm wish about "advancing the friendship that our nations share."[4]

Unnatural Allies

What struck me most when I broke this story was not that the Saudis would make a fuss over being targeted for antiterrorist screening, but that the Bush administration waited so long to do it. The U.S. intelligence community had known for nearly a year that three-fourths of the hijackers were Saudis and that Saudi Arabia helped finance al-Qaida operations, in effect making it a state accomplice to September 11. Yet it took the administration that long to agree to just keep tabs on high-risk Saudis entering the U.S. on visas, something many members of Congress had recommended several months earlier. At least through screening and tracking, authorities may be able to stop another fifteen young Saudi males from slaughtering thousands of Americans.

I also was stunned by the administration's response to the Saudi protest. It refused to stand firmly behind a common-sense policy to protect Americans because it was more worried about offending its Saudi "friend." Other media who tried to follow up on the story were told by Justice officials that they could not confirm the expanded fingerprinting policy, claiming the memo was classified, even though it was not. Justice later felt compelled to send reporters a press release stating, "The Department of Justice considers Saudi Arabia an ally in the war on terrorism."[5]

But if Saudi Arabia is an ally in fighting terrorism, it is only because the Bush administration has made it so—much like Pakistan. Americans are forced to suspend disbelief in both cases.

Only Pakistan resents America more than Saudi Arabia does. Nearly two-thirds of Saudis say they dislike this country. The 64 percent unfavorable rating is the second highest among the Muslim nations surveyed by Gallup following September 11.[6] Tellingly, the Saudi government refused to allow Gallup to ask Saudi citizens questions about September 11.

The anti-American hostility flows from their religion. A growing portion of the Saudi population practices an extremist brand of Islam similar to Talibanism. It is called Wahhabism, a form of Islamic supremacy that teaches that Muslims are chosen by the Koran to cleanse society of "impurities"—namely, Judaism, Christianity, and paganism—and establish a global nation of Islam through violence if necessary. The sect evolved from the teachings of Abd el-Wahhab, an eighteenth-century Muslim cleric who wanted to reform Muslims and make them follow more strictly their prophet Mohammed's commands in the Koran. Many adherents of Wahhabism "were and remain open admirers of Hitler and the Nazis," contended Monu Nalapat, director of the School of Geopolitics at Manipal Academy of Higher Education in India.

"During World War II, preachers at many Saudi-influenced places of worship in the Middle East spoke out in support of the Hitlerite armies," Nalapat said, although the Saudi capital of Riyadh joined Allied forces in declaring war on Germany. "Today, some websites and print publications controlled by Wahhabbists describe the Holocaust as a myth and praise the 'discipline and faith' of the Nazis."[7]

Wahhabism counts bin Laden and al-Qaida among its top adherents.

While Saudi apologists insist the royal government is more secular, or at least more moderate, than the masses, facts tell a foggier truth.

"The Kingdom of Saudi Arabia remains the most intolerant Islamic regime in the world. Within Saudi Arabia, the practice of any religion besides Islam is as strictly prohibited now as it was in Mohammed's lifetime," said Islam historian Trifkovic, author of *The Sword of the Prophet*. "While the Saudis continue to build mosques all over the world, thousands of foreign workers for India, Europe, America and the Philippines must worship in secret, if at all. They are arrested, lashed, or deported for public display of their beliefs." Twenty-first-century Saudi women, moreover, are still not allowed to vote or drive.

Crown Prince Abdullah is a devout Muslim who in so many words has praised the "bravery" of Palestinian suicide bombers, whose families have been rewarded with fat Saudi checks.[8] He frowns on the westernization of Saudis living abroad, particularly those among the thirty-thousand-member royal family. Many of them reside in tony communities in Washington, New York, and London. They wear stylish Western clothing, and men *and women* drive fancy cars. An American who recently worked in security for the House of Saud told me that Abdullah is so disgusted with the westernization of Saudi royals living abroad that he plans to recall them to Saudi Arabia when his half brother dies.[9] The ailing King Fahd turned over the reins of power to Abdullah in 1995.

Under Abdullah, moreover, the Riyadh-based monarchy joined Islamabad in bringing the Taliban to power. And it sent thousands of young Saudi men through bin Laden's camps in Afghanistan for jihadi training. Meanwhile, it bankrolled al-Qaida terrorist operations, wittingly or not, through Saudi-based charities, an issue I'll return to in detail further on.

In an attempt to blunt such facts, al-Jubeir and others constantly remind us that the House of Saud long ago banished bin Laden, stripping him of his Saudi citizenship in 1994.

But the distancing may be more symbolic than real. Some in Saudi intelligence, as well as the royal family, allegedly have maintained ties with bin Laden and are reluctant to help the U.S. capture him. "The Saudis preferred to leave bin Laden alone in Afghanistan because his arrest and trial by the Americans could expose the deep relationship that bin Laden continued to have with sympathetic members of the royal family and elements within Saudi intelligence, which could prove deeply embarrassing," said Rashid, author of the bestseller *Taliban*. "The Saudis wanted bin Laden either dead or a captive of the Taliban—they did not want him captured by the Americans." In fact, the former Saudi intelligence chief, Prince Turki bin Faisal, is accused of cutting a deal with bin Laden in 1998 to leave him in Afghanistan and not work with Washington to extradite him, while pumping more money into the Taliban regime sheltering him.[10] This explains why Riyadh maintained diplomatic ties to the Taliban even after their uber-terrorist guest bin Laden blew up the U.S. embassies in Africa in 1998 and USS *Cole* in Yemen in 2000.

Even now, "the royal family knows where bin Laden is," emphasized an American who worked in the House of Saud. "They hold the purse strings to the operation."[11]

It is also a popular notion that bin Laden deliberately stacked the September 11 hijacking team with Saudis to drive a "wedge" between Riyadh and Washington. Al-Jubeir pressed that point at the news conference he was forced to hold in December 2002 to deflect charges that Saudi Arabia was dragging its feet investigating Saudi funding of al-Qaida. He claimed that bin Laden wants to stick it to the Saudi royal government as much as to the U.S. government.

But that theory does not hold up under closer scrutiny. So far al-Qaida has targeted American installations in Saudi Arabia, not the Saudi government. At home in Riyadh, four Saudi terrorists inspired by bin Laden car-bombed a U.S.-run training facility for the Saudi National Guard. The November 1995 blast killed five Americans and two Indians. In June 1996, Saudi terrorists tied to al-Qaida detonated a massive truck bomb at the Khobar Towers apartment compound in Dhahran. Saudis were not their target there, either. The complex was used as barracks for hundreds of U.S. Air Force personnel stationed in Saudi Arabia after the Gulf War. The blast killed nineteen U.S. airmen and wounded hundreds more. A top-secret CIA report implicated bin Laden in the attack.[12] And the three housing compounds that al-Qaida car-bombed in Riyadh this past May were among the most popular with Western defense contractors working in Saudi, many of whom are former U.S. servicemen. Nine Americans died in the simultaneous attacks. Truth is, the Saudi royal government remains relatively safe, despite what al-Jubeir and other Saudi apologists say about its being an enemy of bin Laden. The chances of al-Qaida hijacking a fuel-laden jet and crashing it into the crown prince's palace are fairly slim. America is bin Laden's target—even in Saudi Arabia.

If he attacked Saudi Arabia itself, bin Laden would be destroying the source of most of al-Qaida's fighters, funding, and philosophy. "The Saudis are active at every level of the terror chain, from planners and financiers, from cadre to foot-soldier, from ideologist to cheerleaders," according to a Rand Corporation briefing prepared for a top Pentagon advisory panel. In the July 10, 2002, briefing for the Defense Policy Board, Rand defense analyst Laurent Murawiec concluded, "Saudi Arabia supports our enemies and attacks our allies."[13]

The Bush administration quickly disassociated itself from the report and lavished more praise on the putative ally. "Neither the presentations nor the Defense Policy Board members' comments reflect the official views of the department," said Defense Department spokeswoman Victoria Clarke. "Saudi Arabia is a long-standing friend and ally of the United States. The Saudis cooperate fully in the global war on terrorism and have the department's and the administration's deep appreciation."[14]

Covering for the Saudis

But there is more than a kernel of truth to the charge that Saudi Arabia is the "kernel of evil" in the world today and hardly has America's best interests at heart.

For one, the House of Saud adopted the fundamentalist dogma of preacher el-Wahhab to "legitimize its rule over Saudi Arabia," Nalapat said.[15] The kingdom's founding father, Abdul Aziz Ibn Saud, was an early leader of the Wahhabis. And Saudi Arabia has since spread Wahhabism around the world through missionary teachers, mosques, and schools it has funded. Riyadh has pumped tens of millions of dollars into mosques and Islamic schools in America alone.

In addition, Saudi nationals made up the largest share of al-Qaida fighters captured in Afghanistan among the thirty or so nationalities represented at U.S. detention camps. More than one hundred held by the U.S. at Guantánamo, Cuba, were Saudi citizens.[16] And Saudis are thick among bin Laden's inner circle of leaders. They include his brother-in-law Shaikh Saiid al-Sharif, believed to be al-Qaida's financial director and the chief September 11 paymaster, and Tawfiq Attash Khallad, a Saudi national thought to be one of al-Qaida's top terrorist trainers. Tawfiq Attash Khallad met with two of the Saudi hijackers in Malaysia before September 11.

Most of al-Qaida's principal financial backers, moreover, are wealthy Saudis, who have given the terrorist group tens of millions of dollars over the years by routing the funds through charities, such as the Muslim World League and International Islamic Relief Organization, and through legitimate businesses around the world.[17] Some allegedly are members of the royal family and high-level government officials in Riyadh. A $1 trillion U.S. lawsuit that links Saudi royals to al-Qaida has named as defendants some of the most prominent members of the Saudi royal family, including Prince Sultan bin Abdulaziz al-Saud, the Saudi defense minister, who is accused of steering at least $6 million to al-Qaida through four groups fronting as charities; Prince Naif bin Abdulaziz, the interior minister; and Prince Turki, the former Saudi intelligence chief who conveniently was appointed ambassador to Britain after the suit was filed, giving him the claim of diplomatic immunity. The class action suit, filed last year by Charleston, South Carolina, attorney Ron Motley on behalf of more than five hundred families of September 11 victims, alleges that Prince Sultan, for one, "publicly supported and funded several Islamic charities that were sponsoring Osama bin Laden."[18]

Even the Saudi ambassador to Washington, Prince Bandar, has been at least tangentially linked to al-Qaida—and September 11. Thousands of dollars from a Washington bank account held by Bandar's wife, who lives with the ambassador in a gated mansion in leafy McLean, Virginia, flowed indirectly to two of the hijackers who slammed the American Airlines jumbo jet into the Pentagon. Payments of about thirty-five hundred dollars a month were made to Saudi families who helped the two hijackers pay for rent and other expenses after arriving in the U.S. in 2000.[19] The al-Qaida hijackers—Khalid al-Midhar and Nawaf al-Hazmi—were Saudi citizens. Bin Laden mentioned al-Hazmi by name in the chilling videotape, broadcast in December 2001, in which he praised the September 11 attacks.[20] Al-Hazmi had overstayed his tourist visa and was in the country illegally on September 11. He and al-Midhar arrived in the U.S. from Malaysia, where they had met with Saudi al-Qaida leader Khallad.

Even after it looked as if the Saudi embassy in Washington might be tied up in the September 11 plot, the White House continued to give Saudi Arabia the benefit of the doubt. "The president does believe that the Saudis have been good partners in the war on terrorism," Bush's spokesman Ari Fleischer insisted in response to questions about the Bandar scandal.[21]

But relatives of September 11 victims are not the only ones who have serious doubts about that. Even foreign leaders are wondering. Russian President Putin, for one, put Bush on the spot last fall when he questioned Saudi Arabia's allegiance to the cause of fighting terrorism. "We should not forget about those who finance terrorism," Putin said, noting that fifteen of the September hijackers were Saudi citizens. "We should not forget that."[22]

No matter the evidence, the administration keeps soft-pedaling the Saudi role in financing and supporting terrorism. At times the appeasement is so intense that it looks as if the Bush administration is actually protecting the monarchy.

For example, the White House refuses to make public FBI dossiers on Saudi financing of al-Qaida, despite repeated requests by Congress. A congressional panel investigating September 11, comprised of members of both Senate and House intelligence committees, has pressed for the release of classified reports that lay out the evidence of how money flowed from Saudi-based charities to al-Qaida. But the Bush administration will not declassify the explosive financial records, which are said to be highly embarrassing to the Saudi government.[23]

The stonewalling and blocking for Saudi Arabia do not stop there. The administration may try to delay or even dismiss the $1 trillion suit against members of the Saudi royal family—at least one of whom, Prince Sultan, is represented by Bush family crony James A. Baker III's Houston-based law firm. Reportedly, the case has been brought up in high-level meetings between Bush officials and Saudi officials. "The Saudis have made their concerns known at a senior level," the *New York Times* quoted a State Department official as saying.[24] The news outraged Motley, the lead trial lawyer in the suit. "Families of the victims have had enough grief to contend with. They deserve the full support of their government. They should not have to be confronted with reports that State Department officials have held talks with the Saudis over whether to block the lawsuit on the grounds that it could impair American foreign relations," he said. "In fact, many of the families wish that our government would take a page from that of Spain, which has vigorously investigated and indicted a Saudi businessman, Mohamed Zouaydi, for running a Qaida cell based in Madrid."

He added, "The Bush administration must insist on full accountability from our allies, especially Saudi Arabia."[25]

But it has not insisted—even in the case of the bin Laden family. Within days of September 11, the administration arranged for Saudi Arabia to charter a jet to whisk out of the country bin Laden relatives living in Los Angeles, Orlando, Boston, and Washington, D.C. They were questioned only briefly on the plane, escaping proper FBI investigation. Bush family pal Prince Bandar worked with the State Department, and possibly the White House, to set up their swift and convenient exodus back to Saudi soil.[26]

In yet another example of covering for the Saudis, the Bush administration censored portions of a videotaped conversation between bin Laden and a Saudi visiting him in Afghanistan after September 11. According to the ABC News translation of the tape, aired in December 2001, the Saudi identified as Khalid al-Harbi told bin Laden he was smuggled into Afghanistan with the help of Saudi's religious police. The section was omitted by the Pentagon. ABC's version also had al-Harbi informing bin Laden that religious leaders close to the Saudi government had praised the attacks in their sermons. That part also is missing in the Pentagon transcript. What's more, bin Laden named Atta, an Egyptian national, and two Saudi nationals—Nawaf al-Hazmi and Salim al-Hazmi—as hijackers taking part in the operation. The Pentagon transcript, however, had bin Laden mentioning only Atta. The public never saw the other two names in the government captioning at the bottom of the video, which shows a smiling bin Laden rehashing the toppling of the Twin Towers. ABC at the time reported that the Pentagon, in its transcript, left out snippets of conversation that "could be embarrassing to the government of Saudi Arabia." The White House insists it was not trying to spare its ally. It claims that poor audio quality prevented the government from producing a verbatim translation.[27] But somehow, a TV network managed to do what the government's best Arabic translators could not do.

The same White House kept the State Department's Visa Express program in Saudi Arabia up and running through July 19, 2002—ten months after the September 11 attacks. The program allowed some 97 percent of Saudi applicants to obtain visas without interviews before the attacks.[28] Those applicants included hijackers al-Midhar, Salim al-Hazmi, and Abdulaziz Alomari.[29] When a tenacious reporter exposed the rubber-stamping operation, the Bush administration terrorized him. Joel Mowbray, a reporter for *National Review Online*, was surrounded by four armed guards after leaving a July 12, 2002, State Department briefing in Washington. He was detained for thirty minutes as the guards tried to shake him down for a confidential State cable he had obtained. The cable—which was not sensitive to national security, only embarrassing to the administration—revealed that the U.S. ambassador in Riyadh had sought an end to expedited visa issuance and suggested better screening of applicants. At the briefing, Mowbray challenged State spokesman Richard Boucher regarding the diplomatic cable. Shortly after, Boucher had him detained in a thinly veiled attempt to intimidate the journalist. According to the official federal transcript, here is Boucher's heated exchange with Mowbray at the July 12, 2002, media briefing, just before the reporter was detained:

> MOWBRAY: The ambassador asked in the cable this week to terminate the program formally known as Visa Express and to interview all applicants. Is that correct?
>
> BOUCHER: Well, no.
>
> MOWBRAY: I have the cable here.
>
> BOUCHER: Well, I have read the cable too, and I think if you read it carefully, even though it's confidential, if you happen to have it, you'll find that he says he's asking for resources, he is asking for consular people to go out there, and that's what we are talking to him about. I mean, I do have to point out, sir, that you've written a lot of things and said a lot of things recently. You said that visas are decided by travel agents, and that's not true, is it?
>
> MOWBRAY: I said it was passed on [from Saudi travel agents] to the consular to the embassy.
>
> BOUCHER: You said that [Saudi Arabia] is the only country that we do accept documents from third parties. And that's not true, is it?
>
> MOWBRAY: And that was told to me by the State Department press office. I have the fax.
>
> BOUCHER: You've said that performance of foreign service officers is measured on courtesy. And that's not true, is it?
>
> MOWBRAY: And that was said by, repeated [by], dozens of consular officers.

BOUCHER: You said that applicants are presumed eligible. And that's not true, is it?

MOWBRAY: Again, I have the cables, I have the best practices memos to prove this.

BOUCHER: Let's be careful about the facts.

MOWBRAY: I am being careful. No need to smear the work falsely.

Senator Charles Grassley (R-Iowa) and Representative Dave Weldon (R-Fla.) came to Mowbray's rescue by firing off a letter to Powell complaining about the harassment. They said siccing security guards on a reporter has a chilling effect not just on the working media, but on federal whistleblowers trying to call attention to holes in national security in the wake of September 11. The added attention from Congress effectively killed the Visa Express program.[30]

The Bush administration has got some nerve. It fought to keep a visa program that made it easier for high-risk Saudis to enter the U.S., then implied it was the reporter exposing the program who was jeopardizing national security. Only after it was ripped for being too soft on Saudi visitors did it cancel the program and beef up screening (as far as we know) on the Saudi side—and then, finally, authorize INS inspectors on the U.S. side to screen young Saudi males entering the country as part of an antiterrorist-tracking system that Congress had mandated right after September 11 to help protect Americans from such dangerous foreign visitors. But then it could not even defend the expanded policy when challenged by the Saudis. When it comes to Saudi Arabia, it seems everyone in the Bush administration walks on eggshells—even when American security hangs in the balance.

Ulterior Motives

Letting Saudi Arabia off the hook for its ties to al-Qaida and its likely role in September 11 is one thing. But why would Bush depend on it to help the U.S. beat al-Qaida, even after his own Treasury Department said Riyadh has taken only "baby steps" to choke off financing for al-Qaida and other terrorist groups?[31] Why make it an ally in the antiterror war, let alone a key ally? Tradition is one explanation offered by Bush officials. Saudi Arabia is a long-standing ally, primarily because it is America's biggest foreign supplier of oil next to Canada. They also argue, privately, that Bush needed to butter up the crown prince in order to get the right-of-way to launch an invasion of Baghdad from Saudi bases.

Only, Iraq was scarcely a blip on the radar screen when Bush reflexively partnered with Saudi Arabia in the first weeks after September 11. Back then it was all about Afghanistan. And U.S. forces have built an air base in Qatar to stage such an attack, in lieu of ones in Saudi Arabia.

Ironically, the Saudi bases are the core reason America was attacked on September 11, and is having to fight a global war against terrorism at all. "At various times [after] 1992, Usama bin Laden disseminated fatwahs to other members and associates of al-Qaida that the United States forces stationed on the Saudi Arabian peninsula, including both Saudi Arabia and Yemen, should be attacked," according to the federal indictment of the alleged twentieth hijacker Moussaoui. In 1996, al-Qaida issued a war order from Afghanistan titled "Declaration of Jihad Against the Americans Occupying the Land of the Two Holy Mosques; Expel the Heretics from the Arabian Peninsula." And in October 2001, bin Laden praised the September 11 attacks and vowed that the U.S. would not "enjoy security" before "infidel armies leave" the Saudi Gulf.[32]

Former President Bush stationed the troops in Saudi Arabia—host of Islam's two holiest sites, in Mecca and Medina—to patrol Iraqi no-fly zones and prevent future aggression from Saddam Hussein, whom he left in power after the Gulf War in 1991. That, in turn, led to bin Laden's *fatwahs* calling for their expulsion, and the punishment of America until they were expelled. He started by truck-bombing the World Trade Center in 1993, killing six, and came back in 2001 to finish the job, crumbling both towers and murdering three thousand. And he hit several

U.S. military targets, including two in Saudi Arabia, in between the WTC attacks, and he has continued to attack U.S. military personnel since September 11, most notably in Kuwait, where U.S. forces are gathering to finish the job started by the elder Bush. The former president claims he could not march on Baghdad without UN authority, insisting security resolutions limited coalition action to liberating Kuwait.

But UN Security Resolution 678, passed in November 1990, authorized U.S.-led coalition forces "to use all necessary means . . . to restore international peace and security in the area" in and around Kuwait. It was a pretty broad mandate, as I read it, providing enough latitude to take out Saddam. After all, how could there be "peace and security" with him still in the picture?

According to a former aide to Colin Powell, who was chairman of the Joint Chiefs during the Gulf War, Saudi Arabia was the real reason Bush chose not to advance on Baghdad. "Bush Sr. canceled the final attack at the behest of the Saudis, who didn't want to be in a position to take sides with Americans over Arabs, because the outcry from the Arab world would have been deafening if U.S. troops occupied Baghdad," which was once an important cultural center in the Islamic world, said the former aide, who requested anonymity.[33] More, he said, the last thing the Saudi monarchy wanted was anything resembling a democracy installed next door. (Of course, Powell has been blamed for stopping the war when the U.S. had Iraqi troops on the run. He reportedly lost the stomach to continue to Baghdad after witnessing the slaughter of Iraqi soldiers retreating from heavily armed U.S. forces on a highway from Kuwait back to Baghdad.)

Even when taken together, the strategic interests of securing the Saudi bases and the uninterrupted flow of Saudi oil imports do not go far enough in explaining the administration's warped marriage with Saudi Arabia. Commercial interests in the region also have to be considered. The wealthy Bush family, an oil dynasty in its own right (the elder Bush's Midland, Texas, wildcatting company became Pennzoil), has been in business with the Saudi royal family for years. So have many prominent friends of the Bushes from the Oil Patch. Through business as well as diplomatic contacts, they have forged tight personal bonds that are hard to break, even in the face of betrayal. President Bush's father insists the Saudis are our friends and would never stab us in the back. "What I don't like is demonizing Saudi Arabia," Bush said last fall. "It's not true. They are not enemies of ours. And to come under that kind of criticism, I think, is ridiculous."[34] Son Neil Bush underscored his father's concerns in a speech last year in Jeddah, Saudi Arabia. "American public opinion sees Arabs as terrorists," Bush lamented, advising Saudis to hire more U.S. lobbyists and publicists for a charm offensive. "I wish Americans would see Arabs and Muslims the way I see them."[35]

The Bushes, who are on a first-name basis with the Saudi elite, definitely have a different perspective. They are so close to some members of the royal family that they have nicknames for them. Prince Bandar, for instance, is "Bandar Bush." The ambassador has bonded with the elder Bush on vacations, such as the time he took him on his private Airbus to hunt fowl in Spain. Bandar even donated $1 million to Bush's presidential library at Texas A&M University in College Station, Texas.[36] That's not the only Saudi donation there. Perhaps the main attraction of the library, which is part of a compound of three limestone buildings set off in the southwestern corner of the sprawling Aggie campus, is a three-foot-wide model of a desert fortress made of solid gold. It was a 1993 gift to Bush from King Fahd, with whom Bush has visited in Saudi Arabia in recent years.[37] Barbara Bush, moreover, is close to Bandar's wife, Princess Haifa, whose charitable checks wound up—oops—aiding two of the September 11 hijackers. "Her Royal Highness," as Bush administration officials are told to refer to her, attended the former First Lady's seventy-fifth birthday party at the Bush compound in Kennebunkport, Maine.[38] The cozy relationship sheds some light on why the administration would stonewall Congress over the audit of Saudi financial transactions.

Pretending Saudi Arabia is still America's friend keeps those old personal contacts alive. They also keep contracts alive—lucrative Saudi contracts involving energy, defense, construction, consulting, and investment.

Former President Bush is a senior adviser to the Carlyle Group, a Washington investment bank with deep business connections to the Saudi royal family. Its Saudi clients include Prince al-Waleed bin Talal, nephew of King Fahd, whose $10 million donation to the World Trade Center victims was summarily rejected by then New York Mayor Rudy Giuliani after the prince tried to lecture America about its pro-Israeli policies. Bush advises Carlyle's Asian Partners fund. He also makes speeches for the investment bank, which specializes in buyouts of defense and aerospace companies, at a reported $80,000 to $100,000 a pop. James A. Baker III, Bush's former secretary of state, is senior counselor for Carlyle. George W. Bush, the current president, was a director of a Carlyle subsidiary. When he was Texas governor, the Teacher Retirement System of Texas invested $100 million with the Carlyle Group, marking its first foray into private equity. Bush appointed some of the pension fund's directors who voted for the huge investment.[39]

Believe it or not, Carlyle also handles investments for the bin Laden family, which runs the $5 billion-in-revenue Saudi Binladin Group, a construction contractor. After al-Qaida operatives blew up the U.S. Air Force barracks in Dhahran in 1996, killing nineteen U.S. airmen, Saudi Binladin Group got the contract to build new barracks. (What a deal: the son bombs, the father's company rebuilds.) According to the *Wall Street Journal*, the bin Laden family in 1995 sank an initial $2 million in a Carlyle investment fund.[40] The elder Bush on more than one occasion has made trips to the Binladin Group's headquarters in Jeddah, Saudi Arabia's trade and financial hub on the Red Sea. He met with the bin Laden family in November 1998 and again in January 2000. Baker also has made the pilgrimage in recent years, once traveling on a bin Laden family jet.[41]

The close ties go a long way toward explaining why the FBI, at Prince Bandar's urging, gave bin Laden's relatives a pass right after September 11. The FBI since then has been "remarkably sensitive, tactful and protective" of the family, the *Wall Street Journal* quoted an associate of two of Osama bin Laden's brothers as saying.[42]

George W. Bush, moreover, is at least indirectly linked to the bin Laden family through his old Texas pal and business partner, James W. Bath. Bath brokered U.S. real estate deals and handled other investments for Osama bin Laden's late older brother, Salem bin Laden, until his 1988 death. Bath gave the junior Bush the seed capital to start his own Midland oil firm, Arbusto (Spanish for bush), the forerunner to Spectrum 7 Energy Corp.—which, like Arbusto, flopped and was later folded into publicly traded Harken Energy Corp. Not long after the Harken merger, a Saudi investor took a 17 percent stake in the Dallas-based concern. Not long after that, the little-known Harken, which had no international expertise, landed a potentially lucrative oil production contract with Bahrain in the Persian Gulf. It won drilling rights to an off-shore area squeezed between productive tracts owned by Qatar and—surprise—Saudi Arabia. That same year, 1990, Bush sold a large chunk of his Harken stock for $848,000.[43]

The Saudi investor who helped turn the junior Bush's fortunes around, Abdullah Taha Bakhsh, is a business partner of shady Saudi banker Khalid bin Mahfouz, whose father founded Jeddah-based National Commercial Bank, Saudi Arabia's oldest and largest financial institution. Bush's pal Bath also was bin Mahfouz's U.S. business representative.[44] The bin Mahfouzes are sometimes referred to as the bankers to the Saudi royals. The billionaire bin Ladens also do much of their banking at National Commercial Bank, and they are close to the billionaire bin Mahfouzes.[45] Osama bin Laden is married to Khalid bin Mahfouz's sister, according to U.S. intelligence officials.[46] It should then come as no surprise that the bin Mahfouz family helped create the International Islamic Relief Organization, a charity used by wealthy Saudi businessmen to funnel millions of dollars to al-Qaida. The money was transferred from the sheiks' personal accounts at National Commercial Bank in Jeddah to banks in London and New York, and then deposited in the accounts of Islamic Relief and other charitable fronts for bin Laden's terror network, according to U.S. intelligence.[47] Khalid bin Mahfouz and National Commercial Bank, as well as Saudi Binladin Group, are named as defendants in the $1 trillion suit filed by families of September 11 victims.

The bin Mahfouz clan, interestingly enough, also owns Saudi's Nimir Petroleum Co.—which brings us to the mysterious Delta Oil Co. of Saudi Arabia, a lead partner in the trans-Afghan gas pipeline project. Nimir formed a joint venture with Jeddah-based Delta Oil to develop major oil and gas fields in the Caspian. Its American partners in the Azerbaijan projects are Amerada Hess and Unocal.

Delta Oil was formed early last decade to manage the energy interests of the Delta Investment Company, a group of fifty prominent Saudi investors, most of whom are politically connected to the royal family. Its president, Badr al-Aiban, is very close to Crown Prince Abdullah, whom Bush has entertained at his Texas ranch.[48] The company is shady for several reasons apart from its ties to bin Mahfouz through Nimir. For one, it counts Mohammed Hussein al-Amoudi among its lead investors.[49] He has been investigated by U.S. and British authorities for allegedly transferring money to bin Laden through a London bank he controls.[50] The investment group's Delta-Nimir and Delta-Hess joint ventures, curiously, are registered in the Cayman Islands.[51] What's more, Delta Oil is not known to have much oil and gas experience.[52] Former Unocal Chairman Roger C. Beach admitted the company partnered with Delta in part to take advantage of its "knowledge of the culture and politics of Central Asia."[53]

For its part, Saudi Arabia's Delta seeks equity in as many Central Asian deals as Unocal and other experienced energy producers can broker. Saudi Arabia is the world's largest oil exporter, and it wants to stay that way. The Caspian's mammoth untapped reserves threaten its monopoly, so it is clamoring for a big piece of the action there. Saudi Arabia also has a strategic interest in laying southern pipelines through

Afghanistan and bypassing its cross-Gulf oil rival Iran. If Iran gets in on the Caspian export bonanza through its own pipelines, Saudi Arabia risks losing leverage in the Gulf.

To that end, Delta hired a former UN mediator in Afghanistan. Charles Santos, an American, tried to negotiate a pipeline deal with the Taliban, but did not make much headway. Santos reportedly reached out to Afghan opposition factions at the same time, and the Taliban stopped trusting him.[54] Four days before Bush started bombing the Taliban, Santos went to Capitol Hill to urge the U.S. to replace the Taliban with a broad-based government in Kabul.[55]

He and Delta got their wish. After Kabul fell to U.S.-backed rebels, Delta began dusting off the old pipeline plans. "With political stability, this remains a feasible project," said Phil Beck, a Delta director.[56] Delta took the biggest stake next to Unocal in the CentGas deal, and if Unocal does not return to the project, Delta will likely become a lead equity holder again. The two companies remain partners in Caspian projects exploring oil and gas in Azerbaijan, however, and Unocal would still have a strong interest in a southern pipeline that could export its reserves to fast-growing Asian markets.

Riyadh, which once funded the Taliban, has joined the Bush administration in funding the construction of a highway along the proposed gas pipeline route in Afghanistan, a highway that it hopes will soon be part of a prized Caspian energy corridor. So does the U.S.-backed government of Hamid Karzai. The new Afghan leader visited Saudi Arabia in January 2002 in his first trip to the Middle East. Karzai returned in September, meeting again with Crown Prince Abdullah.

7

THE PUPPET
Installing Karzai's Regime

As part of the effort to bolster moderate Afghans, the United States should lend its support to the convening of a traditional Afghan grand assembly for the selection of a broadly acceptable transitional government.

—Bush adviser ZALMAY KHALILZAD in 2000 policy paper

CAPES HAVE NOT BEEN IN VOGUE IN WASHINGTON SINCE Franklin Delano Roosevelt wore them in the 1940s. Certainly no man has sat next to the First Lady at the State of the Union wearing one—that is, not until Hamid Karzai made history January 29, 2002. "This evening we welcome the distinguished interim leader of a liberated Afghanistan: Chairman Hamid Karzai," said President Bush, recognizing him just minutes into the address that night. A beaming Karzai, looking resplendent in his flowing green robe draped over his trademark gray *shalwar kameez* (a long collarless tunic), stood beside First Lady Laura Bush in the balcony of the House of Representatives chamber to sustained cheers and applause.

By all appearances, his is a rags-to-riches story worthy of a Disney animated movie: a lowly Afghan rebel fighter, a refugee living in exile, returns triumphant to his war-torn homeland to occupy not only the presidential palace there, but also the best seat in the House at the State of the Union in America, the wealthiest and most powerful country in the world. He even gets to hang out with the leader of the free world in the Oval Office. Fade out Elton John musical score.

Except Karzai is no stranger to Washington and hardly a political neophyte. He already knew his way around Capitol Hill, having rubbed elbows years earlier with GOP Senator Brownback of the Silk Road Caucus and other powerful U.S. lawmakers. Turns out the worldly, English-speaking Karzai was part of the U.S. oil lobby. He worked last decade as a Unocal consultant out of Pakistan.[1] He lived there with his late father, a one-time Afghan dignitary, in Quetta, which is on the proposed gas pipeline route.[2] After Unocal began lobbying Washington to recognize the Taliban and help it lay the diplomatic groundwork for trans-Afghan pipelines, Karzai traveled to the U.S. some ten times. "He has made numerous entries to the U.S. dating back to 1996, all for personal business or official government business," an INS official told me, requesting anonymity because of the delicacy of the subject. "And all entries were to the same address of the Afghanistan mission in Maryland."[3] The Afghan embassy in Washington, now being refurbished, had maintained apartments in Maryland while the Taliban were in power. And Karzai's older brother—who serves with Bush special adviser and envoy Khalilzad on the Afghanistan-America Foundation board[4]—lives in the Baltimore area, where he runs an Afghan restaurant called the Helmand, named after Afghanistan's longest river.[5] Karzai had also worked with State Department and United Nations officials on Afghan political matters long before September 11.

According to INS records I obtained, Karzai entered the U.S. for personal business starting on January 23, 1996, and then again on December 9, 1996. The next year he entered on official UN business on August 12 and November 3. In 1998, he arrived on personal business on September 14, and returned the next year for business trips on January 3 and September 15. In 2000, he came to the U.S. on business twice—once on May 8 and again on July 18, two days prior to testifying before

Brownback's Foreign Relations Subcommittee in the Senate. Last year, he made two trips here to visit with President Bush.

Karzai, age forty-five, was not just plucked from obscurity. Turns out fellow Afghan native Khalilzad and the White House had groomed him to lead Afghanistan from the start of the war. He had the right ethnic and political pedigree—and business connections.

The administration counted on the Northern Alliance, the U.S.-backed fighters made up mostly of Tajiks and Uzbeks, to march on the Afghan capital of Kabul from northern Afghanistan after breaking through Taliban defenses in Mazar-e-Sharif. But it needed someone who could rally the Pashtuns in southern Afghanistan to oust the Taliban from Kandahar, Mullah Omar's stronghold, and then join the Northern Alliance in Kabul. Omar and nearly all his former Taliban cabinet members are Pashtuns, the largest ethnic group in Afghanistan. It was critical that fellow Pashtuns had a hand in their removal and then shared power with the northern Tajiks and Uzbeks in Kabul. A post-Taliban government would never hold without Pashtuns at the center of it. "The most useful allies for the United States are members of the Pashtun community who are willing to oppose the Taliban," Khalilzad advised. "If Pashtun support for the Taliban can be reduced, the movement will weaken considerably."[6] Karzai, an ethnic Pashtun, was one of the anti-Taliban leaders from southern Afghanistan.

But he was not the best-known Pashtun opposition leader or the most respected. That distinction belonged to Abdul Haq, the barrel-chested and charismatic Pashtun leader from eastern Afghanistan, who had a much bigger local following, and potentially more anti-Taliban fighters to offer, than Karzai.

Haq Attack

Revered throughout Afghanistan for his brave fighting during the Soviet resistance, the "Afghan Lion," as his countrymen called him, was the local choice for unifying Afghanistan after the removal of the Taliban. While commanding mujahideen fighters in the 1980s, Haq was wounded some seventeen times in battle and nearly lost a foot in a land mine. But his reputation extended beyond that of a fierce warrior. As a member of a prominent Pashtun family with political ties to pre-Taliban governments, the articulate Haq appealed to intellectuals as well as tribesmen. In the 1980s, the Soviet-resistance commander met with President Reagan in the White House and British Prime Minister Margaret Thatcher in London.

Following the September 11 attacks, it was former Reagan National Security Adviser Robert McFarlane who appealed to the Bush administration to throw its support behind Haq. One Bush official buttonholed by McFarlane's group was Armitage, the deputy secretary of state who helped craft war policy. But appeals for support for Haq were turned down by the administration, and Haq decided to go it alone. On October 21, 2001, he gathered some of his guards from his redoubt in the Pakistani border town of Peshawar, where he was living in exile, and crossed into Afghanistan to try to rally Pashtuns in southeastern Afghanistan against the Taliban, who had murdered his first wife and child after seizing power. The mission was short-lived. The Taliban ambushed Haq four days later near his home village of Azra, Afghanistan, and then moved him to a camp near Kabul where they held him captive. At that point, McFarlane asked the CIA for help, and it dispatched an unmanned Predator drone plane armed with Hellfire missiles to attack a Taliban convoy near the ambush site.

But that was as far as the administration was willing to go to help Haq. His supporters, including former U.S. Special Forces, contacted an aide to General Franks to see if CentCom in Tampa would step in and free Haq—but it refused. They were told that no one even knew who Haq was. "And when that didn't appease the former special forces personnel who pointed out how easy it would be to help Haq, Central Command replied, 'We're worried about civilian casualties,'" noted national security expert Bill Gertz, author of *Breakdown: How America's*

Intelligence Failures Led to September 11. "The only concession made was to provide U.S. air cover if the Taliban attackers used armored personnel carriers (APCs). But the Taliban didn't use APCs, preferring sport utility vehicles and pickup trucks."

So Haq was left stranded at the Taliban training camp near Kabul—completely at the mercy of his brutal captors. On October 26, the Taliban put a metal noose around his neck and hanged him from a maple tree there, then shot his limp body again and again.[7] Haq left behind a pregnant wife.

Karzai, in contrast, got high-level help that month from the Bush administration after he sneaked into Afghanistan from Pakistan. At the same time Haq was battling for his life, and his supporters were begging CentCom to come to his rescue, Karzai and his guards were receiving U.S. ammunition and supplies. Then on November 4, CentCom helicoptered Karzai and his top aides out of Afghanistan, even though they were not in trouble as Haq was. U.S. forces were ordered to taxi them to Pakistan for "consultations" with U.S. officials. Defense Secretary Rumsfeld was in Pakistan at the time.

Asked about the special assistance provided Karzai, Rumsfeld told Pentagon reporters upon returning home from Pakistan: "He has been in Afghanistan with a number of supporters and troops, and we have delivered ammunition and some supplies to him.

"Within recent days—in fact, I think while I was in Pakistan—at his request, he was extracted from Afghanistan with a small number of his senior supporters and fighters, I believe for consultation in Pakistan," he added, "and undoubtedly will be going back in there at that point where those consultations are completed."

Asked later in the same November 6 Pentagon briefing if Karzai had been ambushed by the Taliban, Rumsfeld replied, "To my knowledge, he was not detained or held by the Taliban. No, it was a very sensible arrangement whereby he requested to be extracted for a period, and we cooperated to extract him."

REPORTER: So this was transportation, not a rescue mission?

RUMSFELD: Oh, exactly. No, it was not an extraction in the sense of a military campaign.

The secretary repeated that U.S. forces planned to fly Karzai back into Afghanistan.

Many Afghans believe that Haq, had he lived, would have been a better candidate than Karzai to lead a post-Taliban Afghanistan. Like Karzai, he was an exiled Pashtun tribal chief unaffiliated with the warring factions in Afghanistan. He did not have the reputation for lawlessness that the warlords of the Northern Alliance and other factions gained after the Soviet withdrawal from Afghanistan. He was joined by representatives of the exiled Afghan king to seek paths to unifying Afghans, and like Karzai, he had called for a traditional assembly of representatives of each Afghan tribe, known as a *loya jirga*, to form a new government. Haq, however, had the additional qualification of being a respected military commander and war hero. "Karzai is a political person," Sayed Masood Majrooh, a former journalist from Peshawar now living in the U.S., told the *New York Times*. "Abdul Haq was a commander. He had the confidence of the intellectuals and the tribal people too."[8]

But one key thing held Haq back: he lacked Karzai's connections to the Bush administration and its Caspian oil lobbyists. Both tribal leaders worked for peace and stability in Afghanistan, but only Karzai worked for Unocal, along with Khalilzad, and knew the ins and outs of the proposed trans-Afghan pipelines. His ascent was preordained.

Coronation of Karzai

As soon as the Taliban were driven out of Kabul, the White House dispatched Khalilzad to Bonn, Germany, where he played a crucial behind-the-scenes role in UN talks in late November and December to set up a temporary Afghan government. He persuaded holdouts among both the

Alliance and the Pashtuns to appoint Karzai as their interim leader, and Karzai was sworn in December 22 in Kabul as chairman of the Interim Authority of Afghanistan (which is why Bush referred to him as "chairman" at the State of the Union the following month). Nine days later, Bush quietly named Khalilzad his special envoy to Kabul to make sure Karzai's transition to more permanent power was a smooth one. His first order of business: assembling Afghan delegates from the different tribal, religious, and ethnic groups to formally elect their new leader, a process that would ratify Karzai's ascent and give him an additional two years in office (before he would have to take his chances in a mandatory nation-wide election)—if Khalilzad could engineer their support. The so-called *loya jirga* was one of the Afghan policy recommendations he made in 2000. "As part of the effort to bolster moderate Afghans, the United States should lend its support to the convening of a traditional Afghan grand assembly for the selection of a broadly acceptable transitional government," Khalilzad said.[9]

But as the *loya jirga* neared, support for ex-king Mohammed Zahir Shah grew among Afghan delegates who saw the popular exiled monarch as the only figure capable of unifying the country after decades of civil war. Suddenly, Karzai's election no longer looked like a sure bet. With a crisis brewing, the start of the *loya jirga* was postponed twenty-four hours while Khalilzad met with Zahir Shah and his supporters. The day before the rescheduled opening session of the *loya jirga*, Khalilzad announced that the former king, considered by many Afghans to be the "father of the nation," had not only declined to be Afghanistan's new head of state, but had also indicated he wanted no role in the post-Taliban government whatever. He told a news conference that Zahir Shah would say so for himself in a statement. A few hours later, an aide to the eighty-seven-year-old ex-monarch read a statement announcing his withdrawal from consideration, as the king, Khalilzad, and Karzai looked on. The next day, one-time Afghan president Burhanuddin Rabbani, for whom Karzai had briefly served as deputy foreign minister in the early 1990s, also bowed out of the race. The night before his surprise announcement, Khalilzad reportedly lobbied delegates to back Karzai instead.

With his two major opponents out of the race, Karzai was a shoo-in. On June 13, 2002, when *loya jirga* delegates cast their secret ballots for president, he won easily with 82 percent of the vote. Khalilzad hailed it as a victory for democracy. "It's a great day for Afghanistan—electing a government rather than a government through coups, military intervention or violence," he said after the election. Bush pronounced it "the most broadly representative government in Afghanistan's history."[10]

But delegates and observers say that Khalilzad and the Bush administration manipulated the *loya jirga* process to ensure victory for their man Karzai, whom they had promoted since the start of the military campaign against the Taliban. They say Khalilzad pushed Zahir Shah and other contenders out of the picture, and pressured delegates to vote for Karzai—something Khalilzad has denied. "Khalilzad addressed informal gatherings of delegates to push for Karzai's leadership, and appeared to play a key role in persuading elderly former king Zahir Shah to throw his support to Karzai, effectively scuttling the effort to restore the monarchy that had widespread support among the *loya jirga* delegates," wrote Larry P. Goodson, author of *Afghanistan's Endless War: State Failure, Regional Politics, and the Rise of the Taliban.*[11] The request to delay the *loya jirga* came from Khalilzad, reported Pamela Hess, a UPI correspondent in Kabul at the time. "It looked very much like the U.S. was involved in picking its candidate," she observed.[12] Two delegates, Omar Zakhilwal and Adeena Niazi, charged that "powerful forces inside and outside the country" applied undue influence to secure the election of Karzai over the king, who was supposed to convene and preside over the assembly. "The vast majority of us viewed him as the only leader with enough popular support and independence to stand up to the warlords," they penned in a June 21, 2002, *New York Times* column. "But our democratic effort to nominate Zahir Shah did not please the powers that be. As a result, the entire *loya jirga* was postponed for almost two days while the former king was strong-armed into renouncing any meaningful role in the government."

Goodson pointed to another Afghan-American—Ashraf Ghani—helping Khalilzad twist delegates' arms, and also helping shape Karzai's cabinet. "Ghani was often seen taking second-tier ministers on 'power strolls' behind the big tent where they could press their cases to be considered in the new cabinet," Goodson said. Within weeks of the September 11 attacks, Ghani, then a Washington-area professor, urged the Bush administration to first seek "a change of regime" in Afghanistan before mobilizing troops to strike al-Qaida. Singing from the same hymnal as Khalilzad, he wanted the U.S. to focus, above all, on replacing the internationally unpopular Taliban with a "stable and legitimate government" run by a "younger group of Afghan technocrats who have gained success in industrialized countries." He called for the UN to help Afghans establish a broad-based government. But he asserted that "this process would only be credible if officials in the U.S. government avoided the temptation of giving Afghanistan's octogenarian former king a decisive role in the process."[13]

Ghani, an ethnic Pashtun, ended up Karzai's powerful new finance minister. He was recommended for the position by Karzai's older brother and trusted adviser, Qayum Karzai,[14] the Baltimore restaurateur who sits with Khalilzad on one of the Afghanistan-America Foundation's advisory boards in Washington. On the same board is S. Frederick Starr, chairman of the Central Asia-Caucasus Institute, which is part of the School for Advanced International Studies at Johns Hopkins University in Washington. Starr has been a tireless cheerleader for the development of a Caspian energy corridor through Afghanistan. Ghani was an adjunct professor at Johns Hopkins before returning to Kabul, where he once lectured at Kabul University. He also is a former World Bank official, conveniently enough. In his role as finance minister, Ghani is shepherding through Afghanistan's reconstruction projects, and he has voiced support for the construction of trans-Afghan pipelines.

As long as warlords can be controlled, Ghani is optimistic about their prospects, conveys Qayum Karzai's wife, Patricia, who recently hosted Ghani at her Maryland home. "We've always thought that as long as the pipelines are still there, we know there is a future for Afghanistan and the Afghan people," she told me.

As mentioned earlier, the massive and costly pipeline projects require political stability. Ground will more than likely never be broken until developers and international lenders and insurers are convinced Afghanistan's twenty-three years of civil unrest are behind it. If there is a person who can bring political stability to the war-battered country, it is Karzai, a worldly, Indian-educated Muslim who is considered both a political and a religious moderate in a land of wild-eyed extremists. For example, the secular-minded leader, who is married to a doctor, was saddened by the Taliban order two years ago to blow up two towering fifth-century statues of Buddha outside Kabul. Mullah Omar had found them offensive to Islam. "Afghanistan has been a staunch Muslim country for 1,200 years and the mullahs have never tried to destroy these statues," he said at the time the edict was issued. "Why wasn't the issue of these statues being against Islam raised in 1,200 years?"[15]

Though many Islamic hard-liners think the moderate Karzai has sold out to his American keepers—in fact, some call him a stooge of the U.S. government, which may be closer to the truth than they know—he has not made many bloodthirsty enemies among them, which improves his chances of survival. Karzai has wisely curried favor with warlords by giving them key roles in the government. For example, he made Northern Alliance Gen. Mohammad Fahim Khan, an ethnic Tajik, his defense minister. And he has given Omar and other ex-Taliban leaders little reason to actively seek revenge.

Early last year Karzai let several Taliban ministers go under a general amnesty agreement. They had been captured in Kandahar. But he had vowed not to punish former Taliban who stopped fighting, and they were released. The senior leaders reportedly included Defense Minister

Obaidullah Akhund, who coordinated operations most closely with al-Qaida leaders. U.S. commanders in Afghanistan were dismayed that the high-ranking Taliban were released before they even had a chance to question them.[16] Whenever Karzai is asked about fugitive Omar, who is said to be hiding out with many of his guards north of Kandahar, the president just shrugs and says that local police will "arrest" him if they find him, adding that he no longer considers the Taliban a threat.

Local legend has it that Omar escaped from Kandahar on a motorcycle after Karzai negotiated his surrender.[17] There may be some truth to it. The new Afghan leader originally supported the Taliban and even had an early, low-level position in Omar's regime.[18] "I was among the first to actively support the Taliban movement," Karzai, who speaks polished English, revealed in a Senate hearing three years ago, before the world knew him. "I personally knew and worked with the majority of their leadership during the entire period of jihad."[19] Karzai joined the Soviet resistance at age twenty-five, and he got to know Mullah Omar and other mujahideen fighters. Some of Karzai's cousins in Maryland even hosted Omar in their homes, his sister-in-law Patricia Karzai confided to me.

One of his younger brothers, Ahmed Wali Karzai, who also lived in Quetta before returning to Afghanistan, intimated in a *New Yorker* magazine interview: "In the early days, we did kind of help the Taliban."[20] Once radical elements infiltrated the new Taliban government, however, the Karzais discontinued their support and moved to Pakistan. "There were many wonderful people in the Taliban, many moderate and patriotic people, but the control from the outside, the interference from Pakistan and the radical Arabs made it hard for the moderates to stay there and help," explained Hamid Karzai.[21]

And in late 1998, after Taliban guest bin Laden blew up the U.S. embassies in Africa, the brothers actively campaigned against the regime. That's also when Khalilzad gave up trying to rehab the Taliban and began advising U.S. policy makers to undermine the regime. The next year, Karzai's father was assassinated in Quetta, possibly by Taliban agents. Abdul Ahad

Karzai, who served as deputy speaker in the Afghan parliament in the early 1970s, at the time had openly denounced the Taliban as a cancerous brand of Islam.[22] Despite that tragedy, Karzai seems to have little lust for revenge.

The Taliban are not the only dogs he is letting lie in Afghanistan, however. He apparently has also gone easy on al-Qaida agents and those who still harbor them inside Afghanistan, according to U.S. intelligence officials who shared with me startling CentCom communiqués that are classified as "Secret." One series of internal e-mails last fall tells of an incident in which Karzai asked U.S. forces to release a friend caught up in a sweep of suspected terrorist haunts north of Kandahar. The Afghan president's friend and colleague was among terrorist suspects captured by U.S. Special Forces in a raid on a "suspicious residence" thought to be harboring both Taliban and al-Qaida operatives in Uruzgan province. There, the Special Operations team found a model of a Boeing 747, ammunition, weapons, grenades, and a satellite phone.

Not long after the September 2002 raid, Karzai called a U.S. commander to complain that the team had arrested one of his friends. The suspect initially was held in the Deh Rawod district of Uruzgan province. But the president later vouched for the entire group of twenty-three suspects caught up in the al-Qaida reconnaissance sweep, and they were released at Karzai's request before they could be photographed and interrogated. "We didn't get 23 prisoners," a CentCom officer said. "These guys all got let go." He stated that Tampa immediately put a tight lid on the political mess, described by a colonel as "warlord politics," in an attempt to save the White House from embarrassment, since it essentially hand-picked Karzai to replace Omar and assigned U.S. Special Forces personnel to guard him around the clock at his presidential palace.[23]

One of the secret e-mails, sent to CentCom officers September 21, 2002, from a colonel in Afghanistan, reads as follows:

> Gents the attached emails layout [sic] a situation where ODA 364 [Operational Detachment Alpha or A Team, aka Special Forces

team] was on a recon and acquired 23 PUCs [persons under control] at a suspicious residence. CG [commanding general] then received a call from President Karzai saying the ODA had arrested one of his friends/colleagues. Items found at the resident [*sic*] are outlined in the email. They also include a model of a Boeing 747, ammo, weapons, grenades and a satellite phone. Currently, the CG has asked that the possible colleague of President Karzai not be released until the identity is verified! He will be held in Deh Rawod awaiting disposition and direction from the CG.

In a subsequent e-mail, the colonel added, "Of course the big question is . . . what was he doing in this situation with the model of a Boeing passenger plane?" To which another officer replied, "Trust me, he ought to be treated like any other dirtbag associated with the bad guys. Guilty by association is guilty!"

After talking to Lt. Gen. Daniel McNeill, commander of U.S. forces in Afghanistan, the colonel said, "He wants us to not move the PUCs until he gets to talk to President Karzai. Sounds like a political mess is brewing. OGA [other government agencies] got a call from Karzai who says he is now vouching for the whole group! Sounds like warlord politics. We will take pictures and collect MI [military intelligence] data on the players we have until the disposition is made in the morning here."

As details of the situation moved through the chain of command in Tampa, a senior officer there commented in an e-mail under the subject line, "ODA 364 Sweep in Deh Rawod/PUC/Possible President Karzai Colleague Caught in Sweep": "This has the potential to spin through the ceiling . . . We need to track this very closely and build a story board for the SecDef [secretary of defense] prep in the morning."

The Pentagon declined to comment on the incident. Why would it agree to release bad guys? Isn't that the whole reason our military is halfway around the world—to catch the bad guys? That is what we have been led to believe by the Bush administration. Its overarching goal, however, is to create a stable and durable government in Afghanistan. And, insane as it may seem, releasing some bad guys helps Karzai buy goodwill among political enemies bent on revenge.

Buying Afghanistan

To bring about "stability," which is shorthand for long-term U.S. contracts, it is also important for the U.S.-backed leader to buy goodwill among the Afghan population, who may hold resentment against America and sympathize with a warlord or ex-Taliban leader planning to overthrow the new U.S.-backed government in Kabul. The bombing campaign was not popular among Afghans, and now they see the same U.S. military building what amounts to an occupation force in their Muslim homeland. To help Karzai overcome that resentment, the White House has launched a three-pronged plan for winning over the Afghan people, consisting of a pro-Islam public relations campaign, massive humanitarian aid, and long-term economic commitments.

1. Pro-Islam public relations campaign. Bush has gone out of his way to assure the Afghan people that the U.S. is not waging war against Islam, that they and other Muslims are not the enemy, and that America respects them and their faith. Almost like a broken record, one that has grown particularly annoying to Christian leaders in the U.S., the president intones that Islam is a "religion of peace" that has been "hijacked" by militant extremists like Omar and terrorists like bin Laden—America's true enemies—to further their own radical causes. "Our war against terror is a war against individuals whose hearts are full of hate," Bush reiterated last November. "We do not fight a religion."[24]

The president has said a lot of kind things about Islam since America was attacked by Islamic terrorists, but he seems to save his sweetest comments about the religion for Afghan audiences. Addressing new Afghan government ministers gathered at the White House last fall, he claimed

Islam inspires "compassion" among its adherents. "Islam is a vibrant faith. Millions of our fellow citizens are Muslim. We respect the faith. We honor its traditions. Our enemy does not. Our enemy don't [*sic*] follow the great traditions of Islam. They've hijacked a great religion," Bush stated. "But it's important, as we lift that veil, to remember that they are nothing but a bunch of radical terrorists who distort history and the values of Islam. Islam is a faith that brings comfort to people. It inspires them to lead lives based on honesty, and justice, and compassion."[25] Speaking last year at the Afghanistan embassy in Washington, on the eve of the September 11 anniversary, Bush even went so far as to describe Islam as being based on love. "All Americans must recognize that the face of terror is not the true face of Islam. Islam is a faith that brings comfort to a billion people around the world. It's a faith that has made brothers and sisters of every race," he said, minutes after praising Afghan native Ishaq Shahryar for renouncing his U.S. citizenship to become Afghan ambassador to Washington. "It's a faith based upon love, not hate."[26]

At the same time, Bush has tried to paint the U.S. military as a superhero swooping down to save poor, helpless Afghans from the evil clutches of the Taliban. Time and again he has emphasized how America "liberated" women and children in Afghanistan. "We've got a great tradition of liberating people, not conquering them," he reassured Afghan dignitaries last year.[27]

2. Massive humanitarian aid. As U.S. forces bombed Taliban targets, Bush also had them drop a total of 2.4 million humanitarian food rations, worth about $10 million, across Afghanistan,[28] as Khalilzad had strongly recommended. And Bush called on American kids to donate a buck each to provide food and medical assistance to Afghan kids. "A year ago, the children of Afghanistan were suffering greatly in a nation beset by war. It's not hard to imagine children suffering in a nation beset by war, and it's really sad," he told Afghan leaders last October. "The children of America responded with great compassion. America's Fund for Afghan Children has collected more than $10.5 million. That's a dime at a time, or a dollar at a time; that's a lot of kids working hard to collect money. It has allowed the Red Cross to deliver emergency medical supplies to help serve 60,000 people. This fund has helped provide winter clothes to 8,000 children, to help rehabilitate hospitals in Kabul."[29]

Of course, the volunteer kiddy fund was more publicity stunt than major humanitarian relief. The lion's share of aid to Afghanistan has come from American taxpayers through the State Department and the U.S. Agency for International Development, which has pumped hundreds of millions of dollars into schools, hospitals, and food and refugee-assistance programs in the country. The agencies have spent nearly $200 million just on assisting the nearly 2 million refugees who have returned to Afghanistan from Pakistan and elsewhere. In addition, they have provided about 7,000 metric tons of seed and about 15,000 metric tons of fertilizer, benefiting an estimated 140,000 Afghan farmers in time for the spring planting season. More money still has gone to building some 600 Afghan schools and supplying them with more than 10 million textbooks.[30]

The Defense Department, meanwhile, has built another 127 schools, as well as 26 medical clinics. The U.S. Army Civil Affairs' top project for 2003 is constructing a series of maternity clinics throughout Afghanistan.[31] "Our soldiers wear the uniforms of warriors, but they are also compassionate people," Bush pointed out to Afghan leaders. "And the Afghan people are really beginning to see the true strength of our country. I mean, routing out the Taliban was important, but building a school is equally important."[32] He added that the U.S. will help build and refurbish "several hundred" more schools across Afghanistan through 2004.

But American aid hardly stops with schools, Bush noted. "A year ago, millions of Afghans lived in fear of famine and disease," he said. "In the time since, America has delivered food and medicine to the Afghan people," including 575,000 metric tons of food to nearly 10 million Afghans through a U.S.-supported UN program. In addition, "the United States joined with other nations to support UNICEF's vaccination of more than 8 million children against measles. American health-care officials are helping with other efforts to improve public health, including the fight against polio and malaria, HIV and tuberculosis," Bush stated. "These relief efforts have put hunger and disease on the retreat" in Afghanistan.[33]

The president vowed to continue to provide Afghanistan with such essential short-term relief. However, "we also understand that Afghanistan needs long-term economic reconstruction help," he said, singing from Khalilzad's policy hymnal. "And we will meet this commitment, as well."

3. Long-term economic commitments. On the economic front, the U.S. is leading a group of developed nations that has pledged more than $4.5 billion over five years to the reconstruction of Afghanistan. Construction projects will provide much-needed jobs, especially for ex-combatants roaming the streets with Kalashnikov rifles, and higher living standards for all Afghans—which in turn will work to ease local tensions and quell civil unrest. Kabul has already received 2002's installment of more than $2 billion. "That's a tremendous down payment on stability," said Joseph J. Collins, deputy assistant secretary of defense for stability operations.[34] In 2003, more money will be freed up for Afghan reconstruction projects, he predicted. "The balance between humanitarian assistance and reconstruction will shift very, very strongly in favor of reconstruction," Collins explained, while the "story in 2004 and 2005 is going to be business development and free trade."[35]

The master planner for reconstructing Afghanistan is Ghani, Karzai's new propipeline finance minister, who is "a great believer in free trade and the free market," noted Collins.[36] "To gain the trust of the population, a credible program for reconstruction of the country has to be offered," Ghani impressed upon the U.S. as it was preparing to evict the Taliban in the weeks after September 11.[37]

The finance chief has approved at least 154 Afghan infrastructure projects so far,[38] from wells to bridges, but one project stands out. He and Karzai have assigned top priority to building a major highway connecting the city of Herat in northern Afghanistan, Kandahar in southern Afghanistan, and Kabul. The Herat-to-Kandahar section happens to be on the path of the proposed mammoth Caspian gas pipeline—the sexiest industrial project in Afghanistan, if not the region, and the one on practically everyone's mind there. "The 48-inch diameter pipeline will extend 790 miles from the Afghanistan-Turkmenistan border, generally follow the Herat-to-Kandahar Road though Afghanistan, cross the Pakistan border in the vicinity of Quetta, and terminate in Multan, Pakistan, where it will tie into an existing pipeline," according to a Unocal press release describing the CentGas project.[39] As originally envisioned, the project calls for the construction of a highway, a railroad, and telecommunications lines, in addition to the pipeline, to form a "commerce corridor."[40]

Bush agrees that the highway is "an important project" and has committed $80 million to help finance its construction. Saudi Arabia and energy-poor Japan—the two biggest partners next to Unocal in the CentGas pipeline consortium—have each kicked in an additional $50 million.[41] "The United States and Japan and Saudi Arabia committed $180 million to rebuild the highway connecting Kabul, Kandahar and Herat," Bush told Afghan officials last fall. "It's an important project. President Karzai spoke to me about it in the Oval Office."[42]

About 470 miles, or 52 percent, of the proposed gas pipeline would pass through Afghanistan, almost all of it along the Herat-to-Kandahar highway. And about 42 percent of the proposed 1,040-mile oil pipeline from Turkmenistan to the Arabian Sea would run through Afghanistan. Both would be buried their entire length.[43]

But they would still be vulnerable to damage from factional fighting or terrorism, violence that has plagued Afghanistan in the past and stopped international development agencies from underwriting the huge projects. U.S. humanitarian and economic aid may help stabilize the Afghan government, but it does not guarantee security of new infrastructure and industrial assets, a prerequisite for such big investments. Only a strong military presence can establish law and order in a chronically lawless land—something else the Bush administration has committed to providing Karzai "for a long, long time," as CentCom's General

Franks put it.[44] Afghanistan now has what it never had before: a police force backed by the U.S. Army, with no expiration date. Pipeline investors could not ask for better security.

"Security is an umbrella that overarches both the economic and the political side of reconstruction," said Collins, who is in charge of stabilizing Afghanistan for the Defense Department. "As President Karzai is fond of saying: Security is the first priority. You can't have reconstruction without security, and in the end, you won't have security without reconstruction."[45]

President Bush has echoed Karzai's sentiments. "Security is a requirement for recovery and development. Can't have recovery and development unless there is a secure society," he assured Afghan officials last October. "America and other nations will continue working with the Afghan government to build security."[46]

To that end, the administration has paired U.S. Special Forces and Army civil affairs soldiers with Afghan soldiers to patrol ten regional zones around Afghanistan. "The purpose of these teams will be to facilitate reconstruction and to help spread security," Collins said, singling out the Herat-Kandahar-Kabul highway project as a prime candidate for protection. "They will also work to dampen regional tensions."[47] He added that, starting in 2003, the U.S. military's role in Afghanistan "will shift from being primarily combat to being primarily stability operations." (Ironically, the transition has been slowed by the White House's unholy alliance with Pakistan. Most of the hit-and-run attacks on U.S. troops based in Afghanistan have been launched by al-Qaida fighters entrenched in Pakistan's lawless northern tribal region that hugs the Afghan border. U.S. ground commanders want to chase the attackers back into Pakistan and destroy their bases, but the terms of Bush's partnership with Musharraf prohibit such cross-border raids. That is, the Pakistani strongman won't let them.)

Backing the army's joint regional teams is a five-thousand-man international peacekeeping force. "The International Security Assistance

Force in Kabul means that the Afghan government has not only U.S., but also international protection," Collins said. "The era of changing government by force in Afghanistan is over, and everyone has come to realize that—even the regional warlords will tell you that. It's out of the question. It's beyond the pale. It's not going to happen."[48]

Meanwhile, the U.S. is helping Afghanistan build its own army, something else Khalilzad recommended to crack down on radicals operating inside the country. Special Forces teams are training recruits. "America is helping to form a new Afghan national army. We are committed to an Afghan national army," Bush asserted. "The idea is to train 18 battalions of over 10,000 soldiers and finish the task by the end of" 2003.[49]

That does not mean U.S. troops will be pulling out any time soon. Franks expects they will be in Afghanistan for many years. "We intend to remain engaged with this country for the foreseeable and longer future," he said.[50]

Even if the U.S. were to pull out its eight thousand or so troops in Afghanistan, it would still have forces in the Caspian region it did not have before the war. Two years ago, not a single U.S. soldier was in the region. Now the U.S. has bases and thousands of troops in Kyrgyzstan, Uzbekistan, and Tajikistan, which are all within striking distance of Afghanistan in the event the Taliban or a powerful warlord tries to march on the U.S.-backed government in Kabul—or commandeer, say, a U.S.-backed pipeline or two in western Afghanistan.

The administration originally said that it would keep military forces in the region only as long as necessary to defeat al-Qaida, which is now based in Pakistan where U.S. forces apparently cannot touch it, at least not without Musharraf's permission. Afghanistan-based troops are being used instead for nation building and peacekeeping—things Bush was determined not to get involved in when he came into office.

Afghanistan is a special circumstance, he argues. Pulling out now might create another power vacuum in Kabul that could be filled by another terrorist-sponsoring regime, reverting the situation in Afghanistan to the way it was before September 11. That's why, he says, "America affirms its full commitment to a future of progress and stability for the Afghan people."[51]

That's one reason. Another is that a stable and secure Afghanistan will finally attract international backing for a Caspian energy corridor to Asia—something both the Bush and the Karzai administrations favor. And so do, for that matter, their allies in Saudi Arabia and Pakistan. "Instability and war in Afghanistan [have] been an obstacle to building pipelines to bring Central Asian oil and gas to Pakistan and the world markets," Khalilzad told Washington policy makers as a Unocal consultant last decade. "These projects will only go forward if Afghanistan has a single authoritative government."[52] And that is exactly what Afghanistan now has, and exactly what those projects have done—gone forward, thanks to him and his former Unocal colleague Karzai. I will chronicle in another chapter how the new U.S.-backed leader of Afghanistan has managed to advance the trans-Afghan pipeline projects with the Taliban out of the way.

But first, it is instructive to trace his handler Khalilzad's stealthy rise to international power broker.

8

THE SPECIAL ENVOY
Bush's Point Man in Afghanistan

To implement the changes . . . the administration should appoint a high-level envoy for Afghanistan who can coordinate overall U.S. policy. The envoy must have sufficient stature and access to ensure that he or she is taken seriously in foreign capitals and by local militias. Equally important, the special envoy must be able to shape Afghanistan policy within U.S. bureaucracies.

—One of KHALILZAD'S policy recommendations, written a year before Bush appointed him special envoy to Afghanistan

ZALMAY MAMOZY KHALILZAD WAS BORN IN THE NORTHERN Afghan city of Mazar-e-Sharif on March 22, 1951. When he was a youngster, his ethnic Pashtun family moved to the capital of Kabul, where his educated father, Khalilullah, worked for the Pashtun-dominated government, which at the time was headed by a king—the same one forced into exile years later. Kabul under the monarchy was more affluent and cosmopolitan, and the Khalilzads were considered part of the intellectual elite. During high school, Khalilzad attended the Ghazi Lycee in Kabul, an English-language academy.[1] He won a scholarship to the American University of Beirut in the 1970s, where he reportedly held pro-Palestinian views.[2]

From there he traveled to America to enroll in graduate school at the University of Chicago. It appears from INS records that Khalilzad was supposed to be deported in 1978, but he was able to have the deportation order suspended by a judge and his status adjusted to a permanent resident that year.[3] He became a U.S. citizen a few years later. In 1979—the same year Soviet troops invaded his homeland—he earned a doctorate in political science from the university. His mother, Zahra, followed him to America in 1982, arriving in New York City as an Afghan war refugee, INS records show.[4] At the University of Chicago, Khalilzad studied under Albert Wohlstetter, the late anti-Soviet hard-liner who counted among his acolytes Deputy Defense Secretary Paul Wolfowitz, who has figured prominently in Khalilzad's career.[5]

He also met his wife, Cheryl Benard, there. The Austrian-born author and feminist has championed the cause of Afghan women who suffered under the Taliban. In a book published in 2002, she condemned Taliban clerics as nothing but robed troglodytes who treated Afghan women like chattel. *Veiled Courage: Inside the Afghan Women's Resistance* slams the Taliban mullahs for carrying out what she calls "gender apartheid." Under Taliban rule, Benard notes, women were forbidden to work or go to school, which was a severe hardship on the fifty thousand or so widows in Kabul alone, whose husbands were killed in the war against the Soviets or during the civil war that followed. They also could not leave their homes to run errands without a male chaperone, and when they did go out, they had to wear a head-to-toe covering called a burqa. Of course, the Taliban did not introduce burqas to Afghanistan. Afghan women have been wearing them throughout the last century, and it was not until 1959 that they were first permitted to discard them. Some still choose to wear them—even after the Taliban. Difference is, the Taliban enforced the Islamic dress code with public beatings.

Benard's husband did not seem terribly concerned about such atrocities when he was helping Unocal woo the Taliban as a pipeline consultant. On the same day in 1996, ironically enough, that the *Washington Post* published a front-page report about Taliban militiamen assaulting Afghan women for wearing immodest attire on the streets of Kabul,[6] Khalilzad penned a *Post* column on page 21 calling for the U.S. to engage the

Taliban and help it stabilize Afghanistan by using "as a positive incentive the benefits that will accrue to Afghanistan from the construction of oil and gas pipelines across its territory." He was relatively forgiving in his description of the regime: "The Taliban does not practice the anti-U.S. style of fundamentalism practiced by Iran. The group upholds a mix of traditional Pashtun values and an orthodox interpretation of Islam."[7] Khalilzad clung to the notion that as bad as the Taliban were on human rights, they would finally bring a level of stability and order to Afghanistan that would allow the pipeline deal to go through.

But once it became clear in late 1998 that Washington and the UN would never embrace the Taliban's harsh brand of governance, Khalilzad began attacking the Taliban as medieval brutes who were "hostile" and "dangerous" not only to women, but also to the U.S.; and in a reversal, he began calling for their replacement by a moderate U.S.-backed regime: "If the Taliban cannot be transformed, it must be replaced," he asserted in his 1999 white paper.[8] He further argued in his 2000 policy proposal: "Afghan women face a horrifying array of restrictions, among the most repressive in the world. Washington must weaken the Taliban, support moderate Afghans, and press Afghanistan's neighbors, particularly Pakistan, to work against extremism in the region."[9]

Missiles for the Mujahideen

With his newly minted Ph.D., Khalilzad in the early 1980s taught political science at Columbia University in New York, where he worked with Zbigniew Brzezinski, who was President Carter's national security adviser. Carter reacted to the Soviet invasion of Afghanistan by initiating covert aid to Afghan freedom fighters and Islamic jihad schools in Pakistan with the intent of spreading militant Islamism in Central Asia to destabilize the Soviet Union. Brzezinski in 1998 reportedly lauded the secret CIA operation, code-named "Cyclone," as an "excellent idea."[10]

Then in 1984, Khalilzad joined Wolfowitz at the State Department in Washington, where he actively shaped U.S. cold war policy in Afghanistan as a special adviser to the undersecretary of state for policy and a member of the State Department policy planning staff. Khalilzad helped convince the White House to covertly arm the mujahideen with U.S.-made, highly accurate Stinger missiles. In 1986 alone, the U.S. supplied the Soviet resistance with some 150 Stinger launchers, each with two missiles. The shoulder-fired antiaircraft rockets scored five hits against Soviet aircraft for every eight launches, and substantially raised the cost of war for the humiliated Soviets, who were forced to withdraw from Afghanistan in 1989. Washington declared victory and also went home.[11]

At the time, Khalilzad warned, prophetically, that the U.S. had disengaged Afghanistan too quickly after the Soviet departure, leaving a leadership vacuum that would be filled by warlords and radical Muslim fundamentalists. "The United States aided radical fundamentalists along with more traditional forces and encouraged Arab and Islamic states to support their own anti-Soviet proxies. The implications for a post-Soviet Afghanistan were not considered. After all, our enemy's enemy was our friend," he said.[12]

"But then our enemy departed. With the Soviets gone, the United States saw little reason to focus on this poor and distant land. We left our erstwhile friends to their own devices, assuming that their squabbles and actions would remain confined to the mountains and valleys of Afghanistan," Khalilzad lamented. "As the United States departed, a vicious civil war spread throughout the country . . . Without the glue of the common enemy, the opposition turned their guns on one another."

Somewhat resentful, Khalilzad contended that, to a large extent, the Taliban and al-Qaida rose from Washington's neglect. "Afghanistan has gone from one of Washington's greatest foreign-policy triumphs to one of its most profound failures," he complained nearly three years ago in demanding the U.S. commit to stabilizing his homeland.[13]

But a year after the Soviets pulled out of Afghanistan, the first Bush administration had its own war to worry about—this one in the Persian

Gulf. And during the Iraq conflict, Khalilzad, who left the State Department in 1989, joined the Pentagon as assistant deputy undersecretary of defense for policy planning, working with Wolfowitz, then the Pentagon's No. 3 official. He also got to know Dick Cheney, who was defense secretary, while helping shape U.S. postwar defense strategy.

During the Clinton years, the Bush-connected cold warrior worked as a senior analyst at the Rand Corp., the consulting firm often referred to as the think tank for the Pentagon. While there, he founded the Rand Center for Middle Eastern Studies. Khalilzad also served as program director for strategy, doctrine, and force structure at Rand's Project Air Force, and edited the book *Strategic Appraisal: Aerospace Power in the 21st Century*. His wife, Cheryl, age fifty, is a Rand consultant in Washington. The couple, who live in Potomac, Maryland, and have two sons, cowrote the book *The Government of God: Iran's Islamic Republic*.

In the mid-1990s, Khalilzad also worked as an analyst at the for-profit Cambridge Energy Research Associates, or CERA. The Cambridge, Massachusetts-based consulting firm advises oil clients working in the Caspian, among other regions. Khalilzad conducted risk analyses for Unocal, a big Caspian producer trying to build export pipelines through Afghanistan.[14] In 1997, he even helped Unocal executives in Houston play host to high-ranking Taliban leaders. According to a CERA brochure, its Caspian Energy Advisory Service can help energy companies do the following:

- Develop a framework for anticipating the future of regional politics, economics and markets by understanding the key players, government policies and changing market fundamentals.
- Monitor and evaluate specific investment opportunities in oil, gas, power and transportation.
- Assess the future of the major energy investment projects that will tend to drive the overall investment climate.
- Identify and mitigate political, economic and project risks.

One Caspian analyst at CERA, in a moment of candor during U.S. air strikes against the Taliban, told a *New York Times* business reporter that the Bush administration would be lining up oil companies to build pipelines in Afghanistan after the dust settled. "Once we bomb the hell out of Afghanistan, we will have to cough up some projects there, and this pipeline is one of them," said Matthew J. Sagers, CERA's director of energy economics for Eurasia and Eastern Europe, in early December 2001.

While he was advising Unocal, Khalilzad joined the board of the Afghanistan Foundation, which was founded one month after the Taliban captured Kabul to raise U.S. interest in Afghan reconstruction. As one of its founding directors, Khalilzad drafted the Afghanistan Foundation's position paper. The Washington nonprofit group—which recently changed its name to the Afghanistan-America Foundation and became a 501(c)(4), an IRS designation that allows unlimited lobbying—is a who's who of Caspian oil lobbyists and experts. Its national honorary cochairmen are Brzezinski, a Khalilzad mentor, and former Bush national security adviser Lt. Gen. Brent Scowcroft, mentor of current Bush security adviser Condoleezza Rice, chairman of the President's Foreign Intelligence Advisory Board, and president of the Scowcroft Group Inc., a Washington lobbying firm with Caspian oil clients.[15] Both Brzezinski and Scowcroft are officers in the U.S.-Azerbaijan Chamber of Commerce, along with Cheney and former Texaco lobbyist Richard Armitage, who is part of Bush's war cabinet. Brzezinski lobbied on behalf of Amoco in oil-rich Azerbaijan, before it merged with BP.[16] Amoco, one of the first oil and gas developers to enter Azerbaijan, is a partner in a joint venture with Latin oil giant Bridas, which last decade romanced the Taliban to try to build its own gas pipeline through Afghanistan.

Besides Khalilzad, Brzezinski is tied to foundation adviser Frederick Starr through the Central Asia-Caucasus Institute, which Starr, former Oberlin College president, now chairs. The institute, which promotes the interests of U.S. firms in the Caspian, was created in 1996 with a grant from the Smith Richardson Foundation, which counts Brzezinski as one of its most influential board members. Chevron and Unocal are among the institute's corporate sponsors.[17] Other Afghanistan-America Foundation advisers include Khalilzad's old pal Tom Gouttierre of the University of Nebraska's Center for Afghanistan Studies, who also helped Unocal court Taliban leaders; Barnett Rubin of the Council on Foreign Relations, who has testified alongside Khalilzad about the pipelines; Qayum Karzai, brother of new Afghan president Hamid Karzai, who also consulted for Unocal; and Robert Oakley, the former ambassador to Pakistan whom Unocal also hired to advance its trans-Afghan pipeline project. According to the foundation's tax returns, Gouttierre was originally listed as its vice president.[18]

According to its latest mission statement, the Afghanistan-America Foundation, which has organized congressional "roundtable" discussions on Afghanistan, is "unique in its ability to inform the White House, Congress, and the independent agencies to provide the framework for policy and the planning of the reconstruction of Afghanistan. This role is vital to the progress and rebuilding of Afghanistan." To that end, the foundation—which recently opened an office in Kabul—has created the Afghan-American Chamber of Commerce "to facilitate investments for private-sector based reconstruction."

In January 2001, after George W. Bush was elected president, Khalilzad headed the Bush-Cheney transition team for the Defense Department. He counseled Defense Secretary Rumsfeld as lead coordinator of the Defense Department policy coordination group set up by Bush to help Rumsfeld prepare to run the U.S. military. Bush named Randall Schriver of Armitage Associates and another expert to assist Khalilzad in the effort.[19] Armitage Associates is an Arlington, Virginia-based consulting firm founded by Armitage, the former Caspian oil lobbyist who became Bush's No. 2 State Department official. Armitage worked with Khalilzad and others in Bush's inner circle to oust the Taliban after September 11.

Then in May 2001, Bush appointed Khalilzad special presidential assistant and senior director for Persian Gulf, Southwest Asia, and other regional issues of the National Security Council, where he reports directly to NSC Adviser Condoleezza Rice, the Caspian expert and longtime Chevron director who guided the post–September 11 war strategy. The fifty-two-year-old moderate Muslim has an office in the Eisenhower Executive Office Building across from the West Wing.

In that role, Khalilzad oversees White House security policy toward Afghanistan, Pakistan, and the Middle East—including Iraq and the Palestinian-Israeli conflict. His ideas helped cement Bush's position backing the creation of a Palestinian state. Though he condemns Palestinian suicide bombings in Israel, Khalilzad believes both sides can reach a final peace settlement if Israel withdraws from territories claimed by the Palestinians.[20] When it comes to Iraq, however, Khalilzad is an aggressive hawk. He was one of the earliest hand-wringers over Saddam Hussein. He warned in a 1988 State Department paper that Iraq posed a bigger threat to Gulf peace than Iran, and he advised isolating and containing Iraq, while backing insurgents to overthrow Saddam's regime. In early 1998, he joined Wolfowitz and others in signing an open letter to President Clinton urging him to develop a policy to depose Saddam. Now Khalilzad is spearheading the Bush administration's plan for a post-Saddam Iraq. He has met with opposition leaders to talk about regime change there, just as he did in Afghanistan. He has worked most closely with pro-U.S. Iraqi exile Ahmad Chalabi—nephew of Fadhil Chalabi, a former top official in Iraq's Oil Ministry who has pushed for the privatization of Iraqi oil and a lead role for the U.S. in the country's reconstruction, according to my sources.

Even before the war, Khalilzad, as the only native Afghan in the White House, was its most influential voice on Afghan policy. Back then, however, Afghanistan was not exactly on Washington's A-list of foreign policy hot spots, and few paid attention when Bush appointed him to the National Security Council.

But since September 11, Khalilzad has played a key behind-the-scenes role in the war on terrorism, driving much of Bush's response to the World Trade Center and Pentagon attacks. Few still appreciate the degree of his influence. The president incorporated into his war policy nearly all of the recommendations that Khalilzad made for Afghanistan coming into the White House. It turned out to be a wildly successful plan for removing a regime blocking development of the Caspian energy corridor Bush's Afghan pal, "Zal," was promoting, but a lousy one for nailing bin Laden and the other September 11 mass murderers who still threaten America.

Khalilzad's Strategy

Consider the steps Khalilzad recommended taking in Afghanistan before the attacks, and the steps Bush took there after the attacks. The overlap is stunning—and in light of the poor al-Qaida scorecard, highly unfortunate.

1. *Tear down the Taliban.* "The United States should offer existing foes of the Taliban assistance," Khalilzad proposed. But efforts should not be limited to helping the Northern Alliance, the main military opposition to the Taliban, he said. The U.S. should also try to undermine the Taliban's ethnic base of support. "Washington must emphasize efforts to reduce Pashtun support for the Taliban," he urged, and "seek to fracture the Taliban internally, a step that goes beyond simply supporting the Taliban's existing foes."[21] Bush, in turn, armed the Northern Alliance and helped it smash the Taliban in Mazar-e-Sharif and Kabul, while working through Pashtun tribal leader Karzai to undermine support for the Taliban in the southern stronghold of Kandahar.

2. *Oppose the Taliban's ideology.* "It is not enough to oppose the Taliban on the ground," Khalilzad asserted. "The ideas that they advocate must be opposed as well." So he suggested the White House "expand the Voice of America's Dari and Pashtu broadcasts to Afghanistan, providing airtime to the Taliban's opponents."[22] Bush heeded his top Afghan aide's advice. After the U.S. air strikes began in Afghanistan, the Voice of America added one hour of programming in Afghanistan's two main tongues, Dari and Pashtu. Among other U.S. propaganda, the government-funded radio station broadcast Bush's statements that the strikes were not aimed at Afghans or Muslims. It also criticized the Taliban regime for failing to adequately feed and care for the Afghan people.

3. Aid the victims of the Taliban. Khalilzad argued that humanitarian aid could be used to "weaken" the Taliban's hold. He recommended U.S. food and medical aid be "sent to areas outside the Taliban's control or channeled through the Taliban's opponents."[23] Bush followed Khalilzad's playbook by airlifting tons of aid to Afghan women and children. In a risky war strategy, U.S. forces dropped thousands of food rations over Afghanistan on the first day of bombing, exposing pilots failing to fly at high altitudes to antiaircraft fire from the Taliban.

4. Coordinate anti-Taliban efforts with Russia. Khalilzad recommended enlisting Russia in the campaign to oust the Taliban, since it shares a common interest in halting the spread of Talibanism. The Taliban had directly or indirectly supported Islamic rebels in Chechnya. "As unrest grows in Chechnya, Moscow may recognize the importance of better relations with the United States on the issue of Afghanistan," he said.[24] In the run-up to the anti-Taliban military campaign, Bush dispatched Deputy Secretary of State Armitage and other officials to seek help from Moscow, which came through with intelligence, arms for the Northern Alliance, overflight rights, and troops.[25]

5. Press Pakistan to withdraw its Taliban support. "As the Taliban's most important sponsor, Pakistan bears a responsibility for its misdeeds and can play an important role in transforming the movement," Khalilzad advised. To that end, "the United States should press Pakistan to reduce its support for the Taliban," he added. "Pressing Islamabad now is essential, as its new military leadership consolidates power and seeks to gain the goodwill of the United States."[26] He recommended using U.S. economic aid as leverage. Within hours of the September 11 attacks, the Bush administration pressed Islamabad to end its support for the Taliban. After the regime was ousted from Afghanistan, the administration rewarded Pakistan with $2 billion in economic aid and debt write-offs.

6. Forge closer diplomatic ties with Islamabad. "The United States has let its relationship with Pakistan drift since the end of the Cold War. In recent years acrimony has grown, and Pakistan's nuclear tests further strained

U.S.-Pakistan relations," Khalilzad further advised. "For any progress to occur on transforming the Taliban, however, the United States must repair relations with Pakistan," and "increase the respect shown for Islamabad." He also proposed "developing a strategy for winning over Pakistan."[27] Bush not only patched things up with Pakistan; he made it America's key ally in the war on terrorism, trusting it to hunt down al-Qaida fugitives and crack down on their confederates and money-laundering rings there.

7. *Renew military aid and training for Pakistan.* Khalilzad recommended the White House consider waiving the Pressler amendment, which bans military assistance to Pakistan unless the president can certify that Pakistan is no longer developing nuclear missiles. "The Pressler amendment has, if anything, proven counterproductive in stopping Pakistan's nuclear program. It also has led to a slide in U.S.-Pakistan relations," he argued. "Increasing U.S. leverage may require lifting or modifying the Pressler amendment."[28] Sure enough, Bush on October 16, 2001, awarded Pakistan a one-year presidential waiver under 620 E(e) of the Foreign Assistance Act—the so-called Pressler amendment.[29] The waiver was automatically extended and is still in effect—even though Pakistan was caught last year helping North Korea advance its nuclear weapons program in exchange for missile technology. Military training exercises between the U.S. and Pakistan resumed in 2002. And the Bush administration is reviewing the previous cancellation of a shipment of F-16 warplanes, among other arms, to Pakistan, which is trying to strengthen its forces against India.

8. *Appeal to Pakistan's commercial interests in Afghanistan.* "To achieve progress in Afghanistan, Washington must make it clear to Islamabad that it understands and accepts Pakistan's legitimate interests in the region," Khalilzad said. "These legitimate interests include the existence of a nonantagonistic Afghanistan willing to explore all mutually beneficial relationships, including the opening up of Central Asia to trade with the south and the promotion of economic development."[30] Within two months of the Taliban's removal, new Afghan leader Karzai huddled with Pakistani strongman Musharraf in Islamabad to give his blessing to the

stalled pipeline projects. Later on, Bush also discussed the pipelines with Musharraf. The president has offered Pakistan U.S. financing and political risk insurance to develop its oil and gas sector. On October 16, 2001, Bush signed another waiver lifting economic sanctions under the U.S. Export-Import Bank Act.[31] That same month, the U.S. Overseas Private Investment Corporation extended a $300 million line of credit to Pakistan.

9. Appeal to Saudi's interests in Afghanistan. "The United States should encourage other states with interests in Afghanistan, including our regional friends such as Pakistan and Saudi Arabia, to work together for the same objectives," Khalilzad urged.[32] Bush encouraged his friends in the Saudi royal family to cut off their support for the Taliban and help rebuild Afghanistan, which offers the kingdom a gateway for expanding its oil empire into the promising Caspian frontier. And within weeks of taking office, Karzai met with Saudi Crown Prince Abdullah, who is close to the president of Saudi's Delta Oil, a partner in the trans-Afghan pipeline project. After their meeting, Prince Abdullah pledged $220 million for the reconstruction of Afghanistan, according to the Saudi Information Office, including $50 million to help build a new highway from Herat to Kandahar along the gas pipeline route.

10. Replace the Taliban with a moderate, pro-U.S. regime. "It is not enough to tear down the Taliban," Khalilzad said. "Washington must also create an alternative to their leadership in the long-term"—one that is "more in accord with U.S. regional interests." It should groom "moderate" Afghan leaders "who would embrace U.S. ideals and goals," he stated, while discouraging warlords from vying for the top office. "Support should go far beyond backing the remnants of the Northern Alliance, whose leaders have an unimpressive track record in their previous governance of parts of Afghanistan," Khalilzad emphasized.[33] With Karzai's regime, fittingly, the administration has installed a progressive, pro-U.S. alternative to the backward, anti-U.S. Taliban—and one that shares its Caspian oil-export goals. Northern Alliance leaders, meanwhile, have roles in Karzai's cabinet, but do not run the show, as Khalilzad recommended.

11. Convene a so-called loya jirga. "As part of the effort to bolster moderate Afghans, the United States should lend its support to the convening of a traditional Afghan grand assembly for resolving the Afghan conflict and for the selection of a broadly acceptable transitional government," Khalilzad advised.[34] The Bush administration did more than lend its support; it dispatched Khalilzad to Kabul, and through behind-the-scenes maneuvering, he essentially rigged the election in favor of Karzai.

12. Appoint a special envoy. "To implement the above changes . . . the administration should appoint a high-level envoy for Afghanistan who can coordinate overall U.S. policy," Khalilzad further advised. "The envoy must have sufficient stature and access to ensure that he or she is taken seriously in foreign capitals and by local militias. Equally important, the special envoy must be able to shape Afghanistan policy within U.S. bureaucracies."[35] Khalilzad could not have written a better job description for himself. Sure enough, Bush created the position for him, adding it to his NSC duties in December 2001.

But Khalilzad had a hands-on role in implementing the changes he outlined well before he became the president's intermediary in Kabul. In the weeks after September 11 and before U.S. forces struck Taliban targets, he helped Bush demonize the Taliban by punching up his anti-Taliban rhetoric. In the president's September 20 speech, for example, Khalilzad contributed to the section where Bush cited examples of how the mullah militia was "brutalizing" the Afghan people. "Women are not allowed to attend school. You can be jailed for owning a television," Bush said. "Religion can be practiced only as their leaders dictate. A man can be jailed in Afghanistan if his beard is not long enough." Khalilzad's input showed up elsewhere, as well. "The United States respects the people of Afghanistan—after all, we are currently its largest source of humanitarian aid—but we condemn the Taliban," Bush told Congress that same night. "It is not only repressing its own people, it is threatening people everywhere by sponsoring and sheltering and supplying terrorists. By aiding and abetting murder, the Taliban regime is committing murder," as if the Taliban controlled bin Laden and al-Qaida, and not the other way around.

Within days of the September 11 attacks, moreover, Khalilzad spoke to Abdullah Abdullah, then the designated foreign minister for the opposition Northern Alliance, by Abdullah's satellite phone from inside Afghanistan. The two discussed toppling the Taliban.[36] Abdullah, who is now Karzai's foreign minister, testified alongside Khalilzad at a 1998 hearing before GOP Senator Sam Brownback's subcommittee in which Khalilzad extolled the virtues of building in Afghanistan "a valuable corridor for the export of Central Asian oil and gas to South Asia."[37] Abdullah, speaking on behalf of Northern Alliance leaders at the hearing, complained about the "draconian policies" of the Taliban, and Pakistan's "military, financial and logistical support" for the regime. "The people of Afghanistan will not accept such a repressive regime," he said.[38]

Once bombs began raining on Taliban targets, Khalilzad monitored the war closely with Rice. Rumsfeld called on him for counsel during the U.S.-led campaign. So did the CentCom commander, Gen. Tommy Franks. Clearly, Khalilzad's fingerprints are all over the Afghan war plans.

Yet few even in Washington see his influence because he has been able to operate largely in the shadows. Incredibly, he managed to avoid mention in *Washington Post* sleuth Bob Woodward's 376-page tome *Bush at War*. The number one bestseller—billed as the definitive, "behind-the-scenes" account of how the president and his advisers responded to the September 11 attacks—does not name Khalilzad even in passing (though that may not be all that surprising, given that Bush and his advisers essentially authorized much of what Woodward wrote by granting him exclusive interviews and access to select notes taken during war strategy sessions).

Khalilzad's work remains almost invisible, and it is not because he is a shy or a particularly modest person. On the contrary, he is by all accounts a colorful figure who shuns the gray uniform of the U.S. bureaucracy in favor of suits with a European flair, and he can become boisterous and animated when he talks. His work is invisible, rather, because the White House likes it that way. It has turned down major press requests to interview Khalilzad, and it usually has to clear his remarks as envoy. The White House even timed his announcement as envoy for New Year's Eve, when few Americans were glued to the news. CBS News was the only TV network that broadcast the December 31, 2001, appointment, a transcript search reveals, and polls show most American adults still get their political information primarily from the evening news. The *Washington Post* buried the story on page 13.

By appointing him special assistant and special envoy, moreover, Bush guarded Khalilzad from the klieg lights and intense scrutiny of congressional hearings, which no doubt would have pried into his connections to the Caspian oil lobby and exposed his conflicts of interest. Khalilzad's positions do not require Senate confirmation.

Unocal Zal

Khalilzad has been a tireless promoter in Washington of a Caspian energy corridor through Afghanistan. "Afghanistan is important to the United States [and] the importance of Afghanistan may grow in the coming years, as Central Asia's oil and gas reserves, which are estimated to rival those of the North Sea, begin to play a major role in the world energy market. Afghanistan could prove a valuable corridor for this energy as well as for access to markets in Central Asia," he said. "Instead, Afghanistan has proven an obstacle to the development of this region, as outside investors fear the strife that emanates from Afghanistan."[39] Before and after the war, Khalilzad's chief objective has been to stabilize Afghanistan—so that multibillion-dollar projects like the Caspian-export pipelines could be built in his home country—and not necessarily to rid the world of Osama bin Laden and al-Qaida.

When it became obvious that the Taliban were not the stabilizing influence for U.S. investments he had hoped for, Khalilzad set his mind on deposing them. He demonized them at every opportunity, while giving their truly dangerous guest bin Laden a relative pass. Khalilzad's insouciance regarding bin Laden is noteworthy. In foreign policy journals, he has referred to him not as a terrorist, but as "a Saudi businessman known to sponsor anti-U.S. terror in Saudi Arabia,"[40] and has disregarded him—even after al-Qaida's 1998 attacks on the U.S. embassies and 2000 attack on the USS *Cole*—as "hardly an evil genius or charismatic leader who single-handedly is waging war against the United States."[41] Unfortunately, the oil-friendly Bush administration adopted his Taliban-centric attitude in response to al-Qaida's World Trade Center and Pentagon attacks.

Of course, Bush and his advisers will never admit that exporting Caspian oil had anything to do with their Afghan war strategy, which focused more on replacing a rogue government than on hunting down September 11 terrorists. Less than a month after U.S.-backed forces evicted the Taliban, State Department official Christina Rocca, a Bush appointee, visited Capitol Hill and explained for the record that the administration had to stabilize Afghanistan to prevent it from becoming a "safe haven" again for terrorists—as if the war on terrorism were over geography, and not a network of nomadic killers, or as if it were more important to deny a home to future terrorists than to catch existing terrorists. "The elimination of bin Laden and his associates from Afghanistan will be followed by a long internationally supported process that aims to rebuild and bring lasting stability to the war-torn country to prevent it from being a safe haven for terrorists," she testified in a December 6, 2001, hearing before the Senate Foreign Relations Committee. "Ousting the Taliban leadership and helping the Afghan people form a broad-based, representative government are high priorities in this process."

Rocca, you will recall, was the chief foreign policy adviser to Republican Senator Brownback, architect of the new Silk Road strategy to promote the interests of U.S. energy firms such as Unocal in the Caspian region. After the September 11 attacks, the Bush administration eagerly embraced Brownback's strategy, which included repealing a ban on U.S. aid to Azerbaijan, where Unocal and Saudi's Delta Oil, as well as Condi Rice's ChevronTexaco, are developing large oil and gas tracts and are looking for a southern pipeline route to export their finds to energy-hungry Asian markets. Afghanistan offers the cheapest and fastest route—if it can be stabilized.

But then Rocca knew this. She had helped book the parade of Unocal executives and consultants, including Khalilzad, who lobbied on behalf of the trans-Afghan pipelines before her former boss's Senate Foreign Relations Subcommittee. When you hear her and other Bush officials talk about the need for "stability" in Afghanistan, they are not just talking about preventing terrorism. They are also talking about promoting oil interests. "Stability" is code for the pipelines. Without Afghan stability, there can be no pipelines, and without the pipelines, there can be no highly desirable southern export route for Caspian producers.

But don't take my word for it. Listen to Khalilzad, the man behind the Afghanistan plan: "Stability can allow the construction of the roads and pipelines linking Central Asia through Afghanistan to Pakistan and the world," Khalilzad rhapsodized as a Unocal consultant.[42]

Caspian Sea energy giant Turkmenistan, which already is tied into export pipelines across Russia, has been clamoring for a more-profitable southern export route for nearly a decade. It shares its southern border with Afghanistan. "The Turkmen would like stability in Afghanistan so they can export gas and oil through pipelines that will be built across Afghanistan to Pakistan, the Arabian Sea and possibly India," Khalilzad said.[43]

"An American company, Unocal, in partnership with the Saudi firm Delta Oil, announced plans for building two pipelines, one for oil and one for gas, to bring Central Asian gas and oil to markets through Afghanistan," he added. "These pipelines are not likely to be built unless the [Taliban] conflict is resolved."[44]

Well, the Taliban are no longer a problem (although the same cannot be said for al-Qaida, America's real enemy), and Afghanistan is more stable than it has been in nearly a generation. That part of Khalilzad's mission has been accomplished. The trans-Afghan pipelines, meanwhile, are not far behind.

9

INKING THE DEAL
Karzai, Musharraf Come Through

This [agreement] will provide the shortest route for the transportation of petrochemical resources from Central Asia to the Far East,
Japan and the West. With the gradual return of peace and normalcy
in Afghanistan, we are confident that this project would be realized
in the near future.

—PAKISTANI PRESIDENT PERVEZ MUSHARRAF upon signing
historic pipeline deal with AFGHAN PRESIDENT HAMID KARZAI

PLANS TO BUILD OIL AND GAS PIPELINES ACROSS AFGHANISTAN
had lain dormant since 1998, when project leader Unocal pulled out a few
months after the U.S. fired cruise missiles into the country in a strike
against al-Qaida. Any hopes for international backing for the ambitious
projects were dashed at that point.

But then September 11 gave the oil-friendly Bush administration a
pretext to kick the Qaida-harboring Taliban out of the Afghan capital of
Kabul, install a new regime there, and provide security for the pipelines;
and within months, White House Security Adviser Zal Khalilzad's pet
projects were catapulted back onto the drawing board. The U.S.-backed
government of Hamid Karzai, another Unocal pipeline booster, was
instantly recognized by the United Nations. And in no time international
economic development agencies began loosening purse strings for at least
the proposed natural gas pipeline, which Karzai has formally agreed to
build with the leaders of Turkmenistan and Pakistan. Their historic deal

was signed not long after he and Pakistani strongman General Musharraf met with President Bush in New York to discuss the more than $2 billion project. Construction is expected to start by 2005.

From Pipe Dream to Pipe Reality

Once Bush's special envoy Khalilzad maneuvered Karzai into power, the new Afghan leader wasted no time putting the pipeline plans in motion. Everything came together with impressive dispatch after the Taliban hurdle was cleared. Here is the subsequent flurry of events that escaped America's attention, distracted as it was by Bush hailing the defeat of the Taliban (while asking for "patience" in defeating al-Qaida) and endlessly shaking his saber at Baghdad:

November 13, 2001: Kabul falls to U.S.-led forces.

December 7: The Taliban stronghold of Kandahar also falls.

December 17: The U.S. embassy reopens in Kabul, resuming a U.S. diplomatic presence in Afghanistan for the first time in almost thirteen years.

December 22: Karzai is sworn in as interim leader of Afghanistan with behind-the-scenes help from Khalilzad.

December 31: Bush appoints Khalilzad special envoy to Afghanistan, in a move meant to underscore the administration's commitment to Afghan reconstruction.

January 2, 2002: The Bush administration, through the Overseas Private Investment Corporation, a federal economic development agency, establishes a $50 million line of credit to support U.S. investment in Afghanistan. The money will be available to Afghan reconstruction projects involving U.S. companies. The credit line is announced at an OPIC conference on Afghanistan investment opportunities attended by Don Ritter, the chairman of the Afghanistan-America Foundation, which counts Khalilzad as one of its founding board members.[1]

January 19: Karzai, in his first trip abroad for the administration, travels to the Saudi capital of Riyadh to meet with Crown Prince Abdullah, who is close to the president of Saudi's Delta Oil, a lead partner in the trans-Afghan gas pipeline project. Abdullah pledges $220 million for the reconstruction of Afghanistan.

January 28: Karzai meets with Bush in the Oval Office to discuss the importance of building a new highway from Herat to Kandahar to Kabul.[2] The Herat-to-Kandahar section is on the pipeline route and part of the "energy corridor" envisioned by Unocal and Khalilzad. Building a road alongside the pipeline is critical not only for its construction, but also for maintaining its security. Bush confirms the $50 million credit line to help Afghanistan attract U.S. business investment.

January 30: Bush appointee Elizabeth Jones, assistant secretary of state for European and Eurasian affairs, meets with Turkmen President Saparmurat Niyazov in the Turkmenistan capital of Ashkabad to discuss the proposed $2.5 billion Central Asian Oil Pipeline, which would link oil pipelines in Kazakhstan, Uzbekistan, and Turkmenistan with a new oil export terminal in Gwadar, Pakistan. Like the gas pipeline, it would cross Afghanistan. Jones, former U.S. Caspian envoy, reportedly says the project looks as if it would be lucrative and profitable, and adds that "the U.S. would support private companies that chose to undertake trans-Afghanistan pipeline projects if they were considered to be beneficial and commercially viable," according to a U.S. Energy Department report.[3]

February 8: Just forty-eight days after taking office, Karzai travels to the Pakistani capital of Islamabad for a one-day visit with Musharraf to discuss the proposed gas pipeline, which will bring gas from Turkmenistan across Afghanistan to Pakistan, and possibly on to India. Karzai says that the two leaders "agreed that it was in the interest of both countries."[4]

March 14: Karzai meets with Turkmen President Niyazov in Ashkabad to discuss the gas pipeline.

April 28: A financial reporter asks Defense Secretary Rumsfeld at the Turkmenbashi Airport in Turkmenistan if he thinks "the situation in Afghanistan is now sufficiently under control for American oil and gas companies to come forward and invest in a trans-Afghan pipeline." Rumsfeld responds: "I am not going to comment on what companies might or might not do with this kind of pipeline. I will say that the security situation in Afghanistan is dramatically improved from what it was."[5]

May 15: The World Bank opens offices in Kabul and commits $100 million in grants to Karzai's government. The international lending agency's chief, James Wolfensohn, affirms that a "number of entrepreneurs" are interested in building a gas pipeline through the country. Once a new consortium is formed to build the pipeline, Wolfensohn says, the World Bank "would certainly take a look at" backing it. He mentions that Karzai and his reconstruction adviser, Ashraf Ghani, expressed to him their interest in the project. Afghan-American Ghani happens to be a former World Bank official.[6]

May 30: In a major breakthrough for the long-dormant project, Karzai returns to Islamabad with Turkmen President Niyazov to ink a preliminary deal, called a memorandum of understanding, with Musharraf to build the gas pipeline, along with rail links, to Pakistan.[7] The agreement "will provide the shortest route for the transportation of petrochemical resources from Central Asia to the Far East, Japan and the West," Musharraf announces at the signing ceremony. "With the gradual return of peace and normalcy in Afghanistan, we are confident that this project would be realized in the near future."[8] The Bush administration reportedly sends an unidentified official to the tripartite summit,[9] which comes just days before the *loya jirga* is to decide who will rule Afghanistan for the next two years. That government will be asked to honor any agreements Karzai makes with other heads of state.

June 13: Karzai wins the *loya jirga* and two more years in power after Khalilzad allegedly delays voting to push Karzai's two main opponents out of the race. Karzai names Ghani finance minister of his transitional administration. He also names Juma M. Mohammadi minister of mines and industry, a position that covers the oil and gas sector. He is a World Bank veteran like Ghani.[10]

July 9: A working committee made up of oil ministers from Pakistan, Afghanistan, and Turkmenistan meet in Ashkabad to discuss the proposed gas pipeline running from Turkmenistan to Pakistan across Afghanistan. Pakistan's delegation is led by Usman Aminuddin, the oil minister who met with former U.S. Ambassador to Pakistan Wendy Chamberlin about the pipeline just a few weeks after the September 11 attacks.[11] The Bush administration sends Robert Tansey, the deputy U.S. ambassador to Turkmenistan, and one of his economic officers to attend the meeting as observers.[12] Tansey says the administration supports the project.[13]

July 9: The conservative Asian Development Bank (ADB) agrees to grant $1.5 million to finance a feasibility study for the pipeline.[14] ADB is poised along with the World Bank to take a lead position in financing the overall project. ADB senior economist Rajiv Kumar, who attended the Turkmen meeting, declares, "Our bank has a strong desire to invest in this project. We will make every effort to help develop this project in the shortest period of time and at the highest level."[15] He also vows to "do our best to make this vision come through and to implement this historic project which will bring peace, prosperity and stability to the region."[16]

September 12: Bush and Musharraf meet in New York to talk about additional aid to Pakistan—as well as the gas pipeline project.[17]

September 12: Bush and Karzai also meet in New York to discuss, among other things, building a new highway along the trans-Afghan pipeline route.[18]

September 13: The White House issues a statement with Japan's prime minister and Saudi Arabia's foreign minister announcing the commitment of a total of $180 million from the two nations and the U.S. to rebuild the highway from Herat to Kandahar to Kabul, a three-year project. "This road will connect Afghanistan to its neighbors north and south [and] can set the stage for the establishment of links through Afghanistan from the Indian Ocean to Central Asia and from the Caspian Basin to the Far East," the joint statement reads. "With this vision in mind, we look forward to the day that Afghanistan regains its place along the 'Silk

Road' connecting East and West in a highway of mutual understanding, commerce and peace."[19]

September 16–17: The working committee of oil ministers from Pakistan, Afghanistan, and Turkmenistan meet again, this time in Kabul, to discuss technical aspects of the feasibility study for the pipeline. Representatives of the Asian Development Bank and World Bank attend.

September 27: Karzai meets with Saudi Crown Prince Abdullah again in Riyadh.

October 17–18: Oil ministers from Pakistan, Afghanistan, and Turkmenistan meet in Ashkabad to finalize a draft intergovernmental agreement on constructing the pipeline.

October 22: UN Secretary-General Kofi Annan expresses support for the pipeline in a meeting with Niyazov in Ashkabad.

December 11: The Bush administration, through the U.S. Trade and Development Agency, agrees to fund a survey of oil and gas resources in Afghanistan.[20] Afghanistan will be able to use the trans-Afghanistan gas pipeline to export its own gas.[21]

December 27: Karzai goes to Ashkabad to sign with Niyazov and Pakistani Prime Minister Mir Zafarullah Jamali a key legal document that outlines the principles for setting up a consortium to build and operate the gas pipeline. Inked just twelve months after the Bush administration installed the pipeline-friendly leader in Afghanistan, the accord finalizes the preliminary agreement signed by the three nations in May.

Whew! Messrs. Bush, Musharraf, and Karzai have been very busy— and not just fighting terrorism. They have found time to broker major energy deals behind the scenes. Their synchronized efforts in reviving the pipeline deal, along with the fast pace of developments, further indicate the pipeline was on the agenda from the start of the war. It took them just one year to launch the first phase of a project most had given up for dead. In that time, they signed government-to-government agreements, secured financing for a feasibility study, lined up international backers, got the UN's blessing, obtained funding for a new road along the biggest stretch of the pipeline route, and formed a high-level steering group to set up a consortium of investors to build, operate, and own the pipeline. There is little doubt that the Bush administration and its new allies are determined to make what had been a pipe dream a reality.

The revived pipeline project will be based largely on Unocal's original plans, which were derailed over fears of instability in Afghanistan and lack of formal recognition of the Taliban regime by the international community. Really only the complexion of its CentGas project—now called the Trans-Afghanistan Pipeline, or TAP—has changed. The Asian Development Bank's feasibility study will be modeled after one already done by Unocal a few years ago.[22] Most of the initial technical and engineering work for the project had been completed by the time the giant Caspian energy producer backed out of the consortium. Unocal, for its part, says it is not interested in rejoining the project at this time. But one of its main partners in the previous consortium, Japanese oil conglomerate Itochu, has expressed interest in participating.[23] Saudi's Delta Oil, Unocal's biggest partner, is said to be interested as well. Bids from companies will not be accepted, of course, until after the Asian bank completes its cost analysis, which is expected by July 2003.

Project details should be settled by September, when Karzai is expected to host the leaders of Turkmenistan and Pakistan in Kabul for another pipeline summit.[24] The TAP project at that point is expected to follow Unocal's original timeline, which estimated it would take about one year after commercial contracts are inked to close international financing, and then two more years to build the pipeline.[25] That means crews in Afghanistan could start digging the nearly five-foot-wide channel for the pipeline as early as 2005.

Making It Work

Of course, the project still must clear some big hurdles before any ground can be broken. Its principals must first secure project financing, political risk insurance, and customers for the Caspian gas, as well as demonstrate that they can secure the pipeline itself.

1. Project financing. The Asian Development Bank cannot finance the entire $2 to $2.5 billion project, but the conservative lender's commitment to the project is a major confidence booster to other international lenders, such as the World Bank and the U.S. Export-Import Bank, to which the Bush administration has given the green light to accept applications from American companies involved in energy projects in Afghanistan and Pakistan. So securing international financing should not be a problem.

2. Political risk insurance. The U.S. Overseas Private Investment Corporation provides insurance covering political violence, including sabotage and terrorism, and loss of business income due to damage or destruction of property,[26] which are risks that U.S. businesses could still face in Afghanistan and Pakistan. To qualify for protection against such losses, U.S. applicants must obtain, among other things, foreign government approval and human rights and foreign policy clearance from the State Department.[27] The governments of Turkmenistan, Pakistan and, most important, Afghanistan have already approved the project. And Afghanistan's human rights violations and terrorism-sponsoring are no longer major issues now that the Taliban are gone.

The State Department, as well as the UN, formally recognizes Karzai's regime as the legitimate and permanent government of Afghanistan. For the first time in thirteen years, "the American flag flies over our embassy in Kabul," Bush crowed last year,[28] where the U.S. is expanding its diplomatic presence. Construction has already begun on a new U.S. embassy building adjacent to its existing site in Kabul, says State Department spokeswoman Pam Lewis.[29] And Karzai's three-day U.S. visit last year, which included his Oval Office meeting with Bush and special appearance at the State of the Union, marked the first official visit to Washington by an Afghan head of state since September 1963, when Afghan king Zahir Shah met with President Kennedy.[30]

With respect to Pakistan, Bush has already lifted long-standing economic and military sanctions against the rogue nuclear (and terrorist) state. And to bring Musharraf's military dictatorship more in line with State Department standards for democracy, the general last November agreed to transfer power to a new civilian prime minister. A parliamentary election was held days later, and Jamali, a candidate of the pro-military Pakistan Muslim League Party, won. Musharraf controls parliament and retains the power to dismiss it. The State Department has nonetheless heaped praise on the dictator for "transitioning toward democracy," as spokesman Richard Boucher has said, paving the way for the OPIC to underwrite the pipeline through Pakistan. Musharraf sent his new prime minister Jamali to Ashkabad in December to cosign the pact finalizing the pipeline deal.

OPIC's counterpart at the World Bank—the Multilateral Insurance Guarantee Agency—also offers political risk insurance.

3. *Customers for Caspian gas.* Unocal's proposal called for a nearly 800-mile gas pipeline running from the Afghanistan-Turkmenistan border across Afghanistan, generally following the Herat-to-Kandahar road, to Pakistan's distribution grid in Multan. Plans included a 400-mile extension into India, which has a big demand for natural gas. Turkmenistan agreed to cover the cost of construction of a 105-mile stretch linking the main line at the Afghan border to its Dauletabad gas field.[31] Dauletabad, one of the largest gas fields in the world, produces sweet natural gas, which is low in sulfur and cheap to refine. Turkmenistan has the world's fifth-largest gas reserves, but limited export options—mostly north across Russia—and has long been eager to develop a southern route to sell its immense gas riches to higher-paying customers in Asia. It first became serious about building a trans-Afghan pipeline back in 1995.[32] The land-locked Caspian state also has toyed with the idea of a pipeline route through Iran to India. But it is less attractive for these reasons: (*a*) the U.S. remains opposed to it, according to Bush's Caspian envoy Steven Mann,[33] (*b*) India also opposes it, and (*c*) it carries a heftier $3.2 billion price tag.[34]

Unocal originally projected that India would absorb about half the trans-Afghan gas pipeline capacity.[35] Though India has signaled it will join the project if certain guarantees are added, political tensions with Pakistan remain, and there's always the chance it won't agree to purchase gas shipped through Pakistan. That leaves only Pakistan itself, unless a liquid natural gas export terminal can be built on Pakistan's coast for shipment to energy-hungry Asian customers such as Japan and South Korea. Pakistan produces much of its own gas now. But exploration has slacked off, and the country will have to import gas before 2010, according to industry projections.[36]

Before construction of the project could begin, contractual aspects of the pipeline, such as gas sales and purchase-price terms, would have to be negotiated with the governments of Afghanistan, Pakistan, and India. Turkmen president Niyazov and Karzai have already agreed that 12 percent of the gas shipped via the line would be allocated for Afghanistan.[37]

4. Pipeline security. In the words of Rumsfeld, the security situation in Afghanistan has "dramatically improved." So much so, in fact, that his aide in charge of securing Afghanistan predicted an end to violent coups there. "The era of changing government by force in Afghanistan is over, and everyone has come to realize that—even the regional warlords will tell you that," said Joseph J. Collins, deputy assistant secretary of defense for stability operations. "It's out of the question. It's beyond the pale. It's not going to happen." As for protecting the pipeline, he said that U.S. commandos will guard major infrastructure projects as part of regional patrols. The pipeline will pass through five provinces in western Afghanistan—three of which are controlled by Ismail Khan of Herat, and two of which are controlled by Gul Agha Sherzai of Kandahar. Both governors have voiced support for the TAP project.[38] Karzai, for his part, is confident his government can protect the pipelines, asserting that the security situation in Afghanistan "can be considered one of the best in the region."[39] Of course, his government is backed by some eight thousand U.S. soldiers and their commander in chief, Bush, who has said the mission in Afghanistan will not be complete until the "country [is] secure,"[40] which might as well mean until the pipelines are built, given the keen interest of his administration in them.

Turkmenistan has also signed an agreement with Afghanistan and Pakistan to develop a crude-oil pipeline from Turkmenistan through Afghanistan to an oil-export terminal and/or refineries in Pakistan on the Arabian Sea. The pipeline would transport crude oil from fields inside Turkmenistan and from the surrounding Caspian region. The Bush administration backs this project too.

What a difference a war makes. Before U.S.-led forces booted the Taliban from Kabul, the pipeline projects languished. "Today these projects could well see the light of day," cooed Frederick Starr, the Caspian oil booster who sits on the Afghanistan-America Foundation with Khalilzad and Karzai's big brother.[41]

As chairman of the Central Asia-Caucasus Institute at Johns Hopkins, Starr sees the pipelines as a boon not just for Afghanistan, but for the entire region, since they will finally open up the landlocked Caspian oil countries directly to Asian markets, which have been hard to reach from pipeline routes through Russia. He said the establishment of an "acceptable and competent government in Afghanistan will do more than anything in the past century to overcome the core problem of distance that defines the economic fate of the entire region." Starr, who calls Afghan finance minister Ghani a former colleague at Johns Hopkins, added that access to direct trade with Afghanistan, Pakistan, and possibly India "will vitalize the economies of Central Asia and even the Caucasus, opening new possibilities to foreign investment."[42]

U.S. businesses that stand to benefit the most from the trans-Afghan energy spigot are some of the Caspian's pioneer developers. They also happen to be connected to Bush and his war advisers.

10

THE BENEFICIARIES
Reaping the Spoils of War

There's never been an administration in power in this country that has been so close to a single industry—in this instance, the oil-and-gas industry.

—CHARLES LEWIS, executive director of the Washington-based Center for Public Integrity, on the Bush administration

FOR SOME TWO THOUSAND YEARS, CENTRAL ASIA HAS been a meeting ground between Europe and Asia, the site of ancient East-West trade routes for caravans carrying silk and other luxury goods that were collectively called the Silk Road. With the recent discovery of massive stores of oil and gas in the Caspian Basin, Central Asia is again in a unique position to serve European and Asian markets, particularly ones in fast-growing Asia—if southern export routes can be built. Thanks to the Bush administration's plan in Afghanistan, that now appears to be a real possibility. As in ancient times, centrally located Afghanistan may be the bridge to riches. The landlocked Caspian region above it boasts more than 5 percent of the world's proven oil reserves and almost 40 percent of its gas reserves.

Former Unocal Corp. executive John Maresca has suggested that the proposed trans-Afghanistan pipelines, carrying both crude oil and natural gas, could meet much of the export needs of the two big Caspian oil groups—the Caspian Pipeline Consortium (CPC), led by ChevronTexaco Corp., and the Azerbaijan International Operating Company (AIOC), led by BP Amoco Corp., and featuring Unocal and Delta Oil Co. of Saudi Arabia.[1]

CPC recently completed the construction of a roughly $2 billion pipeline west from ChevronTexaco's huge oil fields in Kazakhstan across Russia. And the AIOC last fall broke ground on a nearly $3 billion pipeline from Azerbaijan across Turkey, in a ceremony attended by Energy Secretary Spencer Abraham. The AIOC consortium will use its link to export crude oil that its members are producing in three giant oil fields off Azerbaijan's shore in the Caspian Sea.

But even when both pipelines are available, "they would not have enough total capacity to transport all the oil expected to flow from the region in the future," Maresca said. "Nor would they have the capability to move it to the right markets" in Asia.[2]

The proposed trans-Afghan pipelines, on the other hand, will offer that capability, transporting oil and gas from the Caspian to Asia. The potential beneficiaries of the pipelines are not just those who will invest in them, but also—and more key—those who will use them. In fact, the big profit in the pipelines will accrue to big-volume Caspian oil and gas producers looking for a shorter and cheaper export route to energy-hungry Asian markets.

Corporations Cash In

Here is a look at some of the big oil companies that have invested in George Bush, the GOP, and the Caspian, and their links to Bush administration officials who have helped put the pipelines back on track by changing out the Taliban regime in Afghanistan that had derailed them.

CHEVRONTEXACO CORP.
Chevron last decade signed a whopping $20 billion joint venture with the government of Kazakhstan to develop, over forty years, the country's

supergiant Tengiz oil field, giving it one of the largest stakes in the region. After it merged with Texaco Inc., which also has Caspian production contracts, it easily claimed the title of the biggest investor and producer in the Caspian. ChevronTexaco, now the second-biggest oil company in the world with more than $104 billion in sales, is also developing gas fields in Kazakhstan.

Before its trans-Caspian pipeline was built from the Tengiz field to the Black Sea, Chevron had a difficult time getting its reserves just to European markets, let alone Asian ones. It had to find export solutions when none appeared to exist, executives recalled, moving oil by Russian pipelines, barges, rail, tankers, and sometimes all four means.[3]

But a direct export route to Asia, as opposed to the existing circuitous ones via the Mediterranean Sea, would provide Chevron higher "netback values," as they call returns in the industry, on the reserves it produces. That said, it is very interested in the trans-Afghan pipelines now moving forward. When Unocal and Delta Oil first formed their consortium to develop an oil pipeline, Chevron Vice Chairman Richard H. Matzke noted the same benefits cited by Unocal's Maresca. "They want to build a $2.7 billion pipeline from the heart of Turkmenistan south through Afghanistan and Pakistan to the Arabian Sea. Oil would then move by tanker to the fast-growing economies of East Asia," said Matzke approvingly in a 1997 speech to oil industry analysts. "This Unocal-Delta concept would create a sort of pressure-relief valve to the south of the Caspian region."[4]

Chevron has led the industry in lobbying Washington for the new Silk Road. Its lobbyists, both in-house and on K Street, are familiar faces, for example, in the offices of Senator Sam Brownback, cochairman of the Silk Road Caucus on Capitol Hill.[5] The Republican senator, a key oil ally of the Bush administration, has authored legislation opening up U.S. investment in the Caspian, as well as Pakistan, and has given trans-Afghan pipeline boosters a regular forum on his Foreign Relations Subcommittee. Chevron has been a campaign contributor.

The company also contributed heavily to Bush. In the 2000 election cycle, before Chevron and Texaco merged, Chevron gave more than $780,000 to Bush and the GOP, while Texaco donated more than $340,000, according to the Washington-based Center for Responsive Politics, which tabulates Federal Election Commission data. Most of the top executives of both energy giants donated individual gifts to Bush, records show.

Ties to Bush administration. Condoleezza Rice, Bush's quiet but powerful national security adviser, was a longtime and highly influential Chevron board member, as well as stockholder. She resigned January 15, 2001, after ten years with the company, including two as head of the board's public policy committee.

In 1993, San Francisco–based Chevron honored Rice by naming an oil tanker in its international fleet for her. But the double-hulled ship, christened the *Condoleezza Rice*, was quietly renamed the *Altair Voyager* a few months after the Bush administration started taking heat from a government watchdog group for its cozy ties to big oil.[6]

Rice's former 129,000-ton tanker "does underscore that there's never been an administration in power in this country that has been so close to a single industry—in this instance, the oil-and-gas industry," Charles Lewis, executive director of the Washington-based Center for Public Integrity, complained in April 2001. "Look at the president and his background, the vice president, [Commerce Secretary] Don Evans and his oil interests . . . and now this."

Because Rice is best known as a scholar, having served as Stanford University provost, "I don't think anyone recognized the extent of her closeness to a major oil company," Lewis added. "It's not every day that someone has an oil tanker named after her."[7]

At the time Rice defended her close relationship with Chevron. "I'm very proud of my association with Chevron, and I think we should be very proud of the job American oil companies are doing in exploration abroad, in exploration at home, and in making certain we have a safe

energy supply," she said, while promising to recuse herself from any decisions directly involving Chevron.[8] (Of course, the trans-Afghan pipeline
projects did not *directly* involve Chevron when Rice was helping make
war against the Taliban, although there is nothing stopping the company
from investing in the pipelines now. New consortia must be formed.)

Rice held Chevron stock valued between $250,000 and $500,000
before selling the shares when she joined the White House. She earned
$60,000 in annual retainer and attendance bonuses her last year as a
director of the company.[9]

Before joining the Chevron board in 1991, Rice served in the first
Bush administration as a White House aide specializing in Russian
affairs. She was an aide to Brent Scowcroft, former President Bush's
national security adviser. Soon after she left the White House, Chevron
appointed her to its board, tapping in to her Russian expertise as it began
exploring ventures in the Caspian after the breakup of the Soviet Union.
Over the next ten years, Rice, who is fluent in Russian,[10] proved a valuable asset in Chevron's dealings in the oil-rich former Soviet republics
there. From 1999 to 2001, Rice chaired the Chevron board's public policy committee, demonstrating her clout as an outside director within the
board itself.[11]

It can be argued that Rice remains valuable to Chevron in the White
House, given the results of the war and her input in war strategy. A key
member of Bush's war cabinet, as well as a close confidante of the president (the two are reportedly as close as brother and sister), she monitored
Situation Room meetings at the White House after September 11.
Dubbed the "Warrior Princess" by aides, she pressed for the broader
strategy of regime change in Afghanistan rather than a focused strike
against al-Qaida—a strategy that finally produced a stable environment
for the Caspian export pipelines, but unfortunately not Osama bin
Laden's head.[12] Rice argued for using Afghan proxy forces to overthrow
the Taliban, matching a plan drafted earlier by her senior aide Zal
Khalilzad, a former Unocal consultant who has been shopping the idea of

trans-Afghan pipelines around Washington for years. Rice's mentor, Scowcroft, it turns out, is affiliated with Khalilzad's Afghanistan-America Foundation. He is the lobbying group's honorary co-chairman.

Then there is Richard L. Armitage, the deputy secretary of state who worked with Rice on the war cabinet and also backed the odd post–September 11 response of first ousting the Taliban, then hunting down al-Qaida leaders. Months earlier, he had lifted a State Department ban on funding the Northern Alliance, the Afghan militia that U.S. forces helped smash the Taliban in Kabul.

What is Armitage's connection to ChevronTexaco? Before joining the Bush administration, he was a longtime Caspian oil lobbyist who called Texaco a client. In fact, he acted as Texaco's emissary in oil-rich Azerbaijan last decade when the company was trying to broker deals with the Azerbaijani government.[13] Armitage was president of Armitage Associates L.C., a ten-year-old consulting firm in Arlington, Virginia. One of his partners there, Randall Schriver, worked with Khalilzad on the Bush-Cheney transition team for the Defense Department.

Armitage is also tied to ChevronTexaco through the U.S.-Azerbaijan Chamber of Commerce (USACC) in Washington. He served on its board of directors with Mike Kostiw, ChevronTexaco's general manager of international government relations.

Vice President Dick Cheney was a USACC officer too. And Cheney served with the heads of both Chevron and Texaco on the twelve-member Kazakhstan Oil Advisory Board.[14]

UNOCAL CORP.

When the incorrigible Taliban forced Unocal to pull out of its CentGas project in 1998, the energy giant said it would "only participate in construction of the proposed Central Asia Gas Pipeline when and if Afghanistan achieves the peace and stability necessary to obtain financing from international lending agencies for this project, and an established government is recognized by the United Nations and the United

States."[15] It took nearly four years, but the company's prerequisites have been met. The U.S.-backed government of Hamid Karzai has the UN's blessing, and international lending agencies are rallying behind the project.

But Los Angeles–based Unocal has no interest in sponsoring the project—at least "not for the foreseeable future," according to Teresa Covington, a spokeswoman in the company's Houston office. Covington qualified the statement by adding, "I don't think it would serve me to say 'forever.'"[16]

Unocal may just be acting coy about its pipeline interest for fear of bad press, suggests Raheem Yaseer, who in 1997 helped Unocal entertain Taliban leaders at the University of Nebraska at Omaha, where he is assistant director of the Center for Afghanistan Studies. "Unocal ran into lots of political scolding a few years ago, and they have kept quiet about it," Yaseer said in a recent interview. "I don't know what their plans are, but they are not coming in the open about it."[17]

After Bush's post–September 11 demonization of the Taliban, it is not surprising that Unocal would want to continue distancing itself from the project. Sustaining memories of how it once courted the Taliban would be, well, courting a public relations disaster. The last thing Unocal wants is the media reminding shareholders so soon after the September 11 tragedy that it tried to cut a deal with a regime that later became America's war enemy.

But do not count Unocal out just yet. It invested at least $15 million in its CentGas project alone.[18] Walking away from such a well-funded trophy project, one that would give it control over a key gateway to the world's last great commercial frontier, will not be easy.

And many of the company's previous statements regarding the pipeline became no longer operative, as they say here in Washington, soon after they were issued.

In October 1996, for example, Unocal expressed support for the Taliban takeover of Kabul, since the establishment of a single authoritative government in Afghanistan would make it easier to negotiate a contract for the pipeline. Unocal later said it was misquoted.[19] Then in August 1998, after the U.S. hit al-Qaida targets in Afghanistan, the company said it was giving up on the project because of "sharply deteriorating political conditions in the region."[20] But it did not formally pull up stakes until more than three months later—and only after oil prices tanked.[21] Then in early 1999, a press report quoted Pakistani officials saying Unocal was considering rejoining the pipeline consortium, a report that Unocal had to quickly shoot down.[22] The next year, however, a Unocal executive reportedly said the pipeline project would be revived as soon as a peace deal was struck in Kabul.[23]

There has been other dissembling too. Unocal, for instance, has repeatedly denied training Afghans for pipeline construction, when it did train them for such work. "Unocal provided humanitarian support and skills training to Afghanistan through CARE and the University of Nebraska at Omaha. Neither program was designed to provide pipeline construction skills training," the company has insisted.[24] Apparently, Unocal Vice President Marty F. Miller, the company's pipeline point man, didn't get the memo, as they say. He swore in a 1997 Senate hearing that, in fact, the University of Nebraska program did teach pipeline skills. "Under the auspices of the University of Nebraska at Omaha, we are supporting a program to train Afghans in the skills necessary for pipeline construction and support," Miller testified.[25]

Asked about the nature of the training, Yaseer replied that the Afghan studies center built classrooms in Kandahar to help Unocal train locals in pipe-fitting and welding techniques. What has become of the schools? "Those buildings are bombarded and gone," he told me. "So, our workshops and tools and facilities and classrooms and guesthouse have been bombarded, because the Taliban, you know, developed their own residence around the compound. They were using our facilities as the official guesthouse and things like that. And it has been bombarded." But according to him, the center has applied to the State Department for another USAID grant to rebuild its vocational-training schools.

Yaseer said he hopes $7 billion-in-sales Unocal leads the pipeline project again, citing its technical expertise and marketing savvy. Karzai, who once consulted for Unocal, is also partial to Unocal heading the project, he noted. So are members of his administration involved in pipeline negotiations. "If Unocal made a bid, it would be hard to beat," said Mohammed Ebrahim Adel, Afghanistan's deputy minister of mines and industry. "We are sure Unocal will win," based on its previous plans and technical edge over other competitors.[26]

And Turkmenistan and Pakistan have always been in Unocal's corner. As early as April 1995, Turkmen officials met with Unocal executives in Houston to talk about the pipeline. And a Unocal delegation, in turn, visited the Turkmen capital of Ashkabad, as well as Islamabad, where executives held talks with aides to former Pakistani Prime Minister Benazir Bhutto. Unocal has been doing business in Pakistan since 1976.[27] In the CentGas consortium, Pakistan held a 3.5 percent stake through its Crescent Group conglomerate, and the Turkmen government held a 7 percent share.

Companies interested in investing in the CentGas project, now called the Trans-Afghanistan Pipeline (TAP), will likely start stepping forward after the Asian Development Bank releases its feasibility study this summer, at which time the TAP steering group is expected to begin entertaining bids. Unocal's intentions won't be plain until after bids are accepted. At this point, no company is formally involved in the project; it hasn't advanced to that stage yet.

Even if Unocal really does give up on its oil and gas pipelines, it still has a vested interest in seeing them built. The company has been active in Azerbaijan since 1991, and is part of a consortium that is developing the country's offshore oil and gas reserves in the Caspian Sea. Unocal knows that the key to Caspian development is export capability—getting oil and gas cheaply to hot markets—and it also welcomes a southern route to Asia. Unocal executives have made it clear that they would prefer to sell the oil and gas they produce from Azerbaijan not to Europe and the U.S., but to Asia—via Afghanistan pipelines. "An export route, south to the Indian Ocean, remains the most economical route to the Asian markets," said Robert Todor, executive vice president of Unocal International Energy Ventures in Houston.[28]

With a 10.5 percent stake, Unocal is the second-biggest private investor in the Azerbaijan International Operating Co., a consortium that has signed an $8 billion contract with the Azerbaijani government to develop three huge oil and gas fields in the Caspian Sea less than one hundred miles off Azerbaijan's shore. It is the largest offshore development in the landlocked waters. "Our participation in the Azerbaijan project is a key element in our growth strategy," said Marty Miller, Unocal vice president for new ventures in Central Asia and the Middle East, in a July 30, 1996, corporate statement. When Unocal first invested in the development group early last decade, through its Unocal Khazar Ltd. subsidiary, the three fields—Guneshli, Chirag, and Azeri—were thought to contain an estimated 4.4 billion barrels of recoverable crude oil (compared with the estimated 6 to 9 billion barrels in Chevron's huge Tengiz field), plus substantial amounts of natural gas.[29] Saudi's Delta Oil and Japan's Itochu Corp., both Unocal partners in the trans-Afghan gas pipeline venture, are partners in the AIOC consortium. And both companies have expressed an interest in rejoining the gas-pipeline project. Though Unocal closed other regional offices after the Taliban PR fiasco, it has kept open its main Central Asian office in the Azerbaijan capital of Baku.

Actually, Unocal would benefit at both ends of the proposed gas pipeline, which would eventually link to India, where Unocal has gas projects. It also has substantial gas reserves and exploration projects in neighboring Burma, along with gas pipeline interests there and in Thailand. Unocal, as part of its Project Energy Renaissance, envisions "a trans-Asia natural gas network that would include existing and proposed pipelines in Thailand and Myanmar (Burma), as well as proposed pipelines in Central and South Asia," the company said in a December 9, 1997, press release.

Unocal is a major donor to the Republican Party, giving more than $42,000 to Bush and the GOP in the 2000 election cycle, the Center for

Responsive Politics reports. Individual donors to the Bush campaign included several executives based in Unocal's Houston office, which runs the company's Caspian operations, including its pipeline projects. Unocal, moreover, has participated in the Silk Road lobbying effort on Capitol Hill, and has supported GOP Senator Brownback's campaigns.

Ties to Bush administration. Khalilzad—Bush's top Afghan adviser and chief architect of the war plan in Afghanistan—was a Unocal consultant, who not only conducted risk analyses for its pipeline projects, but also lobbied Washington on behalf of the politically and diplomatically sensitive projects through congressional testimony and articles in the *Washington Post* and other influential publications. He even helped Unocal wine and dine Taliban leaders in Houston.

Armitage and Cheney, moreover, were officers with Andrew Fawthrop, vice president of Unocal International Energy Ventures, on the U.S.-Azerbaijan Chamber of Commerce.

Commerce Secretary Donald L. Evans is also connected to Unocal through the Denver-based oil and gas concern he headed before joining the Bush cabinet. The $314 million-in-sales Tom Brown Inc. is a partly owned subsidiary of Unocal.[30] Evans worked there for twenty-five years, rising to chairman and chief executive officer. When he left the company, he received a retirement payment of $1.5 million in cash. In addition, the company accelerated the vesting of his outstanding stock options, resulting in a noncash, pretax charge to its earnings of approximately $3.8 million.[31] As a presidential candidate, George W. Bush listed Tom Brown Inc. among his stock holdings.[32]

Evans and Bush have been best friends since their early days in the Texas wildcatting business. Tom Brown Inc. has been developing fields around Midland, Texas, where the company also maintains offices. Evans helped run Bush's two campaigns for Texas governor and his race for the presidency. As Bush's national finance chairman, Evans raised more than $100 million in private donations, smashing all previous fund-raising records, according to the Center for Responsive Politics.

Some Unocal employees, past and present, are tied to this Bush administration through the old one (some joke that the two Bush administrations are really one and the same, given all the holdovers and retreads). Maresca, the one-time Unocal VP who lobbied Congress on behalf of the trans-Afghan pipelines, served as a diplomat in the first Bush administration. He is not the only Unocal official from the Bush family fold. The company includes on its board of directors Donald B. Rice, who served as former President Bush's secretary of the air force after a seventeen-year stint as president and chief executive officer of the Rand Corp.,[33] the defense consulting group where Khalilzad worked as director of its air force project. Khalilzad also worked in the Pentagon with Rice.

HALLIBURTON CO.

The energy-services giant has been doing business in oil-rich Kazakhstan for more than ten years. It has three offices in the former Soviet republic, employing almost three hundred people. Headquartered in Dallas, Halliburton is also active in Turkmenistan, where it has provided a variety of services over the past five years, as well as Azerbaijan, where its Brown & Root Energy Services subsidiary has a contract to build offshore drilling platforms and oil and gas pipelines. Brown & Root has also worked on pipeline projects in Pakistan[34] and Iraq.[35] The Army has awarded another Halliburton subsidiary, Kellogg Brown & Root Engineering & Construction, no-bid projects worth almost a half-billion dollars to build U.S. camps, actually mini towns, in Iraq as part of Operation Iraqi Freedom. (A CentCom official told me that U.S. occupation of Iraq is slated for 10 years.)

Halliburton, with $13 billion in sales, gave big bucks to Bush and the GOP in the 2000 election cycle. The Center for Responsive Politics tallied more than $410,000 in contributions. The company's front office gave individual gifts to Bush. Halliburton, also a Brownback contributor, has been a leading proponent of the Kansas senator's so-called Silk Road strategy, and has joined Chevron and Unocal in their Caspian lobbying efforts in Washington.[36]

It has also lobbied the new U.S.-backed government in Afghanistan. Executives from Halliburton early last year attended a private meeting at a Washington hotel during a reception held for new Afghan leader Karzai, who was in town for Bush's State of the Union address. The deal-making session between Afghan political leaders and several U.S. oil officials was reportedly arranged by Armitage, the former Caspian oil lobbyist.[37]

Ties to Bush administration. Vice President Cheney, former defense secretary and a key member of Bush's war cabinet, was the chairman and CEO of Halliburton and Brown & Root. When he stepped down during the campaign after five years at the helm, Cheney took a resigning bonus of $1.5 million and $18 million in stock profits.[38] His office denies he had any part in Brown & Root landing the fat contracts in Iraq.

Cheney headed Bush's still-secret energy task force, formally known as the National Energy Policy Development Group. Despite being sued by the General Accounting Office, the investigative arm of Congress, as well as the public interest law firm Judicial Watch Inc., the vice president still refuses to make public his task force records. He will not disclose all the names of energy industry officials he and his task force met with while formulating the administration's energy policies.

As Halliburton's CEO, Cheney was a big Caspian booster. "I can't think of a time when we've had a region emerge as suddenly to become as strategically significant as the Caspian," Cheney remarked at a 1998 gathering of several hundred oil industry executives in Washington. "It's almost as if the opportunities have arisen overnight."[39] The previous year, he said the name of the game in the Caspian was finding profitable export routes. "Pipeline routes are obviously a key issue for developing the region's oil," said Cheney. The former defense secretary, who prosecuted the Gulf War, frowned on pipeline routes through Russia, arguing they would only strengthen the country's monopoly over the region's oil-and-gas transport routes.[40]

BP AMOCO CORP.

BP, as the London-based oil conglomerate now calls itself for short, is the biggest investor in the Azerbaijan International Operating Co., which has sunk some $1 billion into an initial phase of its development program in the Caspian. It is also the consortium's operator. Though $174 billion-in-sales BP is in the middle of developing a trans-Turkey pipeline, the route is long and headed in the wrong direction for sales to the fast-growing markets of the future. Like other long-term Caspian investors, BP is still looking for more profitable returns on the oil and gas it produces there vis-à-vis a shorter, southern export route to Asian markets.

It is worth noting that BP is in a joint venture with Argentine oil giant Bridas, which has proposed its own plan for building a gas pipeline across Afghanistan from gas fields it co-owns in Turkmenistan. In November 1996, in fact, Bridas's chairman signed pipeline deals not only with the Taliban, but also with Abdul Rashid Dostum, then a northern-Afghan warlord who became commander of the Northern Alliance.[41] Dostum is now deputy defense minister of Karzai's cabinet.

The Taliban favored Bridas over Unocal because it placed no conditions on its deals. Unocal, Taliban leaders griped, kept bugging them to improve their human-rights image and open talks with the anti-Taliban alliance to form a broader-based government, which would help it win Washington's acceptance, paving the way for project guarantees from Western banks. Put off by Talib intransigence, Unocal eventually reached out as Bridas did to opposition leaders who later formed the Northern Alliance,[42] and who now are part of the new U.S.-backed government in Kabul.

After the Taliban's collapse, General Dostum opposed the interim government until Karzai persuaded him to change his mind in a visit to his northern stronghold of Mazar-e-Sharif. It was then that Karzai offered him a key role in his cabinet and made him Kabul's chief representative in the north, where Afghanistan's own gas fields are located. One of Dostum's top lieutenants was initially made Afghanistan's minister of mines and industries, giving him authority over the pipelines projects,[43] but he has since been replaced by World Bank veteran Juma M. Mohammadi.

BP Amoco gave in excess of $890,000 to Bush and the GOP during the 2000 cycle, according to Center for Responsive Politics data.

Ties to Bush administration. Attorney James A. Baker IV—son of the former secretary of state, an old Bush family crony—represents the AIOC consortium led by BP. He is a partner in the corporate department of the Washington office of Houston-based Baker Botts LLP, his father's law firm.

Both he and his father, James A. Baker III—who represented Bush in the Florida election crisis—are USACC officers, serving on the Azerbaijani lobbying group with Armitage and Cheney before the Bush officials had to resign their board memberships to avoid a conflict of interest (yeah, that solved it). The Bakers also serve with former Carter national security adviser Zbigniew Brzezinski, a USACC adviser who helped Amoco lobby the Azerbaijani government for contracts. Brzezinski is one of Khalilzad's mentors, and is also affiliated with his Afghanistan-America Foundation in Washington. As secretary of state under former President Bush, the elder Baker considered naming Khalilzad a special envoy to Afghanistan after the Soviets pulled out of the country. Khalilzad had traveled to Pakistan for talks with mujahideen leaders during his tenure at the State Department, and had helped convince the White House to arm mujahideen fighters (including a young leader named Osama bin Laden) with U.S.-made Stinger missiles.[44]

Baker, with his Caspian clients and deep Bush connections, does not just wield influence over oil policy issues regarding Central Asia. He also appears to have the White House's ear with respect to Iraqi oil.

Through his James A. Baker III Institute for Public Policy at Rice University in Houston, he commissioned a study of U.S. energy needs and submitted the findings to Cheney in early April 2001. Many of the findings in the Baker report, titled "Strategic Energy Policy Challenges for the 21st Century," made their way into the report released more than a month later by Cheney's secret energy task force.

But perhaps the most controversial part of the Baker report, one not in the official Cheney report, is its recommendation to consider a "military" option in dealing with Iraq, which the report charged was using oil exports as a "weapon," by turning its spigot on and off to "manipulate oil markets." The report advised the Bush administration to, at a minimum, bring UN weapons inspectors back to Iraq, and then, "once an arms-control program is in place, the United States could consider reducing restrictions on oil investments inside Iraq."

"Like it or not," the report continued, "Iraqi reserves represent a major asset that can quickly add capacity to world oil markets and inject a more competitive tenor to oil trade."[45]

In short, the Baker task force was arguing for greater American access to, and control of, the oil fields of a country with the world's second-largest oil reserves. Of course, Bush's invasion of Baghdad and planned installation of a new U.S.-friendly government there, such as the one he installed in Kabul, would guarantee such access and control. Toward that end, Bush has dispatched Khalilzad to work with anti-Saddam factions, as he did anti-Taliban factions, and essentially duplicate in Iraq what he had done in Afghanistan. On December 2, 2002, Bush formally named Khalilzad his special envoy and ambassador at large to the Iraqi opposition. He also ordered U.S. troops to seize and secure the prized Rumaila oil fields in Southern Iraq within hours of the invasion. And he has convinced the United Nations to lift economic sanctions on Iraq, which means its oil can now be exported for cash, rather than just food, and U.S. oil companies can now profit there.

Baker energy task force members included Daniel Yergin, the chairman of Cambridge Energy Research Associates, where Khalilzad did his risk analyses for Unocal's pipelines; David J. O'Reilly, Chevron chairman and CEO and a Bush donor; and Eric Melby, a partner in the Scowcroft Group and former National Security Council energy adviser to former President Bush. Enron Corp.'s Ken Lay also worked on the panel, as did his old gas industry pal Thomas "Mack" McLarty, now vice chairman of Kissinger McLarty Associates, the Washington consulting firm founded by Bush crony Henry Kissinger, another Unocal pipeline lobbyist.[46]

Bush's new Iraq administrator, Paul Bremer, had been managing director of Kissinger's firm, as well as an Afghan diplomat.

Iraq's undiscovered and undeveloped reserves, which analysts believe to be impressively vast, have American oil tycoons champing at the bit. Even though they have publicly mouthed support for oil sanctions against the rogue state, they have not been happy about being banned from doing business in Iraq all these years. "Iraq possesses huge reserves of oil and gas—reserves I'd love Chevron to have access to," admitted Kenneth T. Derr in a speech he gave in 1998 as Chevron's chairman and CEO. Derr, a Bush donor who worked with Condi Rice on the Chevron board, cautioned that he nonetheless supported the Iraqi sanctions.[47] Now retired from Chevron, Derr is an outside director on Halliburton's board—along with former Bush Secretary of State Lawrence Eagleburger, who argued loudly for regime change in Iraq—showing just how interconnected the Bush-Cheney oil family is.

The Baker report also recommended the Bush administration "investigate whether any changes to U.S. policy would quickly facilitate higher exports of oil from the Caspian Basin region," a concern of Chevron's O'Reilly and many other task force members. "The exports from some oil discoveries in the Caspian Basin could be hastened if a secure, economical export route could be identified swiftly," the report added.[48] The reference to "secure" hints at Afghanistan—which, of course, is the most "economical," or cost-effective, route—but the task force stopped short of identifying in its report the route it might have had in mind.

Houston-based Enron Corp. also stood to gain from the pipelines before its epic collapse. Bush, who is close to former Enron chief executive Ken "Kenny Boy" Lay, a top fund-raiser for his 2000 campaign, was nearly finished changing out the Taliban regime when the natural gas giant filed for bankruptcy protection on December 2, 2001. Enron last decade conducted feasibility studies and provided technical assistance for several Caspian projects, including trans-Caspian gas pipelines involving Turkmenistan and Azerbaijan, according to records furnished by the U.S.

Trade and Development Agency, which helped fund the projects through various grants, including ones totaling $637,500 for the Turkmenistan contract alone.[49] Enron, moreover, had gas deals in India, including a $3 billion gas-fired power plant near Bombay. And last decade, senior Enron executives, including Rebecca Mark and Terence Thorn, had scouted deals involving gas development, power plants, and pipelines in Pakistan during official U.S. trade missions, according to copies of Energy Department trip reports I have obtained.[50]

Governments Cash In

The governments of several countries in that part of the world also are poised to cash in on their connections to the Bush administration if the new Silk Road connecting the Caspian with Asia, by way of Afghanistan, is built.

KAZAKHSTAN
Called the New Kuwait, Kazakhstan holds most of Central Asia's oil wealth, and its government would like nothing better than to use Afghanistan as a conduit for exporting its petro to more-profitable Asian markets.

"We are interested in Afghanistan as a transit country for us," reasserted Kazakhstan President Nursultan Nazarbayev in late November 2001, after the Taliban fell to U.S.-backed forces in Kabul, reported the Kazakh news service.[51] The next month, Bush invited Nazarbayev to the White House, where the two discussed building oil and gas export pipelines, among other things. "We affirm our desire to strengthen our energy partnership to diversify export options for Kazakhstan's oil and gas," the two leaders said in a joint statement. "We share the view that a key element of this effort is development of multiple pipelines that will ensure delivery of Caspian energy to world markets, unfettered by monopolies or constrained by geographic chokepoints," which was a subtle slap at Russian export routes.[52]

After meeting with Bush, Nazarbayev flew to Texas to mingle with oil executives.[53]

Ties to Bush administration. As head of Halliburton, Cheney was one of only twelve board members of the Kazakhstan Oil Advisory Board, which was created by Nazarbayev to help his country broker deals with foreign producers. Cheney advised the Kazakh president on developing his oil resources, while lining up prospects for Halliburton.

AZERBAIJAN

The former Soviet republic has the second-largest oil reserves in the Caspian, as well as sizable gas reserves. It also has some very powerful friends in Washington.

Ties to Bush administration. The nexus of the entire Caspian oil lobby in America, in fact, may very well be the U.S.-Azerbaijan Chamber of Commerce in Washington, set up in 1995 to encourage trade and investment in Azerbaijan. And it is a who's who of Bush cronies. Its current and past officers include former Bush chief of staff John Sununu, Scowcroft, Kissinger, Cheney, Baker, and Armitage.

When Cheney was a USACC adviser, he proclaimed, "We in the petroleum industry have an obvious interest in seeing that the word goes out that Azerbaijan and the Caspian region are indeed of vital interest to the United States."[54]

Armitage, former USACC cochairman, was just as ebullient in his promotion, touting Azerbaijan as "the big prize" in the Transcaucasus. "With enormous untapped oil wealth in the Caspian Sea," he said, "Azerbaijan has the potential to become a regional economic powerhouse."[55]

Together, they fought a federal law barring U.S. aid to Azerbaijan. Armitage argued in a 1994 *Journal of Commerce* column that the Clinton administration "should seek a repeal of the ban on aid to Azerbaijan."[56] And Cheney groused at a February 1997 USACC meeting that "our current policy prohibiting U.S. assistance in Azerbaijan is seriously misguided."[57] At that meeting, members prepared the groundwork for

Azerbaijan's president to visit Washington to persuade the Clinton administration to agree to lift the ban. Maresca of Unocal, who is close to Armitage, also worked with the group.[58]

But their efforts fell short, and the anti-Azerbaijan section of the 1992 Freedom Support Act remained on the books. The amendment, known as section 907, was passed after the Azerbaijani government blocked economic aid to Armenia for more than four years, and after thousands of Armenians living in Azerbaijan had fled the country to escape ethnic violence.

The Caspian oil barons found a staunch ally in the Senate, however. And in 1997, Senator Brownback sponsored the Silk Road Strategy Act, which provided presidential authority to waive section 907. Unocal's Maresca voiced his support for the bill in 1998, when he testified about the pipelines before Brownback's subcommittee. As mentioned earlier, Unocal is heavily invested in Azerbaijan, and also wanted the sanctions there lifted. The bill was later adopted as an amendment to the Foreign Operations Appropriations Bill, but the presidential waiver authority was removed by a close vote.

Then after the September 11 attacks, opportunity struck, and Brownback renewed his efforts to get a waiver for Azerbaijan and his Caspian benefactors (ChevronTexaco, Halliburton, and Unocal are all Brownback donors). This time, working closely with Armitage and other oil allies in the Bush administration, he prevailed. In December 2001, the waiver was attached to the fiscal year 2002 Foreign Operations Appropriations Bill. And on January 25, 2002, Bush quietly signed it. He cited the war on terrorism as reason for lifting the long-standing sanctions against Azerbaijan, which had granted blanket overflight rights to U.S. and coalition aircraft. This January, he extended the waiver another year.

The lifting of sanctions makes its easier for U.S. oil companies investing in Azerbaijan to apply for critical Export-Import Bank loans and Overseas Private Investment Corporation insurance for their projects.

Less than two months after Bush repealed the ban on investment there, Armitage received the "Freedom Support Award" from the USACC. At the ceremony, held March 8, 2002, at the Renaissance Hotel in Washington, he could barely contain himself. "This is kind of like old home week for me," the top State Department official said. "I'm delighted to be back with the chamber." Then he gushed, "We've waived section 907 that denied aid to the government of Azerbaijan," and suggested that the door to Ex-Im Bank and OPIC financing would open up to Azerbaijani investors.[59]

As chairman of the Senate Foreign Relations Subcommittee on Near Eastern and South Asian affairs, Brownback also authored the so-called Brownback amendment easing sanctions against Pakistan—something Wendy Chamberlin vowed to push for as U.S. ambassador to Pakistan.[60] It was Bush-appointee Chamberlin who chatted with Pakistan's oil minister about the trans-Afghan pipeline deals right after September 11.

Brownback, no surprise, is also a USACC board member.

SAUDI ARABIA

Delta Oil chairman and chief executive Badr al-Aiban, a close confidant of Saudi Crown Prince Abdullah, had signed a memorandum of understanding several years ago with Turkmen President Niyazov and Unocal to build the gas pipeline across Afghanistan. At the time, Unocal and Delta held 85 percent of the interest in the project.[61] As more investors joined the consortium, Saudi-based Delta's share shrank to 15 percent. But it still ended up the second-biggest investor. And Delta, which also has offices in London, has expressed renewed hope in the project since the fall of the Taliban. "With political stability [in Afghanistan], this remains a feasible project," said Phil Beck, Delta's chief operating officer.[62]

Even if Delta does not invest in the proposed trans-Afghan pipelines, it stands to benefit from their construction. Through a fifty-fifty partnership with Amerada Hess, called DeltaHess ACG, it has stakes in one of the main Caspian oil groups, the Azerbaijan International Operating

Co., which is developing major oil and gas fields in the Caspian and look-ing for export routes to Asian markets.

Through Delta, the Saudi royal government stands to get a bigger piece of the action in the Caspian, broadening its oil reach from the Persian Gulf. Sunni-dominated Saudi also seeks a geopolitical edge in the region over cross-Gulf rival Iran, which has a Shiite Muslim major-ity. Both Saudi and the Bush administration, moreover, do not want Iran monopolizing export of Caspian energy south to the Persian Gulf.

Ties to Bush administration. As detailed in Chapter 6, the Bush fam-ily has been in business with the Saudi royal family for years, and is on a first-name basis with Prince Abdullah and his ailing brother King Fahd. George W. Bush's silent partner in his first oil venture was also the U.S. business representative of shady Saudi banker Khalid bin Mahfouz, who is connected to Delta Oil (as well as bin Laden).

AFGHANISTAN

The pipelines, of course, would be a tremendous boon for the war-wracked Afghan economy. The gas pipeline alone would create an estimated twelve thousand much-needed jobs, which Yaseer says would help take Afghan men off warlord payrolls and increase stability in the country. And transit fees from just the gas pipeline would guarantee revenues of about $300 million a year for Kabul—an amount nearly four times the annual budget of Afghanistan under the Taliban.[63]

"Afghanistan needs it very desperately, and the government is very, very anxious to start it," said Yaseer, an Afghan-American who is work-ing with the Bush and Karzai administrations to rebuild his former coun-try. "Afghanistan will benefit a lot."[64]

Ties to Bush administration. Karzai is tied directly to Bush's inner cir-cle through Khalilzad. Both worked on the pipeline projects as Unocal consultants, and both worked with University of Nebraska's Yaseer to form a broad-based government in Kabul that could represent Afghanistan in commercial negotiations, especially those involving the pipelines. After September 11, Khalilzad groomed Karzai for leadership. Karzai's older brother, moreover, sits with Khalilzad on the Afghanistan-America Foundation board in Washington.

PAKISTAN

Natural gas accounts for nearly 40 percent of Pakistan's energy consumption,[65] and it is always hunting for cheaper sources of gas. The country's own gas reserves have grown in recent years as the government has sold stakes in gas fields to private producers.

But that could change by the end of this decade. According to energy industry analysts, exploration has slacked off in Pakistan, with the number of wells of all types drilled by private developers falling to twenty-six in the fiscal year ended March 2002 from forty-three in fiscal 2000. What's more, Pakistan's commercial success rate has been cut in half—dropping to 15 percent on eleven wells in 2001 from 30 percent on twenty-nine wells in 1997, observes consulting firm Wood Mackenzie. Meantime, Pakistan's vast Sui gas field, its largest, is headed toward depletion, analysts say, while the country's demand for gas is projected to grow at an average annual clip of 6 percent over the rest of the decade. Wood Mackenzie predicts Pakistan will need to import gas before the end of the decade if it does not discover major new domestic fields. A senior Pakistani government official last fall told *World Gas Intelligence* that Pakistan's domestic supply alone cannot satisfy its consumer market. "We are keen on cross-border gas supply projects," he said.[66]

It is not clear at this point what Pakistan would pay for gas piped in from Turkmenistan. But under the CentGas plan, in 1997, it had inked a thirty-year pricing agreement charging it a relatively cheap $2.05 per thousand cubic feet of gas for delivery in Multan.[67]

Despite tensions with India, Musharraf still expresses interest in building a gas link to India, which has even greater demand for natural gas than Pakistan. Musharraf would be able to charge lucrative transit fees for the gas imported by India, which appears nearer to joining the pipeline thanks to a recent visit to Delhi by deputy Secretary of State Armitage.

Pakistan's domestic production of oil, meanwhile, has declined over the last decade, and the country has become a major importer of crude. As a result, it is in search of guaranteed supplies of cheaper crude. The proposed Caspian oil pipeline across Afghanistan would meet that demand. In addition, it would "turn the country into a major hub for Central Asian oil exports to Asian markets," said Ahmed Rashid, a Pakistani-based journalist who wrote the bestseller *Taliban*.[68] Pakistan under such a scenario would be able to collect big port revenues on its Arabian Sea coast, where pipeline oil would be loaded onto tankers bound for Asia.

In addition to raising Pakistan's value as an important link to the rest of Asia, the pipelines would open up a gateway for Pakistani trade to Central Asia. Khalilzad envisions a full-blown "economic corridor," connecting Pakistan, along with Afghanistan, to Turkmenistan and the rest of the Caspian. The corridor would consist not only of fuel lines, but electrical lines, telecommunications lines, rail lines, and highways.

Ties to Bush administration. Pakistan's oil minister met with Bush's former ambassador to Pakistan, Chamberlin, to talk about reviving the pipeline deals just two days after Bush launched air strikes against Taliban targets. Since then, the Bush administration has sent other diplomats to monitor pipeline talks in Islamabad. What's more, former President Bush's ambassador to Pakistan, Robert Bigger Oakley, lobbied on behalf of the pipelines for Unocal. Oakley also sits with Khalilzad on the Afghanistan-America Foundation board in Washington.

In exchange for his "cooperation" with the Bush administration, Musharraf will likely get a cheap source of gas and regional economic clout—on top of U.S. aid, debt forgiveness, military training, and possibly even arms sales, as Khalilzad has recommended. If the gas link to India goes through, he will also be able to collect transit fees and gain economic leverage over rival India, which would strengthen his position among the Islamic masses at home, who hold violent contempt for

Hindu-dominated India, thereby tightening the military dictator's grip on power. If the oil pipeline goes through, furthermore, Pakistan will be able to collect handsome port revenues as a major hub for oil exports to Asian markets.

Not bad for a rogue nation saddled with massive foreign debt and on the verge of bankruptcy before September 11. (Its sudden good fortune at the hands of the Bush administration is actually quite galling when you consider Pakistan is partly to blame for September 11, and has only feigned cooperation in hunting down bin Laden and other al-Qaida leaders who have taken up refuge there.)

Meanwhile, Karzai, if all goes according to plan, will get cheap gas along with hundreds of millions of dollars in transit-fee revenues for his start-up regime, and thousands of badly needed jobs for his impoverished future voters. That, and a steady flow of U.S. humanitarian aid and U.S. military occupation, will secure his grip on power for years to come. Not bad for an exiled former Taliban official.

But the lion's share of the benefits from the proposed pipelines will flow to the multinational energy corporations that seek to exploit the huge oil and gas reserves in the Caspian Basin, and that invested heavily in Bush, a former Texas oil executive. He got more campaign cash from the oil and gas industry during the 1999–2000 election cycle than any other federal candidate *over the last decade*, notes the Center for Responsive Politics. Bush's direct haul from oil and gas companies, excluding their gifts to his party and other Republicans, totaled nearly $2 million. Their investment in the oil-friendly Bush administration, which declined requests to interview principals named in this book, could pay off "big time," as Dick Cheney is fond of saying.

11

HIDDEN AGENDA

Exploiting the Commercial Front

The importance of Afghanistan may grow in coming years. It could become a valuable corridor for the export of Central Asia's oil and gas to South Asia and beyond.

—ZAL KHALILZAD, Bush's top Afghan adviser, in a 1998 prediction[1]

THE TRAGIC EVENTS OF SEPTEMBER 11 CHANGED MANY things. They forever altered the Manhattan skyline, recognized the world over as the symbol of prosperity. They changed the way we look at otherwise benign things like jumbo jets, tall buildings, and box cutters—as well as those smiling Saudi sheiks we thought were our allies. The al-Qaida attacks, in the span of one morning, vaporized our sense of security while living peacefully, freely, and happily in what had been Fortress America. They changed the way we travel and how we let others travel here. They federalized airport security and permanently mushroomed the Washington bureaucracy—and its police powers. They changed the political landscape as well, putting what voters perceived to be the more patriotic and hawkish Republicans in control of both ends of Pennsylvania Avenue for the first time in fifty years.

And, as with most tragic events, they opened up opportunities for commercial exploitation.

Few Americans knew on September 11 that there was much worth exploiting in Afghanistan. Certainly, I didn't. But the Bush administration knew all too well. Before the attacks, it had supported the development of oil and gas pipelines across Afghanistan, connecting landlocked Caspian riches with profitable Asian export markets. "Afghanistan's significance from an energy standpoint stems from its geographical position as a potential transit route for oil and natural gas exports from Central Asia to the Arabian Sea," the Energy Department stated in a report released just before the attacks.[2]

The pipelines also had the personal backing of several senior Bush officials who had a hand in shaping the war strategy in Afghanistan. The officials worked for oil companies that do business in the Caspian and favor the export links across Afghanistan. Just one thing stood in their way: the Taliban regime. September 11, tragic as it was, provided the oil-friendly Bush administration with a golden opportunity to remove the impediment, thereby breathing new life into the pipeline deals. Unfortunately, officials became so preoccupied with regime change in Afghanistan that they lost sight of their main quarry—Osama bin Laden and the rest of the al-Qaida leadership. I do not doubt that Bush and his war advisers hoped to come up with bin Laden in their sweeping assault on the Taliban, misguided as the strategy was.

But I am just as sure they wanted to get export links through Afghanistan, and that desire clouded their judgment in formulating the best strategy to get bin Laden, who remains free. The conspiracy pretty much ends there—although it is a damnable one considering that bin Laden could strike again at any moment, and that Americans trusted their president to, just this once, stick political and personal interests into a deep black hole for as long as it took to protect the nation.

I do not subscribe for a New York minute to the silly conspiracy theory, argued mainly by black-helicopter kooks and Arab hotheads, that Bush had advance knowledge of the September 11 attacks and let them proceed anyway to start a war over oil or against Islam. For one thing, the

First Lady was at the U.S. Capitol that morning, and the Capitol was the likely target of the fourth hijacked plane. Further, Donald Rumsfeld was in the Pentagon when the third plane smashed into it. You would think that the defense secretary, of all people, would be in on such a conspiracy.

Nor do I buy into the equally absurd theory peddled by two French journalists that Bush, impatient for the pipelines, threatened the Taliban with military action before September 11, leading them to launch a pre-emptive strike against us.[3] The September 11 attacks were planned years before Bush took office, and the hijackers began their flight training while Bush was still on the campaign trail. Immigration records show that hijacker ringleader Mohamed Atta, for example, entered the U.S. to start his pilot lessons on June 3, 2000.

The Bush administration obviously drafted its war plan *after* September 11. But as officials gathered around the Situation Room table after the attacks, as shocked and dazed as the rest of us, they grew to realize the rare commercial opportunity that presented itself in the Caspian region. And they eventually came up with a war plan that piggybacked their oil interests onto national security interests. It centered not on taking out bin Laden, at least not initially, but on replacing the Taliban with a pipeline-friendly puppet regime and lining up Pakistan behind it, since the proposed pipelines will run through that country too. Here is a review of just some of the particulars (call it the unauthorized version of Bush at war):

Two days after Bush launched air strikes against the Taliban, his ambassador to Pakistan talked with the Pakistani oil minister about reviving the pipelines projects. Three days after the secret oil talks—shamefully held at a time when the Twin Tower death toll was thought to be as high as seven thousand—the Bush administration extended a $300 million line of credit to Pakistan through the Overseas Private Investment Corporation, effectively ending a ban on U.S. financing of development projects in Pakistan. Two months later, with the Taliban ousted, Bush sent his top Afghan adviser—who happens to be a former Unocal pipeline lobbyist—to Kabul to help install a new regime there. Afghan delegates

accused the envoy, Zal Khalilzad, of rigging last June's presidential election in favor of another Unocal pipeline consultant, Hamid Karzai, as
previously detailed in Chapter 7. A UN economic development official
said the pipelines were at the root of the political maneuvering.[4] A week
earlier, Karzai had struck a pipeline deal with Pakistani leader Musharraf.
As pipeline talks progressed throughout the year, Bush dispatched U.S.
officials to monitor them. Then last September, the president met with
both Karzai and Musharraf in New York to discuss the pipelines; the next
day, he and Saudi Arabia's foreign minister pledged $130 million to build
a new highway along the proposed gas pipeline route through Afghanistan,
calling it part of a new Silk Road. Japan chipped in another $50 million.
Saudi Arabia and Japan were partners with Unocal in the original pipeline
project. By December, a gas pipeline deal was formally inked.

The multibillion-dollar project's breakthrough, after years of sitting
idle due to the Taliban, was not coincidental. It flowered from plans
drafted by Khalilzad before he joined Bush's National Security Council,
back when he was pushing the pipelines. They called for, among several
other measures, replacing the Taliban with a broad-based government
formally recognized by the U.S. The White House dusted off his plans
after September 11 and adopted almost all of his proposals as policy, as
detailed in an earlier chapter. Unfortunately, his plans had no provisions
for taking out bin Laden.

Too often in Washington, policy is driven by the personal interests of
the people making policy, and not the public interest. In this case, many
of the high-level officials making war policy shared Khalilzad's interest in
building a Caspian export route across Afghanistan to Asia, and his ideas
were easily co-opted. As discussed at length in the previous chapter,
Khalilzad's boss, Condoleezza Rice, was a director at Chevron, the biggest
Caspian producer; Vice President Cheney headed Halliburton, another
Caspian operator; Deputy Secretary of State Richard Armitage, also a part
of the war cabinet, was a paid Caspian lobbyist; and Bush took major campaign donations from Caspian producers. People, as they say, are policy.

But after September 11's bloody nightmare, the average American really doesn't care who rules Afghanistan or whether Caspian oil barons will finally get their pipelines. The average American wants one thing—bin Laden, dead or alive. He is still a grave danger to America, and he does not even have to top September 11. So long as he is alive, all he has to do is threaten to attack again, and it will be enough to panic the public and destabilize markets. The average American also wants justice. A stable, Taliban-free Afghanistan may please oil investors, but it is cold comfort to the families of September 11 victims. The Taliban did not attack New York or Washington (though you would never know it listening to Bush's rhetoric); al-Qaida did, and about two-thirds of its leaders are still on the loose. Bin Laden managed to escape to Pakistan—where he has issued new threats against America and launched new attacks against Americans abroad—while Bush has been busy colonizing Afghanistan. "America failed to kill or capture any of the al-Qaida leadership," bin Laden gloated last October, sticking a finger in Bush's eye.

Yet Bush apparently is too preoccupied to notice—this time with regime change in Iraq. In his last State of the Union speech, he again studiously avoided mentioning bin Laden, while mentioning Saddam Hussein an astounding nineteen times.

But Saddam did not murder three thousand people on September 11, either. Bin Laden did, and he is still at large. "We need to finish the job," advised former President Clinton.[5] Of course, he's one to talk. The only time Clinton got tough on bin Laden was in 1998, in the midst of the Lewinsky scandal, when he needed a big media distraction.

Twice in 2000, including one time after the USS *Cole* bombing, Clinton had bin Laden in his sights and failed to pull the trigger, according to a senior Pentagon official familiar with covert counterterrorism operations in Afghanistan at the time. He said the CIA had equipped pro-U.S. factions on the ground in Afghanistan with high-tech surveillance gear from the Defense Department to track bin Laden. They were armed with sniper rifles and shoulder-fired rocket launchers, the official explained, and had the OK to assassinate bin Laden on orders from U.S. intelligence back in Washington. "There were surveillance systems brought in-country, and they were doing observations and watching some of the likely places bin Laden frequented, such as Tora Bora, and guest-houses in the area," said the official, who requested anonymity. "And we were viewing" the satellite images relayed from Afghanistan.

"Some of it was collaborative—some DOD, some CIA—but we were looking," he said. "And Clinton had opportunities to take him out and didn't take them.

"One was more a command-and-control issue—when they should have made a decision to shoot, but it never got out of country, because the bureaucracy of carrying [the order] back [to Afghanistan] through channels was too much, and the opportunity just disappeared," he said. "And then another one when Clinton said 'No.'"

The Pentagon official stated that Clinton feared the paid CIA recruits might hit innocent Afghans. "There was actionable intelligence provided by that gear, by the optics," he said. "But once it went up the chain of command, it got into stuff like, 'How sure are you guys about that 6-5 guy in the middle of that group? It kind of looks like him, but how sure are you?'

"Clinton didn't want to have an accidental shot kill innocent civilians," he added. "But everyone was pretty certain it was Osama bin Laden. We had images of his face."[6]

Clinton certainly deserves his share of blame for failing to take out bin Laden when he had the chance. However, that was before September 11. Bin Laden did not attack American civilians on American soil when Clinton was commander in chief. That happened on Bush's watch, and he essentially blew a prime opportunity to take out bin Laden when U.S. intelligence had a fix on him in his Tora Bora rats' nest. He blew it because he and his oil cronies were preoccupied with another opportunity—taking out the pipeline-blocking Taliban in Kabul and Kandahar.

September 11 should have been the last straw. Everyone counted on

Bush to decapitate the al-Qaida leadership once and for all. He had a clear national mandate. CentCom officers have told me that they had hoped for a narrowly defined and concentrated search-and-destroy mission against al-Qaida in Afghanistan—go in, get bin Laden, and get out. What they got instead was a broadly defined, long, complicated mission that has included Afghan proxy forces, humanitarian airlifts, regime change, nation building, economic development, and occupation—all the things that Bush's pal, Unocal Zal, had on his wish list for his native country, a list that became the White House's operating manual in Afghanistan. The plan was so comprehensive and complex that it virtually guaranteed finding bin Laden would slip down the priority list.

To be sure, presidents throughout history have been accused of putting business interests first, even ahead of national security. In the most recent example, Clinton was accused of being in the pocket of U.S. aerospace-defense contractors, such as Loral and Hughes, that were hungry for deals in Communist China, which has nuclear-tipped missiles aimed at American cities. He even had his own Caspian pipeline scandal. Millionaire Lebanese oil man Roger Tamraz gave the 1996 Clinton-Gore reelection effort some $300,000 in exchange for White House access.[7] He was trying to get U.S. backing for the development of an alternate pipeline route from Azerbaijan to a Mediterranean port in Turkey—this one through Armenia, Azerbaijan's enemy. Despite warnings from a conscientious NSC aide, the White House hosted him at several events. The shady Tamraz got his access, if not his pipeline.[8]

Sleazy as it was, the funds-for-access deal was not tied to an American war. And this is by no means just any war. This is an epic battle to protect your family and mine, where we live, from the most dangerous and effective network of terrorists in the history of terrorism. As I have articulated earlier, bin Laden may be the most formidable foe—bar none, including Hitler—that America has ever faced. September 11 was hardly a time to play pipeline politics with national security.

The hidden oil agenda that governed the Bush administration's response to September 11 in Afghanistan, and its related monumental failure in ferreting out bin Laden, demands a full and formal investigation, particularly in light of the fact that the administration continues to stonewall media efforts to document its pre– and post–September 11 meetings, here and abroad, and its oil connections. After September 11, Attorney General John Ashcroft directed federal agencies to reject journalists' Freedom of Information Act requests for documents even if there was only a modicum of legal justification for doing so, vowing to back up the document gatekeepers in court.[9] And Cheney still refuses to cough up records of his secret energy task-force meetings.

Just about any seasoned member of the Washington press corps, whether liberal or conservative (I voted for Bush, and against Clinton twice), will tell you that this administration is one of the most secretive in modern memory—and it was that way before September 11. "Control freaks, absolute control freaks," as one senior White House correspondent privately put it. Yes, the Clinton administration was extremely guarded and deceitful, and even had a habit of bullying press corps members it did not like (as I experienced firsthand on more than one occasion covering it),[10] but Clinton officials would at least *engage* reporters during scandals. Though you knew you were being spun, and spun hard, at least your calls were returned. And even though they often redacted salient portions of FOIA (Freedom of Information Act) documents, claiming national security or other specious reasons, they at least turned *something* over to reporters.

The Bush administration, in contrast, completely shuts itself off to the press when it wants to dodge an issue. Officials are sequestered, and records are locked up. Reporters are not the only ones who have witnessed this arrogance of power. The Bush White House has repeatedly snubbed congressional committees and watchdog agencies seeking information. For instance, Cheney fought Congress's investigative arm, the GAO, to keep records of his energy task force secret until the watchdog agency earlier this year threw in the towel, dropping its lawsuit. Even Republican lawmakers, such as Senators John McCain and Charles Grassley and Representative

Dan Burton, have complained about White House "stonewalling." They have cited, for instance, its efforts to suppress key financial and other records linking members of the Saudi royal family to September 11.

McCain, in fact, coauthored legislation creating the special commission now investigating the September 11 intelligence breakdown, after he said the Bush administration "slow-walked and stonewalled" last year's joint inquiry by the Senate and House Intelligence Committees. The probe suffered, he said, because key officials such as Rice and Rumsfeld had not been questioned directly about issues surrounding September 11. He wants the investigation to go at least as far back as 1989, when U.S.-armed mujahideen fighters drove the Soviet army out of Afghanistan.[11] That would most certainly rope in Khalilzad—the behind-the-scenes architect of post–September 11 policy in Afghanistan—as a witness; he worked with the mujahideen as a State Department official.

But should the commission even call such officials to testify under oath, don't count on it asking them any prying questions about the Caspian oil agenda. As it was written, the legislation authorizing the outside probe let Bush pick the commission's chairman, and he settled on someone with his own Caspian connections.

His first choice was Henry Kissinger, an old Bush family crony and a Unocal consultant. That's right; to give cachet to its trans-Afghan gas pipeline, Unocal brought Kissinger to New York in 1995 to lay hands on the deal, which was first signed with the president of gas-rich Turkmenistan, the pipeline's origination point, and announced during the United Nation's fiftieth anniversary celebration.[12] Kissinger, who also is an adviser to the U.S.-Azerbaijan Chamber of Commerce, a top Caspian lobbying group, begged off the September 11 panel when critics cited his ties to big business (though no one even mentioned his ties to Unocal and the proposed pipeline).

So Bush turned to Thomas H. Kean, the former Republican governor of New Jersey, to head the panel. Largely unknown, he did not attract controversy and was left to preside over the investigation.

But his appointment should have raised a red flag too. Kean serves on the board of directors of Amerada Hess Corp., along with former Bush Treasury Secretary Nicholas F. Brady. New York–based Hess, a $13 billion-in-sales oil and gas giant, has a stake in one of the main Caspian oil groups, the Azerbaijan International Operating Co., through a fifty-fifty partnership with Delta Oil Co. of Saudi Arabia. Their venture, called DeltaHess ACG, profits from development of huge offshore oil and gas tracts in the Caspian Sea. Delta Oil was Unocal's main partner in the trans-Afghan gas pipeline, and has expressed an interest in rejoining the project. Hess, moreover, is a member of the U.S.-Azerbaijan Chamber of Commerce—the very nexus of the Caspian oil lobby in Washington. Besides Kissinger, USACC officers include executives from ChevronTexaco and Unocal, and former officers include Armitage and Cheney. USACC is registered as a 501(c)(6) trade association, which is allowed to lobby and endorse candidates. To say Kean is conflicted as the lead September 11 investigator is an understatement.

Perhaps an august and powerful foreign-policy body, such as the Senate Foreign Relations Committee, will take it upon itself to conduct a separate investigation into the role that Caspian oil politics played in shaping the administration's September 11 war policy. But don't hold your breath. Not only is the Senate Foreign Relations Committee now controlled by Republicans, its subcommittee for South Asian affairs, which covers Afghan policy, is run by none other than the cochairman of the Silk Road Caucus, formed just weeks after September 11 to promote Caspian investment on Capitol Hill. Senator Sam Brownback (R-Kan.) cofounded the Caspian caucus with Representative Joe Pitts (R-Pa.) on October 17, 2001.[13] In the wake of the September 11 attacks, "you have an alignment of the constellations," a Brownback aide at the time remarked candidly, and anonymously, in a *Legal Times* interview. "Business interests and national security interests have come together, and we're hoping members respond and sign on."[14] And they have responded in a big way: twenty-five members of Congress, in addition to Brownback and Pitts, have already joined the group.[15]

Brownback, you'll recall, gave voice to Unocal's pipeline projects through his subcommittee hearings. Witnesses included Unocal's pipeline point man, Marty Miller, president of Houston-based Unocal International Energy Ventures, as well as Unocal consultants Khalilzad and Thomas Gouttierre, director of the University of Nebraska's Center for Afghanistan Studies and Khalilzad's Afghan high school chum. Newly installed Afghan leader Karzai, another Unocal consultant, also appeared before Brownback's panel years ago. Brownback, a USACC director, has been a powerful ally of the Caspian oil lobby in Congress, and his efforts have been handsomely rewarded. He ranks among the top fifteen recipients of oil and gas industry money in Congress, according to the Center for Responsive Politics. A review of contributions received by Brownback since he filled out the unexpired term of former Senate Majority Leader Bob Dole, who left the Senate to run for president in 1996, shows that the oil and gas industry has given him more money than any other industry. It stuffed $222,734 into Brownback's campaign war chest in the 1995–2000 Senate election cycle alone. Further analysis shows that key Caspian players tied to the Bush administration have been among his top contributors within the industry. In just the 1995–2000 cycle, Unocal gave Brownback $3,000; Texaco donated $4,500; Chevron, $7,000; BP Amoco, $10,500; and Halliburton, $7,000. For a senator with a safe seat, as Brownback enjoys, they are generous gifts.

And the Kansas lawmaker, who campaigned for Bush's father in 1988, has been a key ally of this Bush administration in its efforts to exploit the Caspian commercial front after September 11. Following the terrorist attacks in New York and Washington, Brownback not only established the Silk Road Caucus, but also teed up pro-Caspian legislation for Bush to sign, including a bill waiving economic sanctions against Azerbaijan and encouraging trade and infrastructure projects in the region. This was a favorite hobbyhorse of Armitage, a former Caspian lobbyist and USACC cochairman, who worked closely during the war with Brownback's former chief foreign policy adviser, Christina Rocca, at the State Department, where she heads the bureau of South Asian affairs. Bush appointed her to the high-level position, which represents White House policy in Afghanistan and Pakistan, in May 2001 (her former boss Brownback presided over her nomination hearing in the Senate, quaintly enough). In that capacity, she met with Taliban and Pakistani officials. Rocca's and Khalilzad's paths crossed in the 1980s. As a CIA operative back then, Rocca coordinated secret deliveries of Stinger missiles to the Afghan mujahideen.[16] Khalilzad, as a State Department official in the 1980s, helped convince the White House to arm the mujahideen with U.S.-made Stingers, and coordinated efforts with mujahideen leaders during powwows in Pakistan. It's another link in the circle of influence among powerful Republicans in Congress and the Bush administration in shaping and carrying out the Afghan war strategy.

Brownback also helped deliver Pakistan to the administration's Afghan cause by authoring legislation lifting economic sanctions against Musharraf's rogue regime, which seized power in a military coup in 1999. Thanks to a Brownback-sponsored bill Bush signed shortly after September 11, U.S. oil and gas companies that want to invest in Pakistani projects can now get financial aid from the Export-Import Bank, the U.S. Trade and Development Agency, and the Overseas Private Investment Corporation. After the terrorist attacks, the Republican senator drafted legislation authorizing Bush to suspend U.S. tariffs on Pakistani textiles and textile products to further reward Musharraf for agreeing to end support for the Taliban—which stood in the way of Brownback's and Bush's Silk Road. "Pakistan is providing invaluable basing rights and intelligence assistance to the United States as we continue to degrade and dismantle the Taliban regime in Afghanistan," Brownback said November 13, 2001, in announcing his Pakistan Emergency Economic Development and Trade Support Act. The senator, who has traveled to Pakistan numerous times, met with Musharraf in Washington early last year.

All this in the name of fighting terrorism. Of course, the full scope and purpose of the war is not just terrorism, as it should be. The American people have been deceived, and their collective will has been subverted by a secret agenda to exploit the Caspian's estimated $4 trillion in potential riches. It seems unfathomable that elected leaders would mortgage Americans' security to further their oil lobby's interests halfway around the world.

But circumstances and associations combine with deeds and documents to paint a picture of an administration using the war on terrorism to secretly carry out such an agenda. Only when viewed through the prism of the Caspian export pipelines across Afghanistan does the administration's odd Afghan war strategy—the obsession with the Taliban, the early grooming of Karzai for leadership, the unholy alliances with Pakistan and Saudi Arabia, the rebuilding of Afghanistan, the permanent basing of U.S. troops in neighboring oil-rich Caspian countries, and on and on—make any sense. The prospect of landlocked Caspian hydrocarbons finally having a direct outlet to hot Asian markets corrupted the judgment of White House war planners, corrupted their war strategy, and corrupted the war's outcome. This was supposed to be a war to eradicate al-Qaida terrorists, not to replace a rogue Afghan regime blocking oil and gas export routes with a UN-approved, U.S.-friendly regime more amenable to such routes (or, likewise, to change a rogue Iraqi regime blocking U.S. oil and gas investment).

Sad to report, America was not the only thing on our commander in chief's mind after September 11. Competing for his attention were Afghanistan and Pakistan—not just because they shelter much of the al-Qaida enemy, but because they also lie between vast oil and gas fields and Asian-bound tankers in the Arabian Sea. Securing their help in laying the pipelines meant getting more tangled in local Muslim politics than would have otherwise been necessary, leading to missed opportunities in capturing bin Laden. Many times, the two missions—securing the pipelines and ferreting out bin Laden—have worked at cross-purposes. Afghan tribal fighters have betrayed us again and again. Some even escorted al-Qaida leaders safely across the border to Pakistan. Now Pakistan won't let our troops in Afghanistan chase marauding al-Qaida fighters based in northern Pakistan back across its border. The overall mission was so complicated, it collapsed of its own weight. It backfired. Bin Laden had long escaped by the time U.S. commandos showed up for the critical Tora Bora battle against al-Qaida. Gen. Tommy Franks, Bush's Midland, Texas, pal, had other priorities; he was busy waiting on Northern Alliance and other proxy forces to take Kabul and Kandahar from the Taliban.

Bush now seems content to leave the hunt for bin Laden and other al-Qaida leaders up to Pakistan, his pipeline ally, yet Pakistan won't admit that the al-Qaida leaders have found sanctuary there. This is a dereliction of duty writ large, yet no one seems willing to talk about it. Or perhaps concerns are drowned out by the incessant media drumbeat over Iraq. Saddam Hussein has proved a valuable diversion for a president trying to distract the media from the specter of bin Laden. Clinton spinmeister and news-manufacturer Dick Morris would be proud.

Right after September 11, Bush stressed the uniqueness of the war on terrorism in asking for Americans' patience in capturing bin Laden. There are no borders, no fronts in this war, he asserted; it's a tireless manhunt for shadowy killers. There will be "no decisive liberation of territory" or antiseptic "air war" like the one above Kosovo in 1999, he said in his drawl, eyes squinting like Clint Eastwood.[17]

Yet now Bush brags of "liberating" and "stabilizing" Afghanistan, as if they were the original war objectives. He has fought the war as if it were indeed a conventional battle over geography, with fronts and antiseptic air strikes and bases. That's because it secretly is—only, the fronts are not just military; they are commercial. If Bush could have tamed a new oil frontier for America and at the same time caught bin Laden, I might have saluted him and said, "More power to you, Mr. President" (although I question the wisdom of enmeshing America any deeper in a part of the world, one dominated by Muslims, that already hates us, and I wonder about quid pro quos with oil donors). But so far he has accomplished only the former. If bin Laden survives to launch another attack on American soil—heaven forbid—Bush's strategy in Afghanistan will go down as one of the biggest military blunders in history.

The Caspian interests of Bush and his oil cronies may be more secure there, but Americans' lives here at home are not. Bush's cronies have hijacked the war on terrorism, and the American people, who trusted Bush to defend them from al-Qaida, may be the victims yet again.

AFTERWORD

WE ALL HOPE AND PRAY THAT OSAMA BIN LADEN AND HIS
senior advisers are caught soon. If it happens today, and America dodges
another major al-Qaida attack, we have nonetheless paid a price for
President Bush's hidden oil agenda in Afghanistan.

If Bush had zeroed in on bin Laden in Afghanistan when he had a
chance, instead of wasting time overthrowing the pipeline-blocking
Taliban, we might have more money left in our mutual funds, and more
civil liberties left in our Bill of Rights. There is also a good chance we
would have a smaller federal bureaucracy and budget.

Though the U.S. and its allies thinned al-Qaida's senior ranks last
year, the bulk of the organization's leadership remained free, including
the masterminds behind the September 11 plot. Their threat of new
attacks against America cast a cloud of uncertainty over the stock market,
which contributed to the worst bear market since the Great Depression.
The Dow Jones industrial average plunged 17 percent in 2002—despite

a budding economic recovery. That was the worst year on Wall Street since 1974. Coming on the heels of sell-offs in 2001 and 2000, it marked the first three-year decline in the Dow since 1939-1941, and made for the nastiest bear, as measured by both duration and depth, since the 1929-1932 crash.[1]

To be sure, several factors other than the threat of terrorism hurt the market last year. They include the corporate accounting scandals and new federal regulations, fear of war in the Mideast and higher oil prices, and threats by Democrats to repeal the 2001 tax cut.

But the devastating al-Qaida bombing at a Bali resort unnerved stocks in October, and so did bin Laden's audiotaped message praising the attack the next month. It was the first hard evidence in a year that the al-Qaida leader was still alive, and the news was said to have contributed to halting a rally on Wall Street.[2] The shocking blasts in Bali, as well as Kenya, made clear that, despite the fall of the Taliban, the war on terrorism was far from over. Though the Taliban and al-Qaida no longer controlled Afghanistan, the threat persisted.

Fresh al-Qaida threats against Americans in February of this year also were blamed for killing a Wall Street rally. Stocks climbed early on February 7 on news the jobless rate fell in January from an eight-year high, but then they turned south after Attorney General John Ashcroft warned that terrorist attacks on Americans were planned and raised the domestic threat alert to the second-highest level.[3]

Last year's stock losses may not have been so brutal had bin Laden been caught. More big money would have flowed into the market from the sidelines. The threat of terrorism is the ultimate uncertainty, and investors, whether long or short on the market, hate uncertainty above all.

So do CEOs. The lingering al-Qaida threat also put a crimp in business plans last year. Companies were less inclined to expand their businesses and add workers. Retailers even hired fewer workers than normal during the busy Christmas holiday season. In fact, last year was the worst hiring slump in almost twenty years. A surge in the number of discouraged workers in the final months of 2002 mimicked the joblessness trend seen in the months immediately following the September 11 attacks.[4]

Economists mainly blame uncertainty over the war on terrorism for the flagging economy. The fourth quarter's anemic 0.7 percent growth in real GDP held overall 2002 growth to 3.2 percent—"well below the normal rate of the first year of a recovery," observed Brian Wesbury, chief economist with Griffin Kubik Stephens & Thompson Inc., a Chicago-based investment banking firm. "Uncertainties over war in Iraq, terrorism, a dockworker lockout and D.C. snipers held back business decisions, contributing to a soft spot in the fourth quarter," he explained.[5]

So last year, as bin Laden continued to haunt America, the economy, the job market, and the stock market all slumped back toward the bottoms they made right after September 11. The rebound stalled—in spite of continued interest-rate cuts and proposed additional tax cuts. It's no coincidence that the relapse came along with the collective realization of business leaders, investors, and consumers that nothing had really changed since September 11, that the nation was just as vulnerable to al-Qaida attack as ever.

By the end of last year, it had become plain that Bush's self-declared victory in Afghanistan was premature.

There may be another, longer-term economic repercussion from Bush's failed Afghan war strategy. Though it doesn't look like it now, with deflation fears still lingering, some are predicting a reflation hangover from loose monetary policy. The Federal Reserve, desperately trying to reignite consumer spending, has continued to flood the economy with money since September 11. But once the economy fully recovers, some financial analysts warn, there will be too much money chasing too few goods. And all the excess money floating around the economy will likely rekindle commodity prices faster than the Fed can cool them. It took decades for the central bank to wring the 1970s inflation premium out of the economy. Will stubbornly high inflation rear its ugly head again now that the Fed has virtually abandoned its credit discipline? And, have historically low interest rates caused a housing bubble, as overeager lenders have enticed otherwise unqualified borrowers to grab risky mortgage and equity loans?

Some money managers say the recent rise in gold prices in part reflects worries over such a post-September 11 liquidity bubble. And they blame Federal Reserve Chairman Alan Greenspan for creating it. They say he has forsaken his earlier sound-money principles, acting more like a politician than a central banker in this crisis and lesser ones in the past.

As a budding economist in the 1950s, Greenspan sat with other young New York intellectuals at the feet of novelist and cold-eyed capitalist Ayn Rand, soaking up her views on economic policy. She preached that federal deficit spending and its attendant inflation were the root of economic evil, and she argued for a return to the gold standard. Later, Greenspan wrote articles for Rand's *The Objectivist* magazine echoing her call for a pure gold standard to rein in government spending.[6]

"Everything he said in the 1950s and 1960s he hasn't pursued in the last five years. He was an advocate of the gold standard and also very much of the view excessive monetary and credit growth had led to the boom of the late 1920s and the subsequent collapse," said former Hong Kong-based investment banker Marc Faber, author of *Tomorrow's Gold: Asia's Age of Discovery*. "But basically what he has done is created this huge liquidity bubble, first by bailing out Mexico and then bailing out U.S. hedge fund LTCM in 1998, and later he flushed the system with liquidity ahead of Y2K, which led to the last Nasdaq bubble," added Faber, now a Swiss economist. "And once again we have a monetary explosion, which I think is highly dangerous."[7]

Even if Greenspan has "grown in office," as they say, and is now more apt to compromise, it's still doubtful he would have continued easing rates last year had bin Laden been caught and the cloud of uncertainty removed from the economy and markets. Greenspan's stated goal since he took the reins of the Fed has been zero inflation; he doesn't want a legacy of reflation if he can help it.

Bloated Budget

Speaking of deficit-spending, the Bush administration is posting record federal deficits, reversing record surpluses. The budget gap in fiscal year 2003 ballooned to $307 billion, eclipsing the historic high of $290 billion set in 1992 when Bush's father was president. At $304 billion, the projected deficit for fiscal 2004 is no real improvement, despite the economic recovery.[8]

Yes, the recession and bear market have shrunk the tax base and cut into revenues. But don't overlook the spending side of the ledger, which has also created the yawning budget gaps. Since September 11, Bush and Congress have been on a spending spree. They claim it's all in the name of the war on terrorism—even though most of the new outlays have little to do with fighting terrorism. Reportedly only about one-third of the recent budget increases can be attributed directly to homeland-security costs.[9]

Bush in his fiscal 2004 budget proposed almost $100 billion more in nondefense discretionary spending than former President Clinton, who was pilloried by Republicans for overspending on social programs and pork-barrel projects.[10] Historically, Congress spends even more money than presidents request, piling on their own pork, so Bush can count on getting his discretionary outlays and then some.

If bin Laden had been captured and al-Qaida neutralized as a threat, American taxpayers more than likely would have paid more attention to the tab Washington's big spenders have run up since September 11. But they have been willing to overlook the Potomac pork-out in the hopes it will protect them as advertised.

The needlessly prolonged hunt for the brains and inspiration behind the al-Qaida network has also given the big-government types in Washington ample opportunity to grow the federal bureaucracy. Last year's creation of the Homeland Security Department is the largest new federal agency since the formation of the Defense Department in the 1940s.[11] Some 170,000 federal employees from twenty-two U.S. agencies—from the INS to FEMA to the newly created Transportation Security Administration (TSA)—will be folded into the monstrous new security bureau.

Its first budget will be at least $35 billion. As with most federal agencies, there will be annual requests for more personnel, offices, furniture, equipment and other things, and its budget will mushroom each year. And if it's anything like other agency budgets, including ones it has inherited, much of the spending will be wasteful.

After TSA took over airport security early last year, its director splurged on new office digs. TSA chief John W. Magaw, who later resigned, spent more than $410,000 just renovating his own office suite. He also engaged in what looked to be a bit of old-fashioned featherbedding, asking Congress for funds to hire, among other employees, 3,407 "shoe bin runners" and 1,430 "ticket checkers" at airport security checkpoints.[12]

Will the Homeland Security Department make you safer? Did the Education Department improve SAT scores? Did the Energy Department solve the energy crisis? Did HUD and the Health and Human Services departments wipe out poverty? You get my point.

Bigger Brother

Since September 11, government is not only larger and costlier, it's also more intrusive. The Homeland Security Department will have new powers to monitor citizens, thanks to the USA PATRIOT Act. Congress passed it in October 2001, before bin Laden escaped Afghanistan, but it was rushed through without much deliberation.

"From its initial draft to its final adoption, the PATRIOT Act zipped through in six weeks—less time than Congress typically spends on routine bills that raise no constitutional concerns," complained Robert A. Levy, a senior fellow at the libertarian Cato Institute in Washington. "Congress' so-called deliberative process was reduced to this: Closed-door negotiations, no conference committee, no committee reports, no final hearing at which opponents could testify, not even an opportunity for most of the legislators to read the 131 single-spaced pages about to become law."[13]

Perhaps if Bush had dispatched U.S. ground troops to corner bin Laden in southern Afghanistan in October 2001, when U.S. intelligence had a fix on him, lawmakers would have actually debated the bill instead of rubber-stamping it. Certainly some of the wind would have been taken out of the Orwellian proposal. Even if the terrorist overlord had not been captured until after its passage, lawmakers might have reconsidered the need for expanded domestic spying powers with the brains of the terrorist operation gone, and amended or repealed the more egregious parts of the law by now.

The PATRIOT Act gives law enforcement officers broader authority to conduct electronic surveillance and wiretaps in the name of fighting terrorism. According to the language of the law, they can now:[14]

- obtain e-mails, voice mails and computer information, including "records of session times and durations," as well as "any temporary assigned network address," with a search warrant, which is easier to get than the previously required wiretap warrant;
- monitor and intercept e-mails—without first obtaining court authority—from any "computer trespasser," broadly defined as anyone who "accesses a protected computer without authorization"— which could include individuals behind in their AOL payments or employees who use their company's e-mail account for personal business;
- tap every phone line a suspect uses by obtaining just one warrant, instead of separate warrants for each line, as previously required.

But the government's civil-rights incursion does not stop there. The USA PATRIOT Act—which is actually an acronym that stands for Uniting and Strengthening America by Providing Appropriate Tools Required to Intercept and Obstruct Terrorism—also lets police enter homes or businesses and search materials without notifying their owners, if authorities can convince a judge that prior notice of the "sneak-and-peek" invasion might jeopardize the search. "No knowledge means no opportunity to contest the validity of the search, including such obvious infractions as rummaging through office drawers when the warrant authorizes a garage search, or even searching the wrong address," Levy warned.[15] What's more, the antiterrorism law makes it easier for police to collect information on customers of banks, credit-card companies, libraries, bookstores, and hospitals.

The Bush administration argues that while the expanded powers may encroach on individual rights, they are needed to protect Americans against future terrorist attacks. Only through greater intelligence gathering and surveillance of U.S. terrorist cells will the government be able to preempt such attacks, it says.

However, Levy points out that the PATRIOT Act does not just apply to terrorists. "The new rules are defended as a necessary instrument of antiterrorism," he said. "If so, why do many of the provisions apply not only to suspected terrorist acts, but also to everyday national security investigations and even ordinary criminal matters?" Levy concluded that, in effect, "our government has used the event of September 11 to impose national police powers that skirt time-honored constraints on state."[16]

In the wake of renewed al-Qaida threats, the administration has secretly proposed expanding the PATRIOT Act, further trampling civil liberties.

On January 9, 2003, Ashcroft's staff drafted a bill, entitled the Domestic Security Enhancement Act of 2003 (aka "the Patriot Act II"), that would give the feds sweeping new powers to increase domestic spying and restrict public access to government information, according to the Washington-based Center for Public Integrity, a government watchdog group that first revealed the secret draft of the bill.

Besides further undermining the Freedom of Information Act, which journalists commonly use to obtain sensitive government papers, the proposed law "would radically expand law enforcement and intelligence-gathering authorities, reduce or eliminate judicial oversight over surveillance, authorize secret arrests, create a DNA database based on unchecked executive 'suspicion,' create new death penalties, and even seek to take American citizenship away from persons who belong to or support disfavored political groups," said David Cole, Georgetown University law professor and author of *Terrorism and the Constitution.*[17]

And who knows what secret orders and findings the president has signed that further expand and broaden the government's power over citizens.

After last fall's al-Qaida bombing in Bali, Bush's own CIA director said the terrorist network was just as threatening as it was before September 11, and that, essentially, America was no safer. "The threat environment we find ourselves in today is as bad as it was last summer, the summer before 9-11," CIA Director George Tenet told Congress last October. "They've reconstituted. They are coming after us. They want to execute attacks. You see it in Bali."

The Homeland Security Act was signed into law not long after the attacks, and then Justice Department lawyers began drafting the enhanced spying powers. The pretext was that the al-Qaida threat was still very real and the government needed greater power to deal with it.

Even if bin Laden is finally taken out of the picture, the bigger Big Brother he spawned while on the lam will likely remain. Forget about sunsetting the PATRIOT Act, as Levy and others have proposed. Once Washington gives itself more powers, it is next to impossible to take them back. We may be doomed to live in a semi-police state in which political enemies will be monitored as suspected "terrorists."

Was it really all necessary? Not if bin Laden had been caught when Bush had the opportunity to catch him.

Unfortunately, he was preoccupied with other opportunities in Afghanistan, which distracted him from the enemy at hand. As his father's former special envoy to the Afghan opposition advised the previous year, narrowly targeting bin Laden would only miss the broader goal of securing U.S. commercial interests in the region.

"It was only after the 1998 Osama bin Laden–instigated bombings of U.S. embassies in Africa that U.S. policy on Afghanistan began to stir. The resultant, single-minded 'get Osama bin Laden' approach has missed the point. Seizing one terrorist, however odious, does not address the broad and important U.S. interests at stake in Afghanistan," said Peter Tomsen, who was former President Bush's Afghan ambassador in the early 1990s. "A comprehensive American policy is required to . . . lay the basis in a positive way for revival of Eurasian trade routes through Afghanistan."[18] Tomsen said the real problem was the "rigid, orthodox, anti-Western Taliban." They were standing in the way of progress, he said, and had to go.[19]

He made the remarks at a July 2000 Senate hearing as a professor of the International Studies Programs at the University of Nebraska at Omaha. The department's dean is none other than Thomas Gouttierre, longtime chum of Zal Khalilzad, Bush's top Afghan adviser. After the Taliban fell in Kabul in November 2001, the two old friends met at the White House. Gouttierre had been invited to speak to Bush officials about Aghan policy.[20]

Bush has described America's mission in Afghanistan as making sure the Taliban is "gone," and the country "secure" and "stable." Rounding up al-Qaida came third.[21] Commercial interests, such as those "Eurasian routes" Tomsen cited, may require the existence of a secure and stable government in Kabul, but America's security interests do not. They just require the *nonexistence* of bin Laden and other al-Qaida leaders.

After defeating the Taliban, Bush asked the American people for "patience" in doing the same to al-Qaida.[22] While waiting, we forfeited some of our civil liberties and lost even more of our 401(k) nest eggs. Meanwhile, Bush and his cronies secured their Caspian oil interests and sweetened their investment opportunities. Sounds a lot like the Enron fleecing, but on a larger scale. Call it corporate government, Bush-style.

APPENDIX A

1. Chronology of Recent Afghan Political History

1933: Mohammed Zahir Shah crowned king of Afghanistan.

1946: Afghanistan joins United Nations.

1964: Afghanistan adopts constitution prohibiting the royal family from participation in the government, while permitting the lower house of the legislature to approve a prime minister.

1973: President Mohammed Daoud assumes the presidency of Afghanistan after a military coup, and abolishes the monarchy. King Zahir Shah goes into exile.

1974–1978: Opposition to Daoud increases among a range of Islamic and communist factions.

April 1978: Daoud is assassinated and replaced by a junta led by Hafizullah Amin.

December 1979: Soviet troops invade Afghanistan, install government.

1980: Armed tribal groups begin a jihad against the Soviet-installed government.

1980–1989: Armed mujahideen groups fight Soviet and government forces; hundreds of thousands of Afghans die in the struggle, and millions more become refugees.

1986: U.S. government begins covertly supplying Stinger missiles to mujahideen.

1986: President Mohammed Najibullah takes office.

1988: Geneva Accords signed, outlining a plan for the withdrawal of Soviet troops.

February 1989: Soviet troops complete withdrawal.

February 1989–April 1992: Conflict between government and opposition forces escalates.

April 1992: President Najibullah is replaced by a four-member council under a U.N. plan.

Late April 1992: An interim government led by Professor Sebghatollah Mojadedi takes power.

June 1992: An interim government led by Borhannudin Rabbani takes office.

December 1992: Borhannudin Rabbani is elected president, Gulbuddin Hekmatyar prime minister, and Ahmad Shah Massoud minister of defense. Hamid Karzai also joins the new government as a diplomat.

1992 to early 1995: Fighting spreads to all major cities as the Shura-e Nezar (Supervisor Council) and the Shura-e Hamahangi (Supreme Coordination Council) compete for control.

Late 1994: The Taliban emerges as a major force, taking control of Kandahar.

January 1, 1995: Some 3,000 Pakistani Taliban from Peshawar leave for Afghanistan.

May 31, 1995: Saudi intelligence chief Prince Turki visits Kabul and Kandahar.

September 27, 1996: The Taliban gains control of Kabul. Karzai initially supports and works for new government. U.S. signals it may reestablish diplomatic relations with Afghanistan.

Late 1996–early 1997: Militia leaders Gen. Dostum and Rabbani, along with the Hezb-e Wahdat and Harrakat-e Islami factions, form the Northern Alliance to resist the Taliban. The Taliban, however, continues to make gains and conquer Herat and Jalalabad.

May 1997: Dostum goes into exile in Turkey for four months after one of his lead commanders, Gen. Malik, defects to the Taliban. Pakistan, Saudi Arabia, and the United Arab Emirates recognize the Taliban.

June 1997: Thousands of Pakistani madrassas students join the Taliban.

September 1997: Dostum returns to his stronghold in Mazar-e Sharif with strong backing from Uzbekistan.

November 18, 1997: In visit to Pakistan, Secretary of State Madeleine Albright scolds Taliban for human-rights abuses.

March 1998: U.N. withdraws international workers from southern Afghanistan, citing physical abuse by Pakistan.

April 17, 1998: Washington's U.N. Ambassador Bill Richardson visits the region and discusses Afghanistan, reaching an agreement among key parties to negotiate their differences. The Taliban breaks the agreement in May.

June 18, 1998: Saudi intelligence chief Prince Turki visits Kandahar.

July 9, 1998: Taliban leader Mullah Mohammed Omar issues edict to deport all Christians from Afghanistan.

July 31, 1998: Some 5,000 more Pakistani madrassas students leave to join up with Taliban in Afghanistan.

August 7, 1998: Al-Qaida bombs U.S. embassies in Kenya and Tanzania.

August 8, 1998: Taliban forces capture key Northern Alliance stronghold of Mazar-e Sharif.

August 20, 1998: U.S. launches cruise-missile strikes in Afghanistan in response to terrorist attacks by Osama Bin Laden on U.S. embassies in Africa.

August 1998: Taliban continues military advances. Iranian Revolutionary Guards deploy along Afghan border following killing of Iranian diplomats in Afghanistan and mass killings of ethnic Hazaras by Taliban troops.

September 1998: The Taliban captures Bamian. Forces led by Massoud shell Kabul and continue resisting Taliban advances. Massoud's forces later recapture Bamian, and fighting continues.

September 6, 1998: Taliban repeats an appeal to the U.N. for formal recognition.

December 9, 1998: U.N. passes tough resolution against Afghanistan.

January 12, 1999: Family of leading former mujahideen commander Abdul Haq gunned down by Pakistani Taliban in Peshawar.

February 1999: The Taliban rules out bin Laden's extradition. The Taliban subsequently claims he is missing.

April 15, 1999: President Clinton slams Taliban for human-rights violations.

May 14, 1999: The Clinton administration warns Pakistan not to support the Taliban, and backs the return of former King Zahir Shah to power in Afghanistan.

July 15, 1999: Karzai's father murdered in Quetta, Pakistan, after meeting with Zahir Shah.

October 12, 1999: Gen. Pervez Musharraf seizes power in Pakistan in a military coup, drawing Pakistan's military intelligence even closer to Taliban, which it helped create.

October 15, 1999: U.N. Security Council imposes new sanctions against the Taliban.

July 1, 2000: Northern Alliance repels a Taliban offensive north of Kabul, inflicting heavy Taliban casualties.

September 11, 2001: Al-Qaida launches terrorist attacks on New York and Washington.

Mid-September 2001–early October 2001: Pakistani intelligence chiefs meet with Taliban leaders in Afghanistan.

October 7, 2001: U.S. forces launches air strikes against Taliban targets.

November 13, 2001: Kabul falls to U.S.-backed Northern Alliance and other anti-Taliban forces.

December 7, 2001: Kandahar, where Mullah Omar conducts most of his business, falls to opposition forces.

December 22, 2001: Hamid Karzai sworn in as interim leader of Afghanistan.

December 31, 2001: President Bush appoints Zalmay Khalilzad his special envoy to Afghanistan.

June 13, 2001: Karzai elected Afghan president in *loya jirga*. Former King Zahir Shah, who backed out of contest after behind-the-scenes maneuvering by Khalilzad, is given no role in new government.

————

Sources: Afghanistan-America Foundation, Ahmed Rashid's *Taliban*, author.

2. Major Caspian Energy Deals

Azerbaijan International Operating Company (AIOC)
Consortium developing offshore oil and gas fields in Azerbaijan. The oil fields are expected to produce 650,000 barrels per day by 2007. AIOC is also developing a 42-inch-diameter pipeline from Baku, Azerbaijan, to Ceyhan, Turkey, on the Mediterranean Sea. First oil delivery is planned for 2005.
AIOC shares are held as follows:

- BP Amoco (UK)* 34.14 percent
- Unocal Khazar Ltd. 10.5 percent
- LUKoil (Russia) 10 percent
- Socar (Azerbaijan) 10 percent
- Statoil (Norway) 8.56 percent
- ExxonMobil 8 percent
- TPAO (Turkey) 6.75 percent
- Pennzoil 4.82 percent
- Itochu (Japan) 3.92 percent
- DeltaHess (Saudi/U.S.) ACG 2.08 percent
- DeltaNimir Khazar Ltd. (Saudi) 1.68 percent

Note: Shares may not total 100 percent due to rounding.
*Consortium leader and project operator.

CASPIAN PIPELINE CONSORTIUM (CPC)

Consortium operating crude oil pipeline recently built from western Kazakhstan to a terminal near the Black Sea port of Novorossiysk in Russia. CPC shares are held as follows:

- Russian Federation 24 percent
- Republic of Kazakhstan 19 percent
- Chevron CPC Co.* 15 percent
- LUKARCO B.V. (Russia/U.S.) 12.5 percent
- Rosneft-Shell Caspian Ventures Ltd. (Russia/UK) 7.5 percent
- Mobil Caspian Pipeline Co. 7.5 percent
- Sultanate of Oman 7 percent
- Agip International (Italy) (N.A.) N.V. 2 percent
- BG Overseas Holdings Ltd. (UK) 2 percent
- Kazakhstan Pipeline Ventures L.L.C. 1.75 percent
- Oryx Caspian Pipeline L.L.C. 1.75 percent

*ChevronTexaco and the Republic of Kazakhstan are developing the giant Tengiz and nearby Korolev oil fields. The partnership is called Tengizchevroil (TCO).

SHAH DENIZ

Consortium formed to develop gas and gas condensate in Azerbaijan. Deal ratified in 1996. Iran a partner. No U.S. participation.

- BP Amoco (UK) 25.5 percent
- Statoil (Norway) 25.5 percent
- TotalFina Elf (France) 10 percent
- LukAgip (Russia/Italy) 10 percent
- OIEC (Iran) 10 percent
- SOCAR (Azerbaijan) 10 percent
- TPAO (Turkey) 9 percent

NORTH ABSHERON OPERATING CO. (NAOC)

Consortium formed to explore and develop oil and gas fields in the Caspian Sea's Northern Absheron ridge. Under the contract signed with the government of

Azerbaijan in 1996, NAOC's exploration program was set to last until March 2000. But a year earlier, it was halted due to insufficient discoveries and low energy prices.

NAOC shares were held as follows:

- BP Amoco (UK) 30 percent
- Unocal Corp. 25.5 percent
- Itochu (Japan) 20 percent
- Socar (Azerbaijan) 20 percent
- Delta Oil Co. (Saudi) 4.5 percent

CENTRAL ASIA GAS PIPELINE LTD. (CENTGAS)

Consortium formed to develop and operate a natural gas pipeline from Dauletabad field in Turkmenistan to growing markets in Pakistan and India. The 48-inch-diameter line would also cross Afghanistan. Consortium leader Unocal pulled out of the project in December 1998 due to low oil prices and political difficulties involving the ruling Taliban militia in Afghanistan. But the project, renamed the Trans-Afghanistan Pipeline (TAP), is back on the drawing board now that the Taliban is gone.

CentGas shares were held as follows:

- Unocal Corp. 46.5 percent
- Delta Oil Co. (Saudi) 15 percent
- Government of Turkmenistan 7 percent
- Indonesia Petroleum Ltd. (Japan) 6.5 percent
- Itochu Oil Exploration Co. (Japan) 6.5 percent
- Hyundai Engineering & Construction (S. Korea) Co. 5 percent
- The Crescent Group (Pakistan) 3.5 percent

Note: The remaining 10 percent equity was reserved for Russia's RAO Gazprom, but it decided not to formally join the consortium.

CENTRAL ASIA OIL PIPELINE (CAOP)

Consortium formed to develop a crude oil pipeline from Turkmenistan across Afghanistan to an export terminal on Pakistan's Arabian Sea coast. The 42-inch-diameter line would tie into the existing Caspian pipeline network and gather oil from other Caspian countries. The Unocal-led project also was shelved in December 1998, mainly because of the Taliban, but the project has since been revived.

CAOP-related agreements were signed by:

- Unocal International Energy Ventures Ltd.
- Government of Turkmenistan
- Government of Pakistan
- Republic of Uzbekistan
- Uzbekneftegaz
- Delta Oil Pipeline Co. (Uzbekistan) Ltd.
- Delta Oil Co. (Uzbekistan) Ltd.
- Delta Oil Co. (Saudi)

Sources: Unocal and ChevronTexaco annual reports, press releases; author.

3. Members of the Silk Road Caucus

Congress' twenty-seven-member bicameral, bipartisan body formed after the September 11 terrorist attacks to develop legislative policy for promoting trade and investment in the greater Caspian Sea region, including Afghanistan and Pakistan.

Congressman Joe Pitts (R, PA-District 16), Co-Chairman
Congressman Gary Ackerman (D, NY-5), Co-Chairman
Senator Sam Brownback* (R, KS), Co-Chairman
Senator Mary Landrieu (D, LA) Co-Chairwoman
Congressman Doug Bereuter** (NE-01)
Senator Robert Bennett (R, UT)
Congressman Marion Berry (D, AR-01)
Congresswoman Judy Biggert (R, IL-13)
Congressman Joseph Crowley (D, NY-07)
Congressman Lloyd Doggett (D, TX-10)
Congressman Phil English (R, PA-21)
Congressman Maurice D. Hinchey (D, NY-26)
Congressman Joseph Hoeffel (D, PA-13)
Congressman Mark Steven Kirk (R, IL-10)
Congressman Joe Knollenberg (R, MI-11)
Congresswoman Karen McCarthy (D, MO-05)
Congressman Jim McDermott (D, WA-07)
Congressman Donald Payne (D, NJ-10)
Congressman Mike Pence (R, IN-02)

Congressman Pete Sessions (R, TX-05)
Congressman Brad Sherman (D, CA-24)
Congressman Mark Souder (R, IN-4)
Congressman Tom Tancredo (R, CO-06)
Congresswoman Ellen O. Tauscher (D, CA-10)
Congressman Todd Tiahrt (R, KS-04)
Congressman Robert Wexler (D, FL-19)
Congressman Albert Russell Wynn (D, MD-04)

*Chairman of the Senate Foreign Relations subcommittee on Near Eastern and South Asian Affairs, who invited Unocal executives and consultants to testify about the proposed trans-Afghanistan pipelines last decade.

**Former chairman of the House International Relations subcommittee on Asia and the Pacific, who also invited Unocal executives and consultants to testify about the pipelines.

APPENDIX B

U.S. Department of Justice
Immigration and Naturalization Service

HQINS 70/28

Office of the Executive Associate Commissioner

425 I Street NW
Washington, DC 20536

SEP 5 2002

MEMORANDUM FOR REGIONAL DIRECTORS
                          SERVICE CENTER DIRECTORS
                          CHIEF PATROL AGENTS
                          DIRECTOR OF INTERNATIONAL AFFAIRS
                          OFFICER DEVELOPMENT AND TRAINING
                             FACILITY, GLYNCO
                          OFFICER DEVELOPMENT AND TRAINING
                             FACILITY, ARTESIA
                          DIRECTOR, LAW ENFORCEMENT SUPPORT CENTER

FROM: Johnny N. Williams
                Executive Associate Commissioner
                Office of Field Operations

SUBJECT: Identification of Nonimmigrant Aliens Subject to Special Registration, or the
                National Security Entry Exit Registration System

    A policy memorandum will be sent to the field addressing the recent changes to Title 8 of the
Code of Federal Regulations, part 264.1(f), [8 CFR 264.1(f)]. This section of the Code of
Federal Regulations relates to the "special registration" of nonimmigrant aliens, more recently
referred to as the National Security Entry Exit Registration System (NSEERS). The special
registration policy memorandum contains information relating to the new processing protocols
for special registrants. The purpose of this memorandum is to outline specifically who will be
subject to special registration.

    Arriving nonimmigrant aliens subject to special registration, or NSEERS, will be registered
(unless exempt) at the arriving ports-of-entry (POE). When fully implemented there will be four
different methods by which a nonimmigrant alien will be identified for special registration. The
four methods are: citizens or nationals of countries designated through publication of a notice in
the Federal Register, notification through the Interagency Border Inspection System (IBIS), pre-
existing criteria as defined by the Attorney General and officer discretion. This information,
excluding the countries published by the Attorney General in the Federal Register, is for law
enforcement use only and is not to be discussed or shared with the media or the public. The
special registration criteria will be implemented in a phased approach beginning on
September 11, 2002, and expanded on October 1, 2002.

    These criteria may be updated routinely in the future based on current national security,
law enforcement or intelligence information. Therefore, managers and supervisors should

"LIMITED OFFICIAL USE ONLY"

Memorandum for Regional Directors, et al   Page 2
Subject: Identification of Nonimmigrant Aliens Subject to Special Registration, or the
   National Security Entry Exit Registration System.

disseminate and discuss the updated criteria at staff meetings, as well as directly with the officers.

Phase 1 – September 11, 2002, through September 30, 2002

The Attorney General, in consultation with the Secretary of State (SOS), may designate that nonimmigrant aliens who are citizens or nationals of certain countries will be subject to special registration by way of a publication of a notice in the Federal Register (FR). In addition, an inspecting officer will subject a nonimmigrant alien to special registration if the officer has a reason to believe that the alien is a citizen or national of a country designated by the Attorney General as being subject to special registration and published via a notice in the FR. For example, a case that might warrant such a registration could be: a nonimmigrant alien who is a dual national and is applying for admission as a national of a country that is not subject to special registration, but the alien's other nationality would subject him or her to special registration.

Currently, there are four countries (Iran, Iraq, Sudan, and Libya) subject to special registration requirements pursuant to 8 CFR 264.1(f), based on an existing FR notice. On or before September 11, 2002, the Attorney General will publish a notice re-designating those four countries and further requiring that nonimmigrant aliens, other than those applying for admission under 101(a)(15)(A) and (G) of the Act, from Syria will be subject to the registration provisions of 8 CFR 264.1(f), as amended. Therefore, on September 11, 2002, any nonimmigrant alien 14 and older, other than those applying for admission under 101(a)(15)(A) and (G) of the Act, who is a citizen or national of Iran, Iraq, Sudan, Libya or Syria, will be registered pursuant to the new special registration procedures. If the inspecting officer learns that a nonimmigrant possesses dual nationality from one of these five countries and is applying for admission using another nationality not cited in a FR notice, the officer *shall* refer the nonimmigrant for special registration.

Phase 2 – October 1, 2002

Inspecting officers will continue to register nonimmigrant aliens applying for admission to the United States from Iran, Iraq, Sudan, Libya and Syria. Commencing October 1, 2002, inspecting officers are also required to specially register nonimmigrant aliens in accordance with the following guidance.

The inspecting officer will receive "special registration" lookouts via the IBIS during their primary inspection of certain nonimmigrant aliens who have been identified by the Attorney General or SOS as being subject to special registration. In addition, nonimmigrant aliens who have been exempted from the special registration requirements by the Attorney General or SOS will also be identified through the lookout system. These alerts will be placed in IBIS by a Department of State consular officer. The consular officer will identify such aliens through the Consular Lookout And Support System (CLASS), which will in turn notify

APPENDIX B

Memorandum for Regional Directors, et al   Page 3
Subject: Identification of Nonimmigrant Aliens Subject to Special Registration, or the
        National Security Entry Exit Registration System.

IBIS through the National Automated Lookout System (NAILS). The lookout will direct the officer to register the nonimmigrant alien or to exempt the nonimmigrant aliens from special registration. A lookout will either bear the code "NSER" and will contain remarks stating that the nonimmigrant alien should be referred to secondary for special registration, or it will bear the code "EXMT" and will contain remarks stating that the nonimmigrant alien should not be referred to secondary for special registration.

The Attorney General has determined under his authority set forth in 8 CFR 264.1(f)(2)(iii) to established pre-existing criteria warranting special registration of certain nonimmigrant aliens, other than those applying for admission under 101(a)(15)(A) or (G) of the Act, who are citizens or nationals, or who an inspecting officer has reason to believe are citizens or nationals, of **Pakistan, Saudi Arabia,** and **Yemen** who are males between 16 and 45 years of age. It is imperative that the officers remain vigilant and verify the age of all males from these three countries in order to properly identify those who are subject to special registration.

Finally, any nonimmigrant alien, regardless of nationality, must be specially registered when the inspecting officer has determined or reason to believe that a nonimmigrant meets pre-existing criteria, as determined by the Attorney General, that would indicate that such alien's presence in the United States warrants monitoring in the interest of national security. In determining whether to exercise his or her discretion to require a nonimmigrant alien to comply with the special registration requirements of 8 CFR 264.1(f) the inspecting officer may only consider the following pre-existing criteria established by the Attorney General:

1. The nonimmigrant alien has made unexplained trips to Iran, Iraq, Libya, Sudan, Syria, North Korea, Cuba, Saudi Arabia, Afghanistan, Yemen, Egypt, Somalia, Pakistan, Indonesia, or Malaysia, or the alien's explanation of such trips lacks credibility.

2. The nonimmigrant alien has engaged in other travel, not well explained by the alien's job or other legitimate circumstances.

3. The nonimmigrant alien has previously overstayed in the United States on a nonimmigrant visa, and monitoring is now appropriate in the interest of national security.

4. The nonimmigrant alien meets characteristics established by current intelligence updates and advisories.

5. The nonimmigrant alien is identified by local, state or federal law enforcement as requiring monitoring in the interest of national security.

6. The nonimmigrant alien's behavior, demeanor, or answers indicate that alien should be monitored in the interest of national security.

Memorandum for Regional Directors, et al   Page 4
Subject: Identification of Nonimmigrant Aliens Subject to Special Registration, or the
       National Security Entry Exit Registration System.

7. The nonimmigrant alien provides information that causes the immigration officer to
     reasonably determine that the individual requires monitoring in the interest of national
     security

    The officer's discretionary determination to refer a nonimmigrant alien to special registration
must be concurred on by a supervisory immigration officer, at a level to be determined by the
district director.

    Please disseminate this guidance to all districts, ports, sectors, and asylum offices in your
jurisdiction. Please refer questions regarding this memorandum to Assistant Chief Inspector
Stephen M. Dearborn at (202) 305-2970.

Office of the Attorney General
Washington, D. C. 20530

September 23, 2002

Mr. Adel Al-Jubeir
Foreign Policy Advisor to
Crown Prince Abdullah
Office of the Ambassador
Royal Embassy of Saudi Arabia
601 New Hampshire Avenue, NW
Washington, DC 20037

Dear Adel:

It was wonderful to have the opportunity to spend some time with you on Friday afternoon. After hearing so many good words about you, I was impressed to see that you lived up to these expectations.

During our visit, you provided me with copies of some documents from the internet. As you may recall, I did not review these documents in our meeting. I later learned that the documents, if they were legitimate, would have been classified as law enforcement sensitive. Therefore, it would have been inappropriate for me to comment on the specific documents which you provided from the internet in any way.

I do want to reiterate, however, my comments on the Department of Justice's role in the immigration system of the United States and the enhanced security measures we will take to protect against the threat of terrorism. As we discussed, all citizens of only five countries which are designated as state sponsors of terrorism will be required to be registered and fingerprinted under the National Security Entry Exit Registration System (NSEERS). Any citizen of any nation visiting the United States can be included in the NSEERS, but all citizens of no other nation, including Saudi Arabia, will be subject to NSEERS as required by current U.S. law. We do expect all citizens visiting the United States from other nations to be included in our border security system.

As we discussed, the NSEERS will be targeted from intelligence and will change as conditions dictate. Any intelligence that Saudi Arabia shares about specific individuals of concern will be greatly appreciated and will assist our targeting. We should also work on mutually beneficial agreements to facilitate immigration, security and exchange for our nations.

I look forward to continuing our relationship in hopes of advancing the friendship that our nations share.

Sincerely,

David T. Ayres
Chief of Staff to the Attorney General

APPENDIX C.

Zalmay M. Khalizad, left, with Defense Secretary Donald H. Rumsfield, in a 2001 meeting. Khalizad, a member of the White House National Security Council, also headed the Bush-Cheney transition team for the Defense Department.
(Credit: Department of Defense file photo by R. D. Ward.)

Khalizad, Bush's special envoy to Afghanistan, and Rumsfield at Bagram Air Base in Afghanistan, April 27, 2002.
(Credit: Department of Defense file photo by R. D. Ward.)

President George W. Bush and Afghanistan President Hamid Karzai walk along the colonnade in the Rose Garden after their joint press conference Jan. 28, 2002. "The United States is committed to building a lasting partnership with Afghanistan," said President Bush.
(Credit: White House photo by Tina Hager.)

NOTES

To avoid redundancy, in most cases sources have not been endnoted when time, place, or publication are cited in the text.

INTRODUCTION

1. White House transcript of remarks by Bush, "U.S. Humanitarian Aid to Afghanistan," Eisenhower Executive Office Building, 11 Oct. 2002.
2. Ibid.
3. Associated Press (AP), 10 Oct. 2002.
4. State Department "Worldwide Caution," 10 Oct. 2002.
5. Update to State Department "Worldwide Caution," 6 Nov. 2002.
6. "Caution" update, 20 Nov. 2002.
7. Bush remarks, 11 Oct. 2002.
8. Senate testimony of Tenet, 17 Oct. 2002.

CHAPTER 1

1. Latest data on potential and proven reserves, by country, American Petroleum Institute, U.S. Department of Energy. Also, opening remarks by Rep. Doug Bereuter (R-Neb.), then chairman of House International Relations Subcommittee on Asia and the Pacific, in hearing on U.S. interests in the Central Asian republics, 12 Feb. 1998.
2. Cited by John J. Maresca, Unocal Corp.'s vice president of international relations, in prepared testimony before House International Relations Subcommittee on Asia and the Pacific, 12 Feb. 1998.
3. Ibid.
4. Transcript of speech by Richard H. Matzke, then president of Chevron Overseas Petroleum Inc., to the National Association of Petroleum Investment Analysts, 21 May 1997.

5. "Discoveries Alter Caspian Region Energy Potential," *Oil & Gas Journal*, 17 Dec. 2001, 18. Also, "Key International Players Inside the Beltway," *Legal Times*, 24 Sept. 2001.

6. Maresca's House testimony, 1998.

7. Ibid.

8. Ibid.

9. Unocal 1997 annual report, and Unocal news release, "Consortium Formed to Build Central Asia Gas Pipeline," 27 Oct. 1997, from Ashkhabad, Turkmenistan.

10. Ibid.

11. Maresca's House testimony, 1998.

12. Prepared testimony of Marty F. Miller, Unocal's vice president of Central Asian operations, before Senate Foreign Relations Subcommittee on the Near East and South Asia, 22 Oct. 1997.

13. U.S.-Azerbaijan Chamber of Commerce Web site <http://www.usacc.org/chamber/prof-officers.htm>.

14. Zalmay Khalilzad, "Afghanistan: Time to Reengage," *Washington Post*, 7 Oct. 1996, A21.

15. Zalmay Khalilzad, "Anarchy in Afghanistan," *Journal of International Affairs*, summer 1997.

16. Ibid.

17. Michael Daly, "Oil Firm Wooed Taliban Chiefs," *New York Daily News*, 28 Oct. 2001, 25.

18. Ahmed Rashid, *Taliban* (New Haven, Conn.: Yale University Press, 2000), 174.

19. Daly, "Oil Firm Wooed Taliban Chiefs."

20. Paul Watson, "Afghanistan Aims to Revive Pipeline Plans," *Los Angeles Times*, 30 May 2002, A5.

21. Michael J. Berens, "University Helped U.S. Reach Out to Taliban," *Chicago Tribune*, 21 Oct. 2001, 1.

22. Rashid, *Taliban*, 171.

23. Daly, "Oil Firm Wooed Taliban Chiefs."

24. Jim Crogan, "The Oil War," *L.A. Weekly*, 30 Nov. 2001, 16.

25. Berens, "University Helped U.S. Reach Out to Taliban."

26. Joe Stephens and David B. Ottaway, "Afghan Roots Keep Adviser Firmly in the Inner Circle," *Washington Post*, 23 Nov. 2001, A41.

27. Berens, "University Helped U.S. Reach Out to Taliban."

28. Rashid, *Taliban*, 240.

29. Watson, "Afghanistan Aims to Revive Pipeline Plans."

30. Rashid, *Taliban*, 171.

31. "Oil Giant Hires Seasoned Diplomat," *Intelligence Newsletter*, 11 Sept. 1997.

32. Miller's Senate testimony.
33. Berens, "University Helped U.S. Reach Out to Taliban."
34. Paul Starobin, "The New Great Game," *National Journal*, 13 March 1999.
35. Afghanistan-America Foundation Web site <http://www.afghanistanameri-cafoundation.org/internat.htm>.
36. IRS Form 990 for Afghanistan Foundation, 1997. Also, "U.S. Policy in Afghanistan: Challenges and Solutions," white paper, Afghanistan Foundation, 1999.
37. Rashid, *Taliban*, 173.
38. Berens, "University Helped U.S. Reach Out to Taliban."
39. Rashid, *Taliban*, 171–72.
40. Afghanistan-America Foundation Web site <http://www.afghanistanameri-cafoundation.org/diplomatic.htm>.
41. Ilene R. Prusher, Scott Baldauf, and Edward Girardet, "Afghan Power Brokers," *Christian Science Monitor*, 10 June 2002, 1A.
42. Author interview by phone, 22 Jan. 2002.
43. Author interview with INS immigration inspector, who searched federal databases.
44. Rashid, *Taliban*, 160.
45. "Suspension of Activities Related to Proposed Natural Gas Pipeline Across Afghanistan," Unocal news release, 21 Aug. 1998.
46. Agence France-Presse, 3 Aug. 2001.
47. Jane Perlez, "After the Attacks: The Diplomacy; Powell Says It Clearly: No Middle Ground on Terrorism," *New York Times*, 13 Sept. 2001, A17.
48. "U.S. Ambassador Calls on Petroleum Minister," Pakistan Press International, 9 Oct. 2001.
49. *Frontier Post*, 10 Oct. 2001.
50. "Talks Begin on Oil, Gas Pipelines from Turkmenistan to Pakistan," *Asia Pulse*, 18 Sept. 2002.

CHAPTER 2
1. Khalilzad, "Afghanistan: The Consolidation of a Rogue State," *Washington Quarterly*, 23, no. 1 (winter 2000).
2. Ibid.
3. Christopher Ogden, "Good News/Bad News in the Great Game; Afghanistan's New Regime May Prove Both Stabilizing and Disruptive," *Time*, 14 Oct. 1996, 28.
4. Testimony of Khalilzad before the Senate Foreign Relations Subcommittee on Near Eastern and South Asian Affairs, 8 Oct. 1998.

5. Ibid.

6. Khalilzad, "Afghanistan: The Consolidation of a Rogue State."

7. Ibid.

8. Ibid.

9. Ibid.

10. Bob Woodward, *Bush at War* (New York: Simon & Schuster, 2002), 35, 36.

11. Pakistan Press International, 18 Aug. 2001.

12. Khalilzad, "Afghanistan: The Consolidation of a Rogue State."

13. Woodward, *Bush at War*, 32.

14. David B. Ottaway and Joe Stephens, "Diplomats Met with Taliban on bin Laden; Some Contend U.S. Missed Its Chance," *Washington Post*, 29 Oct. 2001, A1.

15. Ibid.

16. Agence France-Presse, 2 Aug. 2001.

17. Rashid, *Taliban*, 259–60.

18. "Christina Rocca," *Intelligence Online*, 4 Oct. 2001.

19. Kate Clark, "Revealed: The Taliban Minister, the U.S. Envoy and the Warning of September 11 That Was Ignored," *Independent* (London), 7 Sept. 2002.

20. Agence France-Presse, 28 Dec. 2001.

21. Transcript of National Public Radio interview with Khalilzad, 18 Jan. 2002.

22. Transcript of remarks by General Franks, press conference, Marriott Waterside Hotel, Tampa, FL, 18 Jan. 2002.

23. Julian Borger, "White House 'Exaggerating Iraqi Threat,'" *Guardian* (London), 9 Oct. 2002.

24. Bush remarks, Eisenhower Executive Office Building, 11 Oct. 2002.

25. Ibid.

26. *USA Today*/CNN/Gallup nationwide poll of 1,032 adults, conducted 14–15 Sept. 2001.

27. *USA Today*/CNN/Gallup poll taken 11–14 Jan. 2002.

28. Woodward, *Bush at War*, figure 13.

29. FBI Web site <http://www.fbi.gov/mostwant/terrorists/fugitives.htm>.

30. Paul Sperry, "Pentagon Suspects Osama bin Laden," WorldNetDaily.com, 11 Sept. 2001 <http://www.worldnetdaily.com/news/article.asp?ARTICLE_ID=24434>.

31. Gannett News Service, 18 Sept. 2001.

CHAPTER 3

1. Extracts from a reported Oct. 2002 statement signed by bin Laden, AP, 15 Oct. 2002.

2. Remarks by Levin, citing prior testimony of Joint Chiefs of Staff Chairman Gen. Richard B. Myers, at Senate Armed Services Committee hearing, 7 Feb. 2002. Also, White House data on Enduring Freedom sorties and munitions.

3. Michael Barone and Grant Ujifusa, *The Almanac of American Politics 2000*, National Journal Group Inc., Washington, D.C., 1999, 669.

4. Woodward, *Bush at War*, 299.

5. Ibid., 210.

6. "Operation Enduring Freedom: One Year of Accomplishments," White House press release, 7 Oct. 2002 <http://www.whitehouse.gov/infocus/defense/enduringfreedom.html>.

7. Woodward, *Bush at War*, 314.

8. AP, 7 Nov. 2001.

9. Megan K. Stack, "The Afghan Warnings That Went Unheeded at Tora Bora," *Los Angeles Times*, 25 April 2002, A5.

10. Jonathan Weisman and Jack Kelley, "Did He [bin Laden] Get Away?" *USA Today*, 5 Feb. 2002, A1. Also, Stack, "The Afghan Warnings That Went Unheeded at Tora Bora."

11. Transcript of interview by George Stephanopoulos, *This Week with George Stephanopoulos*, ABC News, 17 Nov. 2002.

12. Rashid, *Taliban*, 186.

13. Moussaoui indictment, U.S. District Court for Eastern District of Virginia, June 2002 term.

14. Woodward, *Bush at War*, 210.

15. State of Union, 2002.

16. Bob Drogin, "No Leaders of al-Qaida Found at Guantanamo," *Los Angeles Times*, 18 Aug. 2002, A1.

17. Bill Gertz, "Al-Qaida Leadership Reported Disrupted," *Washington Times*, 13 Dec. 2002.

18. FBI Most Wanted Terrorists list. Also, "Al-Qaida's Most Wanted," AP, 21 Nov. 2002.

19. Ibid.

20. Transcript of interview by Tim Russert, *Meet the Press*, NBC News, 1 Dec. 2002.

21. Ibid.

22. Author interviews by phone and in person, winter 2002.

23. "Operation Enduring Freedom: One Year of Accomplishments," White House.

24. Author interviews by phone, fall 2002.

25. John F. Burns, "10-Month bin Laden Mystery: Dead or Alive?" *New York Times*, 23 Sept. 2002.

26. Stack, "The Afghan Warnings That Went Unheeded at Tora Bora." Also, Philip Smucker, "Tora Bora Falls, But No bin Laden," *Christian Science Monitor*, 17 Dec. 2001.

27. Author interviews by phone and e-mail, fall 2002.

28. Ibid.

29. Author interview by phone, April 2002.

30. Rowan Scarborough, "Rules Loosened for U.S. Troops Chasing Enemy," *Washington Times*, 22 Dec. 2001, A1.

31. Author interview in person, winter 2002.

32. AP, 9 Jan. 2002.

33. Rowan Scarborough, "Soldiers Say U.S. Let Taliban General Go," *Washington Times*, 18 Dec. 2002.

34. Transcript of Bush news conference, the East Room, White House, 11 Oct. 2001.

35. "Operation Enduring Freedom: One Year of Accomplishments."

36. White House news conference, 11 Oct. 2001.

37. "Operation Enduring Freedom: One Year of Accomplishments."

38. Woodward, *Bush at War*, 160.

39. Transcript of Franks's press conference, Marriott Waterside Hotel, Tampa, FL, 18 Jan. 2002.

40. Transcript of Franks's speech in West Palm Beach, Fla., 12 Nov. 2002.

41. "U.S. Authenticates bin Laden Tape," AP, 18 Nov. 2002.

42. Transcript of remarks at Afghanistan embassy, 10 Sept. 2002.

43. *Meet the Press*, NBC News, 8 Sept. 2002.

44. CNN, 23 Nov. 2002.

CHAPTER 4

1. Gallup poll of 9,924 adults in nine Islamic countries taken in Dec. 2001 and Jan. 2002. Pakistan sample: 2,043, with margin of error +/- 2 percentage points.

2. Rashid, *Taliban*, 92.

3. Mohammed Ahmedullah, "Pakistani Mosque Is Harvard for Terrorists," *Defense Week*, 15 Oct. 2001.

4. Ibid.

5. Rashid, *Taliban*, 90.

6. Cited by Robert Marquand, "Pakistan Edging Toward Islamic Rule," *Christian Science Monitor*, 3 Sept. 1998, 1.

7. Owen Bennet Jones, *Pakistan: Eye of the Storm* (New Haven, Conn.: Yale University Press, 2002), 25, 26.

8. "Patterns of Global Terrorism 2000," State Department report released 30 April 2001.

9. Jones, *Pakistan*, 25, 26.

10. Ibid.

11. Author interview by phone, fall 2001.

12. CBS News transcript, *The Early Show*, 5 Nov. 2001.

13. Paul Watson, "Deadly Shooting in Calcutta May Be Linked to al-Qaida," *Los Angeles Times*, 23 Jan. 2002, A11.

14. Dan Eggen and Michael Dobbs, "Danger Persists After Hobbling of al-Qaida," *Washington Post*, 14 Jan. 2002, A1.

15. AP, 24 Feb. 2002.

16. Paul Watson, "Pearl's Killer Boasted of bin Laden Ties," *Los Angeles Times*, 16 July 2002, A5.

17. Manoj Joshi, "India Helped FBI Trace ISI-Terrorist Links," *Times of India*, 10 Oct. 2001.

18. AP, 5 June 2002.

19. Moussaoui indictment.

20. Ahmedullah, "Pakistani Mosque Is Harvard for Terrorists."

21. David Bamber, Chris Hastings, and Rajeev Syal, "London House Linked to U.S. Plot," *Sunday Telegraph* (London), 30 Sept. 2001.

22. AP, 8 Feb. 2002.

23. Moussaoui indictment.

24. Peter Finn and Dana Priest, "Experts: Damage to al-Qaida Has Limited Operations' Scope," *Washington Post*, 15 Oct. 2002. Also, AP, 25 June 2002.

25. Michelle Malkin, *Invasion* (Washington, D.C.: Regnery, 2002), 223.

26. AP, 25 June 2002.

27. Ibid.

28. Ibid.

29. Watson, "Deadly Shooting in Calcutta May Be Linked to al-Qaida." Also, Alex Spillius, "LSE Drop-out Arrested for Reporter's Kidnap," *Daily Telegraph* (London), 13 Feb. 2002.

30. Ahmedullah, "Pakistani Mosque Is Harvard for Terrorists."

31. Finn and Priest, "Experts: Damage to al-Qaida Has Limited Operations' Scope."

32. "What Does the Saga of Richard Reid Tell Us About al-Qaida?" *Time*, 25 Feb. 2002.

33. Watson, "Pearl's Killer Boasted of bin Laden Ties."

34. Agence France-Presse, 19 April 2002.

35. Moussaoui indictment.

36. Susan Schmidt and Douglas Farah, "Al-Qaida's New Leaders," *Washington Post*, 29 Oct. 2002, A1.
37. Tom Vanden Brook, "Bin Laden Audiotape Raises Life-and-Death Questions," *USA Today*, 13 Nov. 2002, A12.
38. "Odyssey in the Shadows," *Newsweek,* 24 June 2002.
39. Author interview by phone, 18 Sept. 2002.
40. "Patterns of Global Terrorism 2000."
41. Ibid.
42. Reuters, 13 Sept. 2002.
43. "Confessions of an al-Qaida Terrorist," *Time*, 15 Sept. 2002.
44. Serge Trifkovic, *Sword of the Prophet: Islam History, Theology, Impact on the World*, Regina Orthodox Press, Boston, 2002, 233.

CHAPTER 5

1. Khalilzad, "Afghanistan: The Consolidation of a Rogue State."
2. Ibid.
3. Khalilzad, Afghanistan Foundation white paper, 1999.
4. Ibid.
5. Woodward, *Bush at War*, 59.
6. Transcript of remarks by Deputy Secretary of Defense Paul Wolfowitz, U.S. Chamber of Commerce, Washington, D.C., 30 Sept. 2002.
7. Transcript of remarks by Rocca to U.S.-Pakistan Business Council, Washington, D.C., 5 Dec. 2001.
8. Ibid.
9. OPIC press release, 12 Oct. 2001.
10. Wolfowitz, U.S. Chamber of Commerce, 30 Sept. 2002.
11. Tomlinson, "Afghans: Enemies Fled to Pakistan."
12. James Dao, "Taliban and Qaeda Believed Plotting Within Pakistan," *New York Times*, 28 May 2002.
13. Arnaud de Borchgrave, "Bin Laden Said to Be Hiding in Pakistan," *Washington Times*, 23 April 2002.
14. Martin Arostegui, "Bin Laden in Hiding Near U.S. Missile Strike," UPI, 13 Feb. 2002.
15. Ibid.
16. De Borchgrave, "Bin Laden Said to Be Hiding in Pakistan."
17. Tomlinson, "Afghans: Enemies Fled to Pakistan."
18. Author interviews by phone, Dec. 2002.
19. UPI, 12 Sept. 2002.
20. Interview by CNN, 18 Jan. 2002.

21. "Hospital Worker: I Saw Osama," CBSNews.com, 28 Jan. 2002.

22. CNN, 18 Jan. 2002.

23. Remarks at Crawford, Tex., news conference, 28 Dec. 2001.

24. Author interview by e-mail, fall 2002.

25. Dao, "Taliban and Qaida Believed Plotting Within Pakistan."

26. James Risen and David Johnston, "Intercepted al-Qaida E-mail Is Said to Hint at Regrouping," *New York Times*, 6 March 2002.

27. White House news conference, 15 Nov. 2002.

28. Richard Wolffe, "U.S. Names Iran As Chief Sponsor of Terror," *Financial Times*, 21 May 2002.

29. Weisman and Kelley, "Did He [bin Laden] Get Away?"

30. Transcript of president's remarks in Cincinnati, Ohio, 7 Oct. 2002.

31. UPI, 14 Nov. 2002.

32. Jim Hoagland, "Nuclear Enabler: Pakistan Today Is the Most Dangerous Place on Earth," *Washington Post*, 24 Oct. 2002, A35.

33. Dao, "Taliban and Qaida Believed Plotting Within Pakistan."

34. Trifkovic, *Sword of the Prophet*, 231.

35. Rashid, *Taliban*, 185.

36. Crawford, Tex., 28 Dec. 2001.

37. NBC News, 8 Jan. 2002.

38. Crawford, Tex., 28 Dec. 2001.

39. "U.S. Had Warned Pakistan to Bridle ISI in 1992: Report," Press Trust of India, 8 Dec. 2001.

40. UPI, 12 Sept. 2002.

41. Trifkovic, *Sword of the Prophet*, 231.

42. Paul Sperry, "U.S., Ashcroft Get Tough with Paki, Saudi Visitors," WorldNetDaily.com, 19 Sept. 2002 <http://www.worldnetdaily.com/news/article.asp?ARTICLE_ID=28999>. See Appendix of this book for INS memorandum marked "LIMITED OFFICIAL USE ONLY."

43. Ibid.

44. "Pakistan Rejects Terrorism in All Forms and Manifestations," Press Trust of India, 7 Jan. 2002.

45. Reuters, 15 Dec. 2002.

46. Ibid.

47. AP, 30 Dec. 2001.

48. Douglas Jehl, "Death of Reporter Puts Focus on Pakistan's Intelligence Unit," *New York Times*, 25 Feb. 2002.

49. AP, 13 Feb. 2002.

50. Douglas Jehl, "Suspect Says Reporter Was Slain in January As Part of Wider Plot," *New York Times*, 23 Feb. 2002.

51. Paul Sperry, "U.S. Delayed Blacklisting Pakistani al-Qaida Group," WorldNetDaily.com, 25 Feb. 2002 <http://www.worldnetdaily.com/news/article.asp?ARTICLE_ID=26601>.

52. "Afghan, U.S. Ambassadors Visit Pakistan Foreign Office," *Business Recorder*, 11 Oct. 2001.

53. AP, 1 Aug. 2002.

54. Transcript of remarks by Chamberlin before Senate Foreign Relations Committee, 26 June 2001.

55. Author interview by e-mail, 27 Feb. 2002.

56. "Taliban and al-Qaida Leaders Being Hunted in Pakistan: U.S. Envoy," Channel NewsAsia, 31 Oct. 2002.

57. Carlotta Gall, "U.S. to Train Pakistanis to Help Bar Terrorist Funds," *New York Times*, 20 Nov. 2002, A10.

58. "ISI Continued to Arm Taliban Well into October: Report," Press Trust of India, 8 Dec. 2001.

59. Bill Gertz, "Pakistan Sends Supplies to Taliban," *Washington Times*, 1 Nov. 2001.

60. Marcus Tanner, "Pakistan Air Force Seen Evacuating Foreign Fighters from Kunduz," *Independent* (London), 26 Nov. 2001.

61. AP, 23 Oct. 2002.

62. Tomlinson, "Afghans: Enemies Fled to Pakistan."

63. Trifkovic, *Sword of the Prophet*, 231.

64. AP, 22 Nov. 2002.

65. David E. Sanger, "In North Korea and Pakistan, Deep Roots of Nuclear Barter," *New York Times*, 24 Nov. 2002, A1.

66. David E. Sanger and James Dao, "U.S. Says Pakistan Gave Technology to North Korea," *New York Times*, 18 Oct. 2002.

67. AP, 17 Oct. 2002.

68. Hoagland, "Nuclear Enabler: Pakistan Today Is the Most Dangerous Place on Earth."

69. Pakistan Press International, 19 Oct. 2002.

70. Ron Moreau and Zahid Hussain, "A Fragile Friendship," *Newsweek*, 15 July 2002, 18.

71. "U.S. to 'Reconsider' Delivery of F-16s," Press Trust of India, 24 July 2002.

72. Moreau and Hussain, "A Fragile Friendship."

73. Khalilzad, Afghanistan Foundation white paper.

74. Ibid.

CHAPTER 6

1. Sperry, "U.S., Ashcroft Get Tough with Paki, Saudi Visitors," WorldNetDaily.com, 19 Sept. 2002. Also, Paul Sperry, "Saudi Arabia 'Shocked' to Be Added to Watchlist," WorldNetDaily.com, 20 Sept. 2002 <http://www.worldnetdaily.com/news/article.asp?ARTICLE_ID=29014>. See Appendix for full memo.
2. Press release, royal embassy of Saudi Arabia, 23 Sept. 2002.
3. Paul Sperry, "Aides of Crown Prince, Ashcroft Huddle over Memo," WorldNetDaily.com, 24 Sept. 2002 <http://www.worldnetdaily.com/news/article.asp?ARTICLE_ID=29053>. See Appendix for Ayers letter.
4. Ibid.
5. Paul Sperry, "Ashcroft: Saudi Arabia Ally in War on Terrorism," WorldNetDaily.com, 26 Sept. 2002 <http://www.worldnetdaily.com/news/article.asp?ARTICLE_ID=29066>.
6. Gallup poll taken Dec. 2001 and Jan. 2002.
7. Monu Nalapat, "The New Appeasement," *Asian Wall Street Journal*, 23 July 2002.
8. Bob Deans, "Saudi Prince's Rising Stature," *Austin American Statesman*, 25 April 2002, 1A.
9. Author interviews in person, summer 2002.
10. Statement announcing class action lawsuit against members of Saudi royal family by families of Sept. 11 victims, PR Newswire, 15 Aug. 2002.
11. Author interviews, summer 2002.
12. Bill Gertz, *Breakdown: How America's Intelligence Failures Led to September 11* (Washington, D.C.: Regnery, 2002), 172.
13. Reuters, 6 Aug. 2002.
14. Ibid.
15. Nalapat, "The New Appeasement."
16. AP, 23 Oct. 2002.
17. "Wealthy Saudis ID'd As al-Qaida Backers," *Singapore Straits Times*, 19 Oct. 2002.
18. Philip Shenon, "U.S. May Ask Court to Dismiss a $1 Trillion Suit Linking Saudis to al-Qaida and 9-11," *New York Times*, 25 Oct. 2002.
19. Michael Isikoff, "9-11 Hijackers: A Saudi Money Trail?" *Newsweek*, 22 Nov. 2002.
20. Agence France-Presse, 21 Dec. 2001.
21. Reuters, 25 Nov. 2002.
22. AP, 22 Nov. 2002.

23. Isikoff, "9-11 Hijackers: A Saudi Money Trail?"
24. Shenon, "U.S. May Ask Court to Dismiss a $1 Trillion Suit Linking Saudis to al-Qaida and 9-11."
25. Allan Gerson and Ron Motley, "Is Saudi Arabia Tough Enough on Terrorism?" *New York Times*, 30 Dec. 2002, 17A.
26. Byron York, "The Great Escape," *National Review*, 30 Sept. 2002.
27. Agence France-Presse, 21 Dec. 2001.
28. Ben Barber, "'Visa Express' Discontinued in Saudi Arabia," *Washington Times*, 20 July 2002, 1A.
29. Deroy Murdock, "Visa Program Lasted Too Long," *Deseret News*, 21 July 2002, 6AA.
30. Ibid.
31. Transcript of testimony of Jimmy Gurule, Treasury Department undersecretary for enforcement, before the Senate Judiciary Committee, 20 Nov. 2002.
32. Moussaoui indictment.
33. Author interview, spring 2002.
34. AP, 9 Sept. 2002.
35. Jake Tapper, "Neil Bush Says Arab P.R. Machine Not As Good As Israel's," Salon.com, 24 Jan. 2002.
36. Maureen Dowd, "A Golden Couple Chasing Away a Black Cloud," *New York Times*, 27 Nov. 2002, 23A.
37. Richard Stewart, "Visitors Will Find a Thousand Points of Interest at the George Bush Presidential Library and Museum," *Houston Chronicle*, 2 Nov. 1997.
38. Tapper, "Neil Bush Says Arab P.R. Machine Not As Good As Israel's."
39. Maggie Mulvihill, Jack Meyers, and Jonathan Wells, "Slick Deals: Bush Advisers Cashed In on Saudi Gravy Train," *Boston Herald*, 11 Dec. 2000, 1.
40. Daniel Golden, James Bandler, and Marcus Walker, "Bin Laden Family Is Tied to U.S. Group," *Wall Street Journal*, 27 Sept. 2001, 3A.
41. Ibid.
42. Ibid.
43. Jeff Gerth, "The Business Dealings of the President's Relatives: What the Record Shows," *New York Times*, 19 April 1992, 14A.
44. AP, 3 Nov. 1994.
45. Golden, Bandler, and Walker, "Bin Laden Family Is Tied to U.S. Group."
46. Transcript of testimony of former CIA Director James Woolsey before the Senate Judiciary Committee, 3 Sept. 1998.
47. Jack Kelley, "Saudi Money Aiding bin Laden; Businessmen Are Financing Front Groups," *USA Today*, 29 Oct. 1999, 1A.

48. Rashid, *Taliban*, 168.

49. Jack Meyers, Jonathan Wells, and Maggie Mulvihill, "Saudi Clans Working with U.S. Oil Firms May Be Tied to bin Laden," *Boston Herald*, 10 Dec. 2001, 8.

50. Kelley, "Saudi Money Aiding bin Laden."

51. "Saudi Arabia: Treading Carefully," *Energy Compass*, 15 Nov. 2002.

52. James Risen, "New Breed of Roughnecks Battles Over Caspian Oil Fields," *Los Angeles Times*, 24 May, 1998, 11A.

53. Roger Beach, Unocal chairman, "Letters Desk," *Los Angeles Times*, 3 June 1998, 6B.

54. Rashid, *Taliban*, 171.

55. David R. Sands, "Terror Panel Urges U.S. to Oust Taliban," *Washington Times*, 4 Oct. 2001, 1A.

56. "Rebuilding Afghanistan Takes on New Urgency," *Seattle Times*, 21 Nov. 2001, 3A.

CHAPTER 7

1. Prusher, Baldauf, and Girardet, "Afghan Power Brokers."

2. Todd Richissin, "Karzai Family's Quest for Peace," *Baltimore Sun*, 1 Sept. 2002, 15A.

3. Author interview by phone, Nov. 2002.

4. International Advisory Board, Afghanistan-America Foundation Web site <http://www.afghanistanamericafoundation.org/internat.htm>.

5. Richissin, "Karzai Family's Quest for Peace."

6. Khalilzad, "Afghanistan: The Consolidation of a Rogue State."

7. Susan Burton, "The Lion in Waiting," *New York Times Magazine*, 20 Jan. 2002, 32.

8. Ibid.

9. Khalilzad, "Afghanistan: The Consolidation of a Rogue State."

10. Remarks by Bush, Eisenhower Executive Office Building, 11 Oct. 2002.

11. Larry P. Goodson, "Inside Afghanistan: A Failed Opportunity," *Newsday* (New York), 21 July 2002, 4B.

12. Interview by Brian Lamb, *Washington Journal*, C-Span, 21 June 2002.

13. Ghani, "The Folly of Quick Action in Afghanistan," *Financial Times*, 27 Sept. 2001, 23.

14. Richissin, "Karzai Family's Quest for Peace."

15. AP, 27 Feb. 2001.

16. "Taliban Leaders Surrender, Go Free," MSNBC.com, 9 Jan. 2002.

17. Agence France-Presse, 6 Dec. 2002.

18. Woodward, *Bush at War*, 314.
19. Prepared testimony of Hamid Karzai before the Senate Foreign Relations Subcommittee on Near Eastern and South Asian Affairs, 20 July 2000.
20. Jon Lee Anderson, "The City of Kandahar, Post-Taliban, Is Full of Reminders That the Taliban Were Not Always What They Seemed to Be," *New Yorker*, 28 Jan. 2002, 62.
21. Pamela Constable, "Terrorist Leader 'Safe,' Afghan Hosts Declare," *Washington Post*, 21 Aug. 1998, 1A.
22. Richissin, "Karzai Family's Quest for Peace."
23. Paul Sperry, "U.S. Snares Karzai Pal in Afghan Terror Sweep," WorldNetDaily.com, 4 Oct. 2002 <http://www.worldnetdaily.com/news/article.asp?ARTICLE_ID=29177>.
24. Transcript of remarks by Bush, photo op with UN Secretary-General Kofi Annan, Oval Office, White House, 13 Nov. 2002.
25. Bush remarks, Eisenhower Executive Office Building, 11 Oct. 2002.
26. Remarks by Bush at Afghanistan embassy, Washington, D.C., 10 Sept. 2002.
27. Bush remarks, Eisenhower Executive Office Building, 11 Oct. 2002.
28. "American Assistance to the People of Afghanistan," White House fact sheet.
29. Bush remarks, Eisenhower Executive Office Building, 11 Oct. 2002.
30. Transcript of remarks by Joseph J. Collins, deputy assistant secretary of defense for stability operations, Pentagon briefing room, Arlington, VA, 19 Dec. 2002.
31. Ibid.
32. Bush remarks, Eisenhower Executive Office Building, 11 Oct. 2002.
33. Ibid.
34. Sydney J. Freedberg Jr., "Rebuilding Afghanistan, and Maybe, Iraq," *National Journal*, 23 Nov. 2002.
35. Collins, Pentagon briefing, 19 Dec. 2002.
36. Ibid.
37. Ghani, "The Folly of Quick Action in Afghanistan."
38. "Operation Enduring Freedom," White House.
39. "Consortium Formed to Build Central Asia Gas Pipeline," Unocal Corp. press release, 27 Oct. 1997.
40. Miller testimony, 22 Oct. 1997.
41. "Operation Enduring Freedom."
42. Bush remarks, Eisenhower Executive Office Building, 11 Oct. 2002.
43. Miller testimony, 22 Oct. 1997.
44. "Long U.S. Stay in Afghanistan Predicted," CBSNews.com, 16 Aug. 2002.
45. Collins, Pentagon briefing, 19 Dec. 2002.

46. Bush remarks, Eisenhower Executive Office Building, 11 Oct. 2002.

47. Collins, Pentagon briefing, 19 Dec. 2002.

48. Freedberg, "Rebuilding Afghanistan, and Maybe, Iraq."

49. Bush remarks, Eisenhower Executive Office Building, 11 Oct. 2002.

50. Transcript of testimony of Gen. Tommy Franks before Senate Armed Services Committee, 7 Feb. 2002.

51. Bush remarks, Eisenhower Executive Office Building, 11 Oct. 2002.

52. Khalilzad, "Afghanistan: Time to Reengage."

CHAPTER 8

1. Elisabeth Bumiller, "Afghan Adviser: The Country's in His Blood," *New York Times*, 28 Oct. 2001, 8B.

2. Khalilzad biography, "Who Is Who?" Afghanhewad.com, one of the biggest Afghan Web sites on the Internet.

3. Author interview with INS immigration inspector, Nov. 2002.

4. Ibid.

5. Bumiller, "Afghan Adviser: The Country's in His Blood."

6. Kenneth J. Cooper, "Kabul Women Under Virtual House Arrest; Afghan Radicals Bar Access to Jobs, School," *Washington Post*, 7 Oct. 1996, 1A.

7. Khalilzad, "Afghanistan: Time to Reengage."

8. Afghanistan Foundation white paper.

9. Khalilzad, "The Consolidation of a Rogue State."

10. Trifkovic, *Sword of the Prophet*, 210, 211.

11. James A. Phillips, "Updating U.S. Strategy for Helping Afghan Freedom Fighters," *Heritage Foundation Reports*, 22 Dec. 1986.

12. Khalilzad, "Afghanistan: The Consolidation of a Rogue State."

13. Ibid.

14. Stephens and Ottaway, "Afghan Roots Keep Adviser Firmly in the Inner Circle."

15. Afghanistan Foundation white paper.

16. Peter H. Stone, "Caspian Wells Come In for K Street," *National Journal*, 13 March 1999.

17. Starobin, "The New Great Game."

18. Afghanistan Foundation's IRS 990s for 1996 and 1997.

19. "Bush Names DOD Transition Coordinators," *Aerospace Daily*, 3 Jan. 2001, 11.

20. Jim Landers, "White House Adviser Criticizes Muslim Countries," *Dallas Morning News*, 15 May 2002.

21. Khalilzad, "Afghanistan: The Consolidation of a Rogue State."

22. Ibid.

23. Ibid.
24. Ibid.
25. Woodward, *Bush at War*, 103, 118–20, 178, 290, 304.
26. Khalilzad, "Afghanistan: The Consolidation of a Rogue State."
27. Afghanistan Foundation white paper.
28. Ibid.
29. Mark Hibbs, "So Far U.S. Skirting Sanctions Issue on Pakistan's Centrifuge Aid to DPRK," *Platts Nuclear Fuel*, 9 Dec. 2002, 4.
30. Afghanistan Foundation white paper.
31. Hibbs, "So Far U.S. Skirting Sanction Issue on Pakistan's Centrifuge Aid to DPRK."
32. Khalilzad, "Afghanistan: Time to Reengage."
33. Khalilzad, "Afghanistan: The Consolidation of a Rogue State."
34. Ibid.
35. Ibid.
36. Bumiller, "Afghan Adviser: The Country's in His Blood."
37. Transcript of testimony of Khalilzad, Abdullah before Senate Foreign Relations Subcommittee on Near Eastern and South Asian Affairs, 8 Oct. 1998.
38. Ibid.
39. Khalilzad, "Afghanistan: The Consolidation of a Rogue State."
40. Khalilzad, "Anarchy in Afghanistan."
41. Khalilzad, "Afghanistan: The Consolidation of a Rogue State."
42. Khalilzad, "Anarchy in Afghanistan."
43. Ibid.
44. Ibid.

CHAPTER 9

1. "Rallying U.S. Business to Afghanistan's Reconstruction," OPIC news release, 2 Jan. 2002.
2. Bush remarks, Eisenhower Executive Office Building, 11 Oct. 2002.
3. "Caspian Sea Region: Oil Export Options," report of the Energy Information Administration, Department of Energy, July 2002.
4. "Pakistan, Afghan Heads Agree to Consider Gas Pipeline," *Asian Political News*, 11 Feb. 2002.
5. Transcript of remarks by Rumsfeld at news conference at Turkmenbashi Airport, Turkmenistan, 28 April 2002.
6. Agence France-Presse, 15 May 2002.
7. "Trilateral Summit on Gas Pipeline Starts," Pakistan Press International, 30 May 2002.

8. "Ambitious $2 Billion Gas Link Plan Revived," *Gulf News*, 31 May 2002.
9. "Development Bank Will Fund Trans-Afghan Gas Pipeline Feasibility Study," *Morning Star*, 10 July 2002.
10. Tariq Saeedi, "Trans-Afghan Pipeline to Be Planted Firmly," *Business Recorder*, 20 July 2002.
11. Pakistan Press International, 9 July 2002.
12. Saeedi, "Trans-Afghan Pipeline to Be Planted Firmly."
13. Agence France-Presse, 9 July 2002.
14. "Development Bank Will Fund Trans-Afghan Gas Pipeline Feasibility Study," *Morning Star*.
15. Agence France-Presse, 9 July 2002.
16. Saeedi, "Trans-Afghan Pipeline to Be Planted Firmly."
17. AP, 18 Sept. 2002.
18. AP, 12 Sept. 2002.
19. "Joint Statement on Road Construction in Afghanistan by the President of the United States, the Prime Minister of Japan and the Foreign Minister of Saudi Arabia," PR Newswire, 13 Sept. 2002.
20. "U.S. Agency to Conduct Survey of Oil, Gas Resources in Afghanistan," BBC Worldwide Monitoring, 11 Dec. 2002.
21. Agence France-Presse, 28 Dec. 2002.
22. "Trans-Afghanistan Pipeline Agreement Signed in Turkmenistan," *Central Asia & Caucasus Business Report*, 31 Dec. 2002. Also, Agence France-Presse, 9 July 2002.
23. "3 Nations Sign Agreement for Afghanistan Pipeline," *Houston Chronicle*, 28 Dec. 2002.
24. "Gas Pipeline Agreement Good Omen for Economy of Region," *Pakistan Press International*, 27 Dec. 2002.
25. Miller testimony, 22 Oct. 1997.
26. Letter from OPIC Vice President and General Counsel Mark Garfinkel to Patrick G. Heck, Democratic tax counsel, U.S. Senate Committee on Finance, 19 Feb. 2002, letter appendix 3, p. 5.
27. Ibid.
28. State of the Union address, 29 Jan. 2002.
29. Author interview by phone, Sept. 2002.
30. Aziz Haniffa, "Khalilzad May Become U.S. Ambassador to Afghanistan," *India Abroad*, 11 Jan. 2002, 4.
31. Unocal press release, 27 Oct. 1997.
32. Ibid.

33. "Afghan Pipeline Route Worries Iran," IPR Strategic Business Information Database, 19 Dec. 2001.

34. "Islamabad, Moscow to Sign MoU on $3.2 Billion Gas Pipeline Project," *Asia Pulse*, 1 July 2002.

35. Miller testimony, 22 Oct. 1997.

36. "Pakistan Might Use a Bit of Trans-Afghan Gas, After All," *World Gas Intelligence*, 17 Sept. 2002.

37. "Trans-Afghan Pipeline Comes Back on Agenda," *Energy Compass*, 14 March 2002.

38. Saeedi, "Trans-Afghan Pipeline to Be Planted Firmly."

39. "3 Nations Sign Agreement for Afghanistan Pipeline."

40. Bush remarks, Crawford Tex., 28 Dec. 2001.

41. S. Frederick Starr, "Investment Climate in Central Asia and the Caucasus," Central Asia-Caucasus Institute, 2002 report <http://www.cacianalyst.org/Publications/Starr_invest.htm>.

42. Ibid.

CHAPTER 10

1. Maresca testimony, House International Relations Subcommittee on Asia and the Pacific, 12 Feb. 1998.

2. Ibid.

3. Transcript of speech by Chevron Vice Chairman Richard H. Matzke before the Houston World Affairs Council, 19 Sept. 2000.

4. Transcript of speech by Matzke, then president of Chevron Overseas Petroleum Inc., to the National Association of Petroleum Investment Analysts, 21 May 1997.

5. "Key International Players Inside the Beltway."

6. Toby Harnden, "Ship Name Changed After Storm Warnings," *Daily Telegraph* (London), 5 July 2001, 19.

7. Carla Marinucci, "Critics Knock Naming Oil Tanker Condoleezza," *San Francisco Chronicle*, 5 April 2001, 3A.

8. Ibid.

9. Joseph Kahn, "Bush Advisers on Energy Report Ties to Industry," *New York Times*, 3 June 2001, 30A.

10. CNN/People, 8 Dec. 2002.

11. Chevron press release, 16 Jan. 2001.

12. Evan Thomas, "The Quiet Power of Condi Rice," *Newsweek*, 16 Dec. 2002.

13. Stone, "Caspian Wells Come in for K Street."

14. Megan Twohey, "Dick Cheney: A Biography," *National Journal*, 29 July 2000.

15. Unocal press release, 21 Aug. 1998.
16. Watson, "Afghanistan Aims to Revive Pipeline Plans."
17. Author interview by phone, 22 Jan. 2003.
18. Rashid, *Taliban*, 171.
19. Ibid., 239.
20. Unocal press release, 21 Aug. 1998.
21. Unocal press release, 4 Dec. 1998.
22. Unocal press release, 16 Feb. 1999.
23. "The Afghan Option," *APS Review Gas Market Trends*, 11 Nov. 2002.
24. Unocal press release, 4 Dec. 1998.
25. Miller testimony, 22 Oct. 1997.
26. Watson, "Afghanistan Aims to Revive Pipeline Plans."
27. Rashid, *Taliban*, 159.
28. Transcript of interview by NPR, 12 Dec. 1997.
29. Unocal press release, 7 June 1993.
30. Unocal fact sheet on its North American operations, updated 16 May 2002 <http://www.unocal.com/northam/tmbr.htm>.
31. Tom Brown Inc. press release, 22 Feb. 2001.
32. Bush's Public Financial Disclosure Report filed with the Federal Election Commission, 7 March 1999.
33. Unocal press release, 7 Dec. 1998.
34. "Halliburton Unit Joins Project," *Oil Daily*, 24 April 1994.
35. Andrew Buncombe, "Russia Fears U.S. Oil Companies Will Take Over World's Second-Biggest Reserves," *Independent* (London), 26 Sept. 2002.
36. "Key International Players Inside the Beltway."
37. "Oil and Telecommunications in Kabul," *Intelligence Online*, 31 Jan. 2002.
38. AP, 1 June 2001.
39. Tyler Marshall, "High Stakes in the Caspian: U.S. Dives into a Sea of Major Rewards—and Risks," *Los Angeles Times*, 23 Feb. 1998.
40. Transcript of Cheney remarks on the future of Azerbaijan, Washington, D.C., 18 Feb. 1997.
41. Rashid, *Taliban*, 159, 168.
42. Ibid., 240.
43. Watson, "Afghanistan Aims to Revive Pipeline Plans."
44. James Ruper, "Baker Favors Envoy to Mujaheddin," *Washington Post*, 18 March 1989, 1A.
45. "Strategic Energy Policy Challenges for the 21st Century," report of the Independent Task Force sponsored by the James A. Baker III Institute for Public Policy at Rice University, and the Council on Foreign Relations, April 2001.

46. Ibid.
47. Transcript of speech by Kenneth T. Derr, then Chevron chairman and CEO, to the Commonwealth Club of California, San Francisco, 5 Nov. 1998.
48. "Strategic Energy Policy Challenges for the 21st Century," Baker Institute.
49. Letter from Thelma J. Askey, director of the U.S. Trade and Development Agency, to Senate Finance Committee, 12 Feb. 2002.
50. "Trip Report: Presidential Mission on Energy Investment to Pakistan Led by Secretary of Energy Hazel R. O'Leary," U.S. Department of Energy, 21–24 Sept. 1994.
51. "Afghan Pipeline Route Worries Iran," IPR Strategic Business Information Database, 19 Dec. 2001.
52. "Joint Statement by President George W. Bush and President Nursultan Nazarbayev on the New Kazakhstan-American Relationship," *Public Papers of the Presidents*, 21 Dec. 2001.
53. Neela Banerjee, "As the War Shifts Alliances, Oil Deals Flow," *New York Times*, 15 Dec. 2001, 1C.
54. Cheney remarks, Washington, D.C., 18 Feb. 1997.
55. Richard L. Armitage and Frederic C. Hof, "Russia's Bad-Neighbor Policy," *Journal of Commerce*, 19 July 1994.
56. Ibid.
57. Cheney remarks, Washington, D.C., 18 Feb. 1997.
58. Murat Acemoglu, "The Impending Visit of Heydar Aliyev to Washington," *Armenian Reporter*, 31 May 1997, 3.
59. Remarks by Deputy Secretary of State Richard Armitage at the Fifth Annual Conference of the U.S.-Azerbaijan Chamber of Commerce, Renaissance Hotel, Washington, D.C., 8 March 2002.
60. Prepared testimony of Wendy J. Chamberlin before the Senate Foreign Relations Committee, 26 June 2001.
61. "Unocal, Delta Sign MoU with Gazprom and Turkmenrusgaz for Natural Gas Pipeline Project," Unocal press release, 13 Aug. 1996.
62. "Rebuilding Afghanistan Takes on New Urgency," *Seattle Times*, 21 Nov. 2001.
63. Saeedi, "Trans-Afghan Pipeline to Be Planted Firmly."
64. Author interview.
65. Rashid, *Taliban*, 168.
66. "Pakistan Might Use a Bit of Trans-Afghan Gas, After All."
67. Rashid, *Taliban*, 240, 241.
68. Ibid., 168.

CHAPTER 11

1. Prepared testimony of Zalmay Khalilzad before the Senate Foreign Relations Subcommittee on Near Eastern and South Asian Affairs, 8 Oct. 1998.
2. "Afghanistan Fact Sheet," Energy Information Administration, Energy Department, Sept. 2001.
3. Jean-Charles Brisard and Guillaume Dasquie, *Forbidden Truth* (New York: Thunder's Mouth Press/Nation Books, 2002), 142.
4. Watson, "Afghanistan Aims to Revive Pipeline Plans."
5. Agence France-Presse, 6 Sept. 2002.
6. Author interview by phone, Dec. 2002.
7. AP, 25 Feb. 1998.
8. Michael S. Lelyveld, "Controversial Oil Entrepreneur Unveils Pipeline Plan," *Journal of Commerce*, 27 March 1997, 3A.
9. Adam Clymer, "Government Openness an Issue As Bush Holds onto Records," *New York Times*, 3 Jan. 2003.
10. Paul Sperry, "My Picnic with Bill: How One Reporter Gave Clinton Heartburn Over Chinagate," *Whistleblower* magazine, 4–11 <http://www.worldnetdaily.com/news/article.asp?ARTICLE_ID=20765>.
11. Timothy J. Burger, "9-11 Probe: Aiming High," *Time*, 26 Jan. 2003.
12. Risen, "New Breed of Roughnecks Battles Over Caspian Oil Fields."
13. "Pitts, Brownback Forming Silk Road Caucus," Congressional Press Releases, 17 Oct. 2001.
14. "Key International Players Inside the Beltway."
15. See Appendix.
16. "Decision-Makers: Christina Rocca," Intelligence Online, 4 Oct. 2001.
17. Remarks by Bush before Congress, 20 Sept. 2001.

AFTERWORD

1. Terry Lee Jones, "Big Year on All Fronts: War, Economy, Politics; Worst Bear in 71 Years," *Investor's Business Daily*, Jan. 2003, 1A.
2. AP, 13 Nov. 2002.
3. *Bloomberg News*, 8 Feb. 2003.
4. David Leonhardt, "U.S. Economy in Worst Hiring Slump in 20 Years," *New York Times*, 5 Feb. 2003.
5. *GKST Economics newsletter*, 30 Jan. 2003.
6. Paul Sperry, "What Makes Greenspan Tick? Fed Chair's Links to Ayn Rand Shaped His Views," *Investor's Business Daily*, 18 Oct. 1993, 1A.
7. Chris Oliver, "Greenspan's Blunders Put Spotlight on Asia," *South China Morning Post*, 12 Jan. 2003, 2.

8. AP, 1 Feb. 2003.

9. Julie Mason, "President presides over burgeoning government, aggravated by concerns over security after 9-11," *Houston Chronicle*, 26 Jan. 2003.

10. "Bush's budget will make him the biggest spender in decades," Cato Institute press release, 6 Feb. 2003.

11. Mason, "President Presides over Burgeoning Government, Aggravated by Concerns over Security after 9-11."

12. Sara Kehaulani Goo, "House Panel Criticizes Request for Airport Security Spending," *Washington Post*, 21 June 2002.

13. Levy, "USA PATRIOT Act and Domestic Detention Policy," *Cato Handbook for Congress: Policy Recommendations for the 108th Congress*, January 2003, 117.

14. A. Jeff Ifrah, Kirby D. Behre and Larry Barcella, "Casting a Wide Net: The Patriot Act Will Ensnare A Lot of Law-Abiding Corporations," *Legal Times*, 19 Nov. 2001, 30.

15. Levy, "USA PATRIOT Act and Domestic Detention Policy," 119.

16. Ibid.

17. Charles Lewis and Adam Mayle, "Justice Dept. Drafts Sweeping Expansion of Anti-Terrorism Act," The Center for Public Integrity, 9 Feb. 2003. Available at http://www.publicintegrity.org/dtaweb/report.asp?ReportID=502.

18. Transcript of remarks by Peter Tomsen, professor of International Studies and Programs at the University of Nebraska at Omaha, before the Senate Foreign Relations Committee, 20 July 2000.

19. Ibid.

20. Stephen Buttry, "UNO Scholar: Moderates Hold Key for Women," *Omaha World-Herald*, 21 Nov. 2001, 8A.

21. Remarks by Bush, Crawford, Texas, 28 Dec. 2001.

22. Transcript of remarks by Bush at the President's Dinner, Washington Convention Center, Washington, D.C., 19 June 2002.

ACKNOWLEDGMENTS

THERE'S AN OLD TRUISM IN THE JOURNALISM PROFESSION that goes something like this: The farther you are from the world's power centers, particularly Washington, the easier it is to be bluntly honest in your reporting of world affairs. In short, truth survives more comfortably at a distance, as the axiom goes.

Tony Lukas, the late Pulitzer-winning *New York Times* foreign correspondent, is credited with the observation. He named his rule, ironically enough, The Afghanistan Principle, picking that country because it is halfway around the world from Washington. The principle holds true in the coverage of the war in Afghanistan and the Bush administration's hidden oil agenda. With few exceptions, the American media played down or completely ignored the Caspian energy-corridor angle, while the foreign press, particularly in France and India, played it up.

Granted, reporting hard truths so close to home in the midst of flamboyant flag-waving is not easy. These are intensely patriotic times, and we are all supposed to rally around our president.

But in the words of one of our most patriotic (and I would argue, heroic) presidents, Ronald Reagan, we also must not be afraid to see what we see. He was speaking of the threat of communism in our hemisphere, but the same applies to ugly truths right in our own backyard—in Washington. Good patriots don't bury their heads in the flag. Civilians can and should question the soundness of their military leaders' war strategy if it runs counter to core objectives, in this case decapitating the al-Qaida leadership—particularly in this war, critical as it is to our very survival and way of life. And good patriots should even feel free to question their leaders' motives when they don't adjust their strategy to compensate for poor results, in this case failing to decapitate the al-Qaida leadership. (Instead of launching a search-and-destroy mission in northern Pakistan, where Osama bin Laden and his top henchmen have found sanctuary, Bush launched an invasion of Baghdad, a military move that looks far more political than strategic.)

What I saw in the opening rounds of the administration's war on terrorism just didn't add up. Beginning in October 2001, I was one of the earliest critics of Bush's strategy of subcontracting out the fighting to Afghans while using our military to drop food rations, cozying up to terrorist-sponsoring Pakistan, and focusing on the Taliban rather than al-Qaida. And I was hammered for it on talk radio, which cited my columns. How dare I question our commander in chief during the war, some hosts scolded. But I smelled something rotten, and dug until I found the source—and the more I dug, the more it smelled.

Having said all that, I would like to thank, first and foremost, WND Books cofounder Joseph Farah, as well as the principals at Thomas Nelson Publishers, for having the courage to take on this controversial project, which does not exactly put a popular Republican president in the best light. Farah, who is also my editor at WorldNetDaily.com, the Internet's largest independent news site, is often accused of having a conservative or Republican bias, in large part because he OK'd so many hard-hitting stories on former President Clinton during his parade of scandals.

But anyone who knows Farah, a veteran newspaperman, knows he is an old romantic when it comes to journalism. He believes, as I do, that the traditional role of the press is to act as a watchdog on government, no matter if it is run by Democrats or Republicans. Both are capable of unmitigated waste, fraud, abuse, and corruption if their power is left unchecked, if they are not held accountable for their actions by a free press.

Farah proved, if his liberal detractors were watching, that he does not play political favorites the very month the administration changed over from Democratic to Republican control. He let me and my colleague Jon Dougherty loose to do a series of stories on Elaine Chao, Bush's nod for labor secretary. We exposed her cozy business and personal ties to the Beijing leadership—and her potential conflict of interest as a Cabinet member. Farah, as a result of the series, which was picked up by the old media, was disinvited to various media-related events by conservative groups in Washington.

I would also like to thank WND Books editor Joel Miller and the production staff at Thomas Nelson for their remarkable patience as I grappled with the fluid subject matter of this book—the changing developments in the pipeline deals, Caspian politics and, of course, the ongoing war on terrorism.

My wife and children, moreover, deserve sainthood for putting up with me, and also doing without me, during the whirlwind months I wrote this book. I love you.

But I am most grateful—particularly in the Era of Terror, with all the anger, frustration, fear and anxiety it brings—for my faith, and for the peace of God, which transcends all understanding.

ABOUT THE AUTHOR

PAUL SPERRY is the Washington bureau chief at WorldNetDaily.com, a position he previously held at *Investor's Business Daily*, where he wrote for 12 years. The Hoover Institution media fellow's reports on national security issues have been picked up by virtually every major news agency in the world. Sperry's journalistic courage and integrity are backed by years of experience, including extensive reporting and editing on national affairs, economics, manufacturing, real estate, and general business. His 1999 expose on a Clinton appointee to the U.S. Export-Import Bank led the Senate Banking Committee to force her to recuse herself from all deals related to the Beijing-tied Lippo Group. The next month President Clinton "banned" Sperry from the White House for asking him tough questions about his role in the Chinagate fund-raising scandal during a press picnic on the South Lawn. Sperry, 39, graduated from the University of Texas at Austin with a Bachelor of Journalism degree.

INDEX

245

Also from WND BOOKS

In *Center of the Storm: Practicing Principled Leadership in Times of Crisis,* former Florida Secretary of State Katherine Harris discusses the behind-the-scenes negotiations and backroom bartering that everyone suspected, but no one dared to disclose, during the infamous 2000 presidential election vote recount. Through never-before-revealed anecdotes, she explains twelve essential principles that helped her not just survive but thrive. She clearly illustrates how we, too, can learn these skills that help us in times of crises. ISBN 0-7852-6443-4

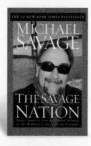

The Savage Nation: Saving America from the Liberal Assault on our Borders, Language, and Culture warns that our country is losing its identity and becoming a victim of political correctness, unmonitored immigration, and socialistic ideals. Michael Savage, whose program is the fourth-largest radio talk show and is heard on more than three hundred stations coast to coast, uses bold, biting, and hilarious straight talk to take aim at the sacred cows of our ever-eroding culture and wages war against the "group of psychopaths" known as PETA, the ACLU, and the liberal media. ISBN 0-7852-6353-5

September 11, 2001, did not represent the first aerial assault against the American mainland. The first came on July 17, 1996, with the downing of TWA Flight 800. *First Strike* looks in detail at what people saw and heard on this fateful night. With an impressive array of facts, Jack Cashill and James Sanders show the relationship between events in July 1996 and September 2001 and proclaim how and why the American government has attempted to cover up the truth. ISBN 0-7852-6354-3

Patricia Roush's girls were kidnapped more than sixteen years ago and taken by their Saudi father, whom they hardly knew, to the kingdom of Saudi Arabia. *At Any Price* is the story of her fight to get them back from a father with a documented history of severe mental illnesses and violent tendencies. In the midst of this tragic set of circumstances was a bigger problem—an ongoing, demoralizing struggle with the U.S. government and the Saudi kingdom to reunite her with her children. This personal story of bravery, courage, and faith will warm and inspire readers. ISBN 0-7852-6365-9

"Joseph Farah has written a thought-provoking recipe for reclaiming America's heritage of liberty and self-governance. I don't agree with all the solutions proposed here, but Farah definitely nails the problems."

—RUSH LIMBAUGH
Host of America's #1 Talk Program,
The Rush Limbaugh Show

"I don't agree with everything Joseph Farah says in *Taking America Back,* but he has written a provocative, from-the-heart call to action. It's a must-read for anyone who wonders how we can expand liberty and reclaim the vision of our founders."

—SEAN HANNITY
Author of *Let Freedom Ring* and
Cohost of *Hannity and Colmes* on Fox News
ISBN 0-7852-6392-6

Gun control has long been a hot topic in the United States, and the controversy has only heightened since the terrorist attacks on September 11, 2001. Now, with a growing focus on homeland security, more and more Americans are asserting their Second Amendment right to bear arms. In *Guns, Freedom, and Terrorism,* NRA executive vice president Wayne LaPierre provides a fact-filled volume and tackles a number of subjects surrounding gun rights. His convincing arguments will cause even the most adamant gun-control supporter to consider the values our forefathers fought to protect: liberty, democracy, and justice. ISBN 0-7852-6221-0

You've heard the saying "Children should be seen and not heard." But teen political writer Kyle Williams is challenging that adage and making a name for himself in the process. As the youngest columnist for WorldNetDaily.com, he has tackled subjects such as abortion, homosexual rights, separation of church and state, and the public school system. In *Seen and Heard* Williams again takes on the establishment, offering clear evidence that a leftist agenda is at work in our nation. His lively, energetic analysis of current events will leave readers with an understanding of the attack on traditional family values that is taking place daily. Williams's writing style—sound logic infused with passion and conviction—makes *Seen and Heard* both informative and entertaining. ISBN 0-7852-6368-3

Pick it up at your favorite bookstore or through www.WorldNetDaily.com

WHISTLEBLOWER MAGAZINE

The Internet's leading independent English-language news site, WorldNetDaily.com, has an amazing sister publication. It's called Whistleblower. This monthly print magazine—described by one prominent reviewer as "printed lightning, searing the facts about important current issues into your brain with the force of a thunderclap"—is very different from other news publications.

Each and every issue is a truly groundbreaking, insightful special report on a single topic of great importance—a topic generally ignored by the rest of the news media, such as: the income tax, guns in America, the deliberate dumbing-down of American education, the radical Islamic threat to America, Christian persecution worldwide, the war between Evolution and Intelligent Design, and the radical environmental movement.

You can subscribe to Whistleblower for only $39.95 (and save $50 off the single-copy price!) by calling toll-free 1-800-4-WND-COM (1-800-496-3266) or by logging on to WorldNetDaily.com's online store, ShopNetDaily.com.